Hiking

New Mexico's
Aldo Leopold Wilderness

Help Us Keep This Guide Up to Date

Every effort has been made by the authors and editors to make this guide as accurate and useful as possible. However, many things can change after a guide is published—trails are rerouted, regulations change, techniques evolve, facilities come under new management, etc.

We would love to hear from you concerning your experiences with this guide and how you feel it could be improved and kept up to date. While we may not be able to respond to all comments and suggestions, we'll take them to heart and we'll also make certain to share them with the authors. Please send your comments and suggestions to the following address:

The Globe Pequot Press
Reader Response/Editorial Department
P.O. Box 480
Guilford, CT 06437

Or you may e-mail us at:

editorial@globe-pequot.com

Thanks for your input, and happy travels!

A FALCON GUIDE®

Hiking

New Mexico's Aldo Leopold Wilderness

Bill Cunningham and Polly Burke

FALCON®

GUILFORD, CONNECTICUT
HELENA, MONTANA

AN IMPRINT OF THE GLOBE PEQUOT PRESS

Maps created by Tony Moore © The Globe Pequot Press

All photos are by the authors.

Library of Congress Cataloging in Publication Data is available.

ISBN 0-7627-1103-5

Manufactured in the United States of America
First Edition/First Printing

Dedicated to the timeless vision of Aldo Leopold,
who started it all; to the memory of Penn Cunningham, Bill's father,
who blazed our trail and set the example for us; and to all of you
with both the desire to explore beyond the roads into the
Aldo Leopold Wilderness and the heartfelt commitment to fight for the
freedom of Wild Country. May your spirit, and it, endure forever.

Contents

Acknowledgments

The Aldo Leopold Wilderness is a vast, complicated landscape with hundreds of miles of trails crisscrossing some of the most rugged terrain in the west. A project of this magnitude, spread over several field seasons, could not have been accomplished without the help of many folks, some of whom we met on the trail. Surely, such encounters were meant to happen, especially when we'd go for days in the wilderness without seeing anyone, and then meet someone special.

One such person was Mark Miller, a helpful, personable landowner on the Mimbres, whom we met along the river a few miles above his place. As a hunter, horseman, and hiker, Mark knows the country intimately. He gladly and accurately shared his knowledge with us. Another encounter, which had to be more than mere chance, was meeting fellow Montanan Maynard Rost atop Emory Pass. Maynard was supervisor of the Gila National Forest in the early '90s. He and his wife, also a native Montanan, are retired in Silver City, New Mexico. We enjoyed talking about mutual friends and learning more about the country.

And then there was the time we ran into Deputy Sheriff Stan Thompson of the Sierra County Sheriff's Office. We were south of Winston on a remote dirt road, wondering about road conditions and distances, when Stan showed up. He pulled out detailed maps and gave us all sorts of good road info that would continue to pay dividends in the ensuing weeks of back roads exploration.

Another wonderful encounter occurred when we reached Hillsboro Peak after five days of tough backpacking. The lookout ranger, Jim Swetnam, had just arrived to open the cabin and the lookout for the season. What was amazing was that Jim had spent eight seasons on Hillsboro, but that had ended thirteen years earlier. After all these intervening years, Jim had just arrived for season number nine, and we certainly felt privileged to be his first "customers" of the year. Jim graciously allowed us to fetch water from the cistern and to use the east cabin, welcome refuge from the wind. We spent the night there, learning much about the land and the history of the lookout from Jim.

This book would not have been possible without the help of some outstanding professionals in the Forest Service. One of our first contacts was with Jim Paxon, District Ranger for the Black Range District. Jim has been on the district for many years, and gave us solid information and advice. His love for the country is contagious.

We are also indebted to Tim Pohlman, who is in charge of wilderness and trails for the Black Range District. Tim has a refreshing, direct way of telling it like it is. He provided accurate, detailed information about trail conditions, road access, threatened and endangered wildlife species, and the reality of infrequent maintenance, trail by trail. Tim was also the principal agency reviewer of this book for the east-side portion of the Aldo that falls within his district.

Tim's counterpart in the Wilderness Ranger District, John Kramer, reviewed the west-side portion of this book that lies within his district. John has a particular interest in wilderness education, and we share a common bond as wilderness field course instructors. It is our fervent hope that this book will serve as an educational tool, for both the managing agency and Aldo visitors.

Carol Charnley, the information specialist for the Wilderness District, was also extremely helpful. Not only did Carol go out of her way to supply us with useful information during our visit, she also responded to our follow-up requests promptly and with professional accuracy.

We are deeply indebted to George Hobbs, Range Technician for the Wilderness District. George spends a lot of time in the field. He generously shared his detailed on-the-ground knowledge of trails, springs, road access, wildlife, and much more.

During our visit to the Wilderness district office, we were warmly greeted by District Ranger Annette Chavez. Her positive attitude and enthusiasm set the tone for the terrific cooperation provided by her staff.

Legend

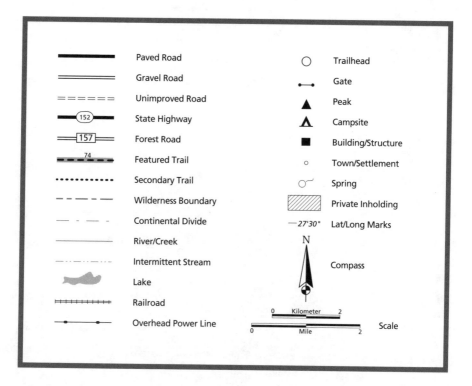

————————	Paved Road
════════════	Gravel Road
= = = = = =	Unimproved Road
——(152)——	State Highway
=[157]=	Forest Road
——74——	Featured Trail
• • • • • • • • • • •	Secondary Trail
— — — — —	Wilderness Boundary
— — · — ·	Continental Divide
———————	River/Creek
— — · — · · —	Intermittent Stream
	Lake
+++++++++++	Railroad
•——•——•	Overhead Power Line

○	Trailhead
•—•	Gate
▲	Peak
⋀	Campsite
■	Building/Structure
○	Town/Settlement
○⌐	Spring
▨	Private Inholding
—27'30"	Lat/Long Marks
N	Compass
0 Kilometer 2 0 Mile 2	Scale

Overview Map

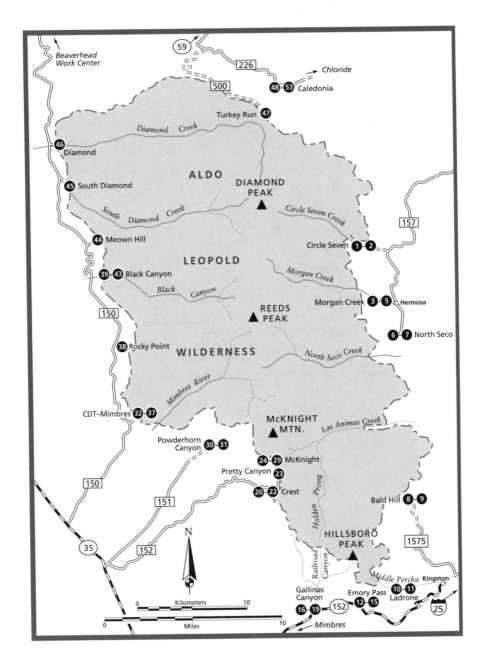

USGS Topographical
Map Index

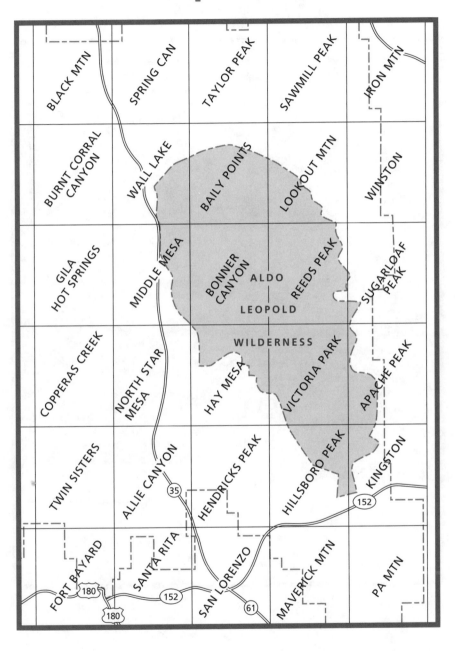

State Locator Map

Introduction

WILDERNESS AND ALDO LEOPOLD

While enjoying the wild majesty of the Aldo Leopold Wilderness, we couldn't help thinking about that remarkable visionary, Aldo Leopold. We wondered if he had axed the blaze on that tree up ahead, or set his tent next to the stream where we were camping. At times his spirit was so strong that we felt his presence at our evening campfire. We could not converse with him, although we longed to, but we hope that he listened approvingly while we talked about the values of the wild country he cared so much about. In his own quiet but persuasive way, Leopold was the driving force behind the notion that we should keep some places wild forever.

It was through the leadership of Aldo Leopold, Forest Service ranger, writer-philosopher, and the nation's pioneer professor of wildlife ecology, that the Forest Service set aside 755,000 acres in the headwaters of the Gila and Mimbres Rivers as the world's first wilderness area on June 3, 1924. This marked the first time that a large expanse of wildland was to be preserved in its natural state, and management was wonderfully simple: "Prohibit roads and hotels, and then leave it alone." In many respects, management hasn't changed all that much since then.

Later on, boundary deletions emphasized the need for the lasting legal protection of wilderness, which was not achieved until forty years later with passage of the 1964 Wilderness Act. Meanwhile, the Gila Wilderness boundary was reduced along its eastern, northern, and western edges in 1930. The following year, the Gila was needlessly bisected by construction of the North Star Mesa Road (Forest Road 150). Ironically, the purpose of the road was to give hunters access to harvest "excess" deer. To Leopold, the road and loss of wilderness added insult to injury, for already he recognized that overpopulation of deer was the result of overzealous predator control. Joining forces with Bob Marshall and other leading conservationists, Leopold cofounded The Wilderness Society, the nation's foremost wilderness conservation group, in 1935.

After being downgraded to a "primitive area" in 1933, additional reductions were made in the Gila in 1936 and 1938.

Upon passage of the landmark Wilderness Act in 1964, the Gila was among the first units in the new National Wilderness Preservation System. Legislation was enacted in 1980 that designated or expanded twelve national forest wildernesses in New Mexico, including an increase of the Gila Wilderness to its present 557,873 acres. Fittingly, the legislation also combined the Black Range Primitive Area just east of the North Star Mesa Road with part of Leopold's original Gila Wilderness, establishing the 202,016-acre Aldo Leopold Wilderness. No doubt, the unassuming professor would be embarrassed to learn that the Black Range portion of his beloved Gila country had been named for him. So, despite the unfortunate bisection of the

Gila country by a road, the wilderness has been restored to the original size envisioned by Aldo Leopold more than seventy-seven years ago.

Today, the 643 units in the National Wilderness Preservation System (NWPS) encompass nearly 106 million acres. New Mexico's share of this wild legacy consists of twenty-three units totaling more than 1.6 million acres. A full appreciation of the meaning and value of wilderness will enhance your enjoyment of the Aldo Leopold Wilderness while lessening your impact on the wildness of this special place.

Those of you who love wild country have your own heartfelt definition of wilderness, as Aldo Leopold did when he defined it as "a continuous stretch of country preserved in its natural state . . . big enough to absorb a two weeks' pack trip." But because Congress has the exclusive power to designate wilderness, it is important to understand the legal meaning of the word.

THE 1964 WILDERNESS ACT

The basic purpose of the Wilderness Act is to provide an enduring resource of wilderness for this and future generations so that a growing, increasingly mechanized population would not occupy and modify every last wild niche. Just as important as preserving the land is the preservation of natural processes that shape the land, such as naturally ignited fires. After suppressing fires for the past seventy years, the Forest Service has been restoring natural fire to the Aldo Leopold Wilderness, which will reduce the threat of catastrophic fire by reducing fuel buildup. Other benefits of natural fires include an increase in secondary ground cover for wildlife and improved moisture retention that will decrease flooding.

The Wilderness Act defines "wilderness" as undeveloped federal lands "where the earth and its community of life are untrammeled by man, where man is a visitor who does not remain." Or, to paraphrase Leopold, the Aldo Leopold Wilderness is meant to play in, not stay in. The word *trammel* means a "net" in Old English, so that "untrammeled" land is "unnetted," or uncontrolled by humans. Congress recognized that no land is completely free of human influence, going on to say that wilderness must "generally appear to have been affected primarily by the forces of nature, with the imprint of man's work substantially unnoticeable."

Further, designated wilderness must have outstanding opportunities for solitude or primitive and unconfined recreation, and must comprise at least 5,000 acres or be large enough to preserve in an unimpaired condition. Lastly, wilderness may contain ecological, geological, or other features of scientific, educational, scenic, or historical value. The moment you set foot in the Aldo Leopold Wilderness, you'll realize that this wild remnant of Leopold's southwest more than meets these criteria.

In general, wilderness designation protects the land from development: roads, buildings, motorized vehicle and equipment use, and most commercial uses. Four federal agencies are empowered to administer land in the NWPS: the National Park Service, the U.S. Fish and Wildlife Service, the Bureau of Land Management, and, in the case of the Aldo Leopold Wilderness, the U.S. Forest Service. These agencies can and do make wilderness recommendations, as any citizen can, but only Congress can set aside wilderness on federal lands. This is where politics enters in, as epitomized by the kind of grassroots democracy that brought about the restoration of much of the original Gila Wilderness in 1980 with the addition of the Aldo Leopold Wilderness. The formula for wilderness conservationists has been, and continues to be, "endless pressure endlessly applied."

Once an area has been designated wilderness, the unending job of wilderness stewardship is just beginning. The managing agencies have a special duty to administer wilderness areas in "such manner as will leave them unimpaired for future use and enjoyment as wilderness." In a speech marking the seventy-fifth anniversary of the Gila Wilderness as the first natural preserve of its kind, it was gratifying to hear Mike Dombeck, former Chief of the Forest Service, call for better management of wilderness areas. Leopold would have been especially pleased to hear Dombeck acknowledge the need for more ecosystems to be preserved as wilderness, from old-growth forests to grasslands to deserts.

Wilderness is the only truly biocentric use of land, a place where the needs of native flora and fauna take precedence over human desires. As such, preservation of wilderness is our society's highest act of humility. It is in places like the Aldo Leopold where we deliberately arrest our impulse to cut down the last great ponderosa pine forest or to dam the chasms of the Mimbres River forks. The explorer of this wilderness can take pride in reaching a remote summit under his or her own power, traversing a narrow serpentine canyon, or walking across the expanse of a high mesa. Hiking boots and self-reliance replace motorized convenience, allowing us to find something in ourselves we feared lost.

NATURAL HISTORY

If you hike several miles or more into the Aldo Leopold Wilderness, you can't help but experience a variety of forest types and landforms. The natural diversity in this vast untrammeled space is mind-boggling. While its 202,016-acre size might not mean much, think of a tract of land without roads or permanent human settlements that is nearly 19 miles square. This rugged, elevated landscape is a mixing zone between the southern end of the Rocky Mountains, the northern extension of the Sierra Madre Mountains from Mexico, and the Sonoran and Chihuahuan Deserts. From a sandy desert floor, the Black Range rises in a complex jumble of steep ridges and peaks separated by deep, narrow canyons. This narrow north-south range is nearly 100 miles long, and the wildest reaches of the range are encompassed by the wilderness boundary.

The Aldo Leopold Wilderness is deeply dissected by the spectacular canyons of Diamond Creek, South Diamond Creek, Black Canyon, Las Animas Creek, North Seco Creek, the Mimbres River, along with their major forks and dozens of twisting tributaries. These deep canyons run east and west from the main divide and crest of the Black Range. Some of this country, without trails or hikable terrain, is so rough, brushy, burnt, and remote that humans never visit it. The major landforms of the wilderness are the

Continental Divide, rising to 10,000 feet through the center to Reeds Peak and from there in a southwesterly direction, and the Black Range Crest that runs south from Reeds Peak to Emory Pass.

Some of the east-side hikes presented in this book begin in upper Sonoran Desert foothills vegetated with cholla, climbing thousands of feet to lush subalpine spruce-fir forests. Along the way, the routes pass by great spires and cliffs, dry pinyon-juniper woodlands, ponderosa parks, meadows, rincons, high mesas, and aspen parklands. Throughout these hikes, rock cliffs, box canyons, and talus slopes alternate with steep to rolling forest.

Sedimentary formations with fossils tell of a time when much of southwestern New Mexico was beneath warm seas. Then came a period of active volcanism about 65 million years ago. A second volcanic period probably took place here 30 to 20 million years ago. As a result, two monumental calderas formed, then collapsed. The resulting volcanic layers from the calderas are blanketed with a thick Gila conglomerate mix of mudstone, sandstone, and alluvial material. In the Black Range, a central core of Precambrian granite is overlain by sediments and covered with volcanics that are up to 3,000 feet thick. They are especially prevalent on the west slope. Meanwhile, flat-topped mesas continue to erode, while some of the mountains are still uplifting. Widespread faulting from earthquakes has produced today's impressive vertical relief.

The most distinctive features of the Aldo Leopold Wilderness include the pinnacles and spires of volcanic escarpments along major streams and rolling virgin ponderosa pine forests. These pine woodlands are by far the most predominant habitat type, and are found mostly in midelevation uplands above canyons, between 6,500 and 8,000 feet. A second major vegetative community includes spruce-fir forests above 9,000 feet, sprinkled with aspen, grassy parks, and wet meadows. Your wanderings through the Aldo will also take you across brushy south slopes, vast mesa grasslands, and woodlands dominated by oak, pinyon-juniper, or deciduous trees along streams. Wherever you hike in the wilderness, look carefully at the surrounding forest and think about how it got there. It is largely determined by exposure to the sun, elevation, available soil moisture, and the presence or absence of fire. Natural fire is especially important to the perpetuation of fire-dependent pine forests that make up most of the Aldo Leopold Wilderness.

Expect to see a blend of Englemann spruce, Douglas fir, and Southwestern white pine high in the Black Range. Midelevation uplands are the home of open pine parks, along with pinyon-juniper woodlands on south-facing hillsides. The greatest plant diversity exists along major fast-moving streams. A typical hardwood mix includes cottonwood, box elder, ash, mountain maple, aspen, and several kinds of willow. Imagine the flourish of colors in early October!

The fauna is correspondingly varied, with a wide variety of birds, mammals, reptiles, amphibians, and fish species. Several threatened and endangered species, such as the reintroduced Gila cutthroat trout and peregrine falcon, find refuge here. Many of the hikes traverse the home of elk, turkey, and blue grouse in the high country, and gila monsters and rattlesnakes in low canyon bottoms. Coyotes and javelinas are commonly seen. Black bears and mountain lions are more reclusive, but chances are they've seen you first from the security of a high rock ledge or dark thicket. Other native critters that you are more likely to see along the trail include foxes, skunks, raccoons, weasels, bobcats, and squirrels. The endangered Mexican wolf, recently reintroduced in the adjacent Gila Wilderness, may eventually regain its rightful place as a key component of the Black Range ecosystem. The presence or absence of wolves is a function of human tolerance, and if ever there was an appropriate place for respect and tolerance for wild nature, it is in Aldo Leopold's namesake wilderness.

So, as you explore the Aldo, think of it as a gigantic patchwork of virtually unlimited forest types, climatic conditions, and topography. As an alert hiker, you'll thrill to the discovery of something new around every bend in the canyon, ridge, or trail.

HUMAN HISTORY

The Black Range has been the scene of human activity for only a few centuries. Its steep slopes and rugged canyons made the area inhospitable for the Paleo-Indian groups that preferred the broad valleys of the nearby Gila. Later groups of Native Americans, most notably the Apache, hunted and fished in the region for centuries, but they left no permanent trace of their presence.

Much of the nineteenth century traffic in the area consisted of Army attempts to eradicate the Apache and their leaders, Victorio and Geronimo. The Apache were skilled at using the difficult terrain to their advantage. Names from this era remain in the wilderness today (Lookout Mountain, Apache Peak), as do the graves on Las Animas Creek below Massacre Canyon.

Miners came also, but found few riches. Evidence of their activities remain near the trails, where you might encounter pieces of equipment rusting in the underbrush.

Ranching remains a commercial activity in the region. According to the Wilderness Act, livestock grazing is permitted in the wilderness where it existed before designation. A few grazing allotments exist in the Aldo. Even if you don't come across cattle, you will frequently encounter corrals, windmills, and stock ponds, dating back eighty years or more. A few feral cattle are still running wild in several east-side canyons.

The wildness of the Aldo has worked in its favor to preserve it from encroachment by human activity. This is land that belongs to the wildlife!

HIKING IN THE ALDO LEOPOLD WILDERNESS

The Aldo Leopold Wilderness has steep rugged mountains, dense brush, deep canyons, broad mesas, and rushing mountain streams. The elevation ranges from below 6,000 feet in east-side canyons to 10,165 feet on McKnight Mountain. Water is a primary concern when planning a trip in this exciting country. There's often too much of it, but usually there's not enough.

Hikes along major stream corridors—the Mimbres and its forks, Diamond Creek, South Diamond, Black Canyon, and Las Animas Creek—involve many wet foot crossings. Flash flooding is a danger in the summer rainy season or during spring runoff if there's a good snowpack in the high country. Before embarking on any trip along main streams, check with the Forest Service office in Mimbres or Truth or Consequences for current and anticipated water levels.

You might be used to streams becoming larger downstream, gathering water from tributaries. This doesn't necessarily happen in the Aldo. During low-water periods, which is most of the time, water often disappears underground wherever the stream gradient levels off. In the deeply incised canyons of the Black Range, the steeper channels are higher up, so surface water is more apt to exist in the headwaters. The lower dry reaches of Diamond and South Diamond Creeks are classic examples of this phenomenon.

The scarcity of water seriously limits your itinerary away from the live streams. Don't be fooled by the springs and stock ponds that appear on Forest Service or USGS quad maps. Not all springs are reliable, and most stock ponds are too muddy and mucky for human use. Again, check with the local Forest Service district office for the status of springs you are counting on. They may have current reports from hikers or their trail crew.

Climate and Weather

The temperature and precipitation graphs show data from Gila Hot Springs, at a lower elevation and to the immediate west of the Aldo, but the information is generally useful for planning your trip to the Aldo.

On the Black Range Crest or the Continental Divide, it could be more than 15 degrees colder, especially at night. Regardless of elevation, nights are cool throughout the Aldo Leopold, even in the summer. The extremely hot weather that's common in surrounding deserts is rare in the Black Range. Temperatures tend to be more moderate. Up-to-the-minute weather reports can be found on the Internet at www.weather.com. Be advised that these lofty mountains create their own microclimate, so local forecasts for a nearby town may be irrelevant.

Average annual precipitation ranges from 12 inches in the lower east-side canyons and foothills to more than 20 inches along and near the crest of the Black Range. Storms from the Pacific typically bring heavy snowfall to the higher country from December through March.

Expect rain during July and August; nearly 3 inches of rain falls in each of those months. Flash flooding, lightning, and wildfires are also dangers during May and June. This summer "monsoon" is caused by a flow of moist air from the Gulf of Mexico, with short and sometimes intense afternoon or evening thunderstorms occurring almost daily.

Climatic Data: The temperatures shown are averages for Gila Hot Springs (Elevation 5,616'). Most of the areas you will travel through will probably be much higher in elevation and therefore cooler. Frost often occurs at higher elevations during the summer months. Always be prepared for the unexpected.

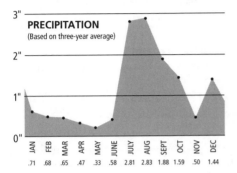

PRECIPITATION
(Based on three-year average)

JAN	FEB	MAR	APR	MAY	JUNE	JULY	AUG	SEPT	OCT	NOV	DEC
.71	.68	.65	.47	.33	.58	2.81	2.83	1.88	1.59	.50	1.44

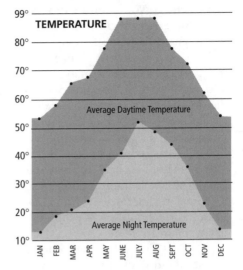

TEMPERATURE

Average Daytime Temperature

Average Night Temperature

September to early November is a delightful time of year in the Aldo, with lower precipitation, warm days and cool nights, and spectacular fall colors on the aspen slopes and along the cottonwood river corridors. Hunting season brings a lot of backcountry users. It is wise to wear hunter's orange when hiking during the fall hunting season. Make sure your pets are properly attired as well. You needn't worry about the spring turkey season in April. Turkey hunters in the Aldo wear camo, and because they make the extra effort to hike into the wilderness, they tend to be quiet and unobtrusive.

Winters are mild at lower elevations, often in the 50s and 60s during the day, but dropping below 20 degrees Fahrenheit at night. Snowstorms can temporarily stop travel on NM 15 from Silver City. The forest roads surrounding the wilderness are not open or maintained until late in the spring.

March through June is prime time for visiting the Aldo Leopold Wilderness. Nights are still cold, especially in the higher country, but the warmer days are excellent for hiking, without insects and without an influx of other hikers. However, spring runoff can make stream crossings more difficult. The Forest Service can provide you with information on river levels. Because springtime is relatively dry, it is also a time of critical fire weather. Summer rains in July bring relief to fire conditions, usually until late September. A fall fire season may then extend through November.

June and July have the highest visitation, with a second spike in use during the fall hunting season. The size of the densely forested wilderness, however, allows you to find ample solitude. Once you've hiked a good distance from the trailheads, you are likely to be totally alone, even during the busiest season.

Wilderness Management, or Management of Visitors

The Wilderness and Black Range Ranger Districts of the Gila National Forest manage the Aldo Leopold Wilderness. To its credit, the Forest Service has adopted a relaxed management policy in the Wilderness. For example, no permits or visitor registration are required, despite what it says on a few old outdated wooden signs that you might run across. For the most part, visitor management consists of random user contacts and educational information about Leave No Trace hiking and camping at trailhead kiosks. This low-key management style is certainly conducive to maintaining the spontaneity of the wilderness experience. It is therefore even more important for hikers and other visitors to help protect wilderness values in the Aldo, so that the wilderness and the freedom to enjoy it remain.

The Forest Service is developing a new trail maintenance schedule for the Aldo. The schedule will probably call for annual maintenance of the popular trails in Railroad Canyon, Emory Pass to Hillsboro Peak, and the Caledonia and CDT Trails to Diamond Peak. The rest of the CDT and Black Range Crest would likely be on a two-year schedule. The remaining trails would be maintained on a three- to five-year basis, but some of these would be stretched out to a seven- to ten-year interval. Even this modest schedule could slip because of the maintenance nightmare of dealing with trails that were originally built on windy ridges and flash flood canyon bottoms.

We spent a lot of time being lost in the Aldo so that you wouldn't be. We were often searching for ghost trails, obliterated by nature and kept that way through lack of maintenance. Some of these trails are intentionally neglected, especially in much of the southeast quarter of the Aldo, because of sensitive wildlife. A good example is the largely brushed-over Trail 117 from East Curtis Canyon to Hillsboro Peak. Others, such as the Flower Canyon portion of Trail 121, are so steep and rough that they have been all but formally abandoned. The basic agency philosophy is to replace and upgrade trails that cause resource damage, which is a large part of the trail system in the Aldo. At the present rate of replacement, based on reduced trail budgets, this will take about sixty years.

What does this mean to you, the hiker? The bottom line is that no one should enter the Aldo expecting a well-maintained trail system. It is far better to relax and slow the pace to fit the rugged terrain and trails. If you've come to the Aldo to be in a hurry, you've made a wrong turn. Vehicular access to trailheads is slow and rough. The trails are also slow and rough, and sometimes abandoned or, at best, neglected. Look at brush, downfall, rock slides, and occasional route-finding as part of a special wilderness experience that has been almost sanitized in our society. Access roads and trails reflect the rough nature of the land itself, and the Aldo gives us a rare chance to slow down our otherwise hectic pace.

Overview of Recreational Use

The Aldo Leopold Wilderness is accessed by twenty-six trailheads that serve several hundred miles of trails. As discussed, some of these trails have been abandoned; while others that haven't been maintained for years may as well be. Back in the early 1980s, visitor-use information was collected from every Gila Wilderness trailhead and some of the Aldo Leopold Wilderness trailheads. This practice has been discontinued, but some interesting visitor-use data were compiled in a 1985 study, Gila Wilderness Visitor Distribution and Use by Scott Steinberg. Some of the general trends and visitor-use data are applicable to the adjacent Aldo Leopold Wilderness.

According to the study, half of the day use originated from 8 percent of the trailheads, most of which were within 2 miles of the Gila Cliff Dwellings. For the Aldo, the same may be said for Emory Pass, which receives a disproportionately high percentage of visitation. In contrast, nearly half of the Gila trailheads showed less than one hundred visitor days per year, which is certainly true of some of the more remote, unsigned trailheads leading to the Aldo. The average group size was three people who stayed an average of three and a half days. The high season of May, June, and July attracted 51 percent of the visitors. In contrast, only 0.3 percent of the annual visitation took place in January. So solitude and snow seem to go together.

Aldo Leopold Logistics, or Front Country Essentials

The Aldo Leopold Wilderness is remote. The nearest cities with major airports are Albuquerque, New Mexico, about 200 miles to the northeast, and El Paso, Texas, about 150 miles to the southeast. There are no cities in the immediate vicinity. Fifty miles east of the Aldo, Truth or Consequences, New Mexico, called Hot Springs until 1950, has a population of 7,000 and a variety of small shops and services, as well as the Black Range District Office of the Gila National Forest. Other towns that are named on the map—Chloride, Winston, and Kingston—flourished in the 1880s silver boom; each has since dwindled to a cluster of homes. Of the three, only Winston has a commercial establishment: a small general store.

The quad maps reveal the plethora of mines and mining claims in the canyons and gulches radiating from these former centers of gold, copper, and silver mining. Hermosa (1884–1929) has vanished completely after evolving from a mining hub to a ranching town. On the southwest of the Aldo, the tiny scattered town of Mimbres has a cafe, a post office, and a small general store with a single gas pump; it is also the location of the Wilderness District Office of the Gila National Forest.

So come prepared. There is little in the way of restocking opportunities around the Aldo. Although the Forest Service offices have the Gila National Forest map and the Aldo Wilderness map for sale, neither office sells USGS quad maps or guidebooks; buy these in advance.

Streams and springs can't be counted on year-round, or even in the spring, for water. The trailheads are dry too, so carry plenty of water in your vehicle. Hospitable merchants in Mimbres, Winston, and Truth or Consequences will let you fill up, but between these towns there are no spigots.

You can buy showers in Mimbres or in Truth or Consequences. For gas, your choices are pretty limited. Both Winston and Mimbres have one-pump gas at tiny general stores, offering regular unleaded and diesel. Only Truth or Consequences has a choice of grades as well as a variety of brands.

The former town site of Hermosa on the east-central edge of the wilderness.

Truth or Consequences and its nearby neighbor to the north, Elephant Butte, have a wide variety of motel accommodations, ranging from those around the historic hot springs in downtown Truth or Consequences to modern chains. Closer to the Aldo, camping is your only option. The official campsites around the Aldo are all no-fee undeveloped camps. Some have pit toilets and maybe a picnic table or two, but none has water, unless the nearby creek is flowing.

On the Forest Service Aldo Leopold Wilderness map, the tepee symbol represents a recreation site, and does not distinguish between a picnic area and a campground. On the eastern side of the Aldo, there are no official campgrounds, but camping is possible at all the trailheads. On the southern perimeter, primitive campgrounds are located at Iron Creek, south of NM 152, about 3 miles west of Emory Pass, and at Gallinas Canyon, 4 miles west of the pass. On Forest Road 150, on the western side of the wilderness, Rocky Canyon and Black Canyon are official but somewhat primitive campgrounds, with pit toilets and picnic tables. Most of the trailheads also are suitable for a quick overnight stay before your outing. To the north, Monument Park is a pleasant location for camping, with its ponderosa pine park and pit toilet.

Safety and Preparedness
Statistically, your backcountry outing is safer than your drive to and from the trailhead. There are, however, hazards you need to be aware of in the Aldo Leopold Wilderness. If you are prepared, you will be much safer.

Water. The biggest challenge to the hiker in the Aldo is water. When the streams are running in the spring, or after heavy summer rains, water is available in many of the drainages. All natural water in the wilderness should, of course, be treated by pumping or boiling, or with iodine tablets. The springs indicated on the maps cannot be counted on to be running, so you will always need a fall-back plan if the spring is dry. When in doubt, carry plenty of water with you and always have plenty in your car. The Aldo is a very dry wilderness.

Stream crossings. Before embarking on any trip along the Aldo's main streams, check with the Forest Service for water levels. Sturdy wading footwear is necessary for backpacking along the Mimbres River, the Forks of the Mimbres, Holden Prong, and Las Animas Creek. A sturdy walking stick is also handy for stability.

Hypothermia. Even in moderate temperatures, hypothermia is a danger. It results from a combination of exhaustion, moisture, and wind, which cool the body faster than it can replace the lost heat. These conditions can occur after a spill in a stream or on a mountain ridge in a summer storm. Symptoms include shivering, slurred speech, lack of coordination, drowsiness, and poor judgment. Keep an eye on your companions when hypothermic conditions exist; the victim will be unaware of his own situation, denying that there's a problem. The solution is immediate warmth. Get the hypothermic hiker out of wet clothes and into warm and dry clothing or a sleeping bag. Seek shelter and administer warm drinks and food.

Heat-related illness. Protect yourself from sun and heat with proper clothing. Avoid exertion during the hottest part of the day, especially if you are not yet acclimated to the heat. Seek shade. Drink plenty of water, both before and during your outing. Avoid alcoholic beverages when exercising in hot weather.

Wildfire. Fires are frequent in the Aldo Leopold Wilderness. If naturally ignited by lightning, wilderness fires are usually allowed to burn unless they threaten structures or are growing too huge. If you encounter a fire, stay upwind from the blaze. In mountainous terrain, fires tend to run uphill, so stay below a fire, out of its path. If a trailhead is closed by fire, which is sometimes the case in August, find an alternate route.

Lightning. Especially during summer months, lightning is a very real hazard in the Black Range. Stay off ridges and peaks when storms threaten. Seek shelter in dense woods, a grove of young trees, or a deep valley or canyon. Avoid large or lone trees. If caught in the open, discard any metal products, such as your backpack, stay away from fences, and sit or lie down separately.

Mountain lions. The Black Range is outstanding habitat for mountain lions. This is their home and you are only visitors. Avoid hiking at night when lions are often hunting. Instruct your children to stay calm when confronted with a lion: Do not run. As a precaution, keep your children in sight.

Rattlesnakes. The Aldo is home to several species of rattlers, which may be out as early as April and as late as October. They are most active in the hot summer months. Do not sit or put your hands anywhere before looking. Use a walking stick to prod a trail covered with leaves or vegetation.

11

Snakes are terrified of humans and will usually flee if you warn them of your approach. If you get bitten, seek help as quickly as possible. Use a venom extractor kit only when you are far from medical assistance.

Hantavirus. Deer mice are carriers of this deadly disease. The virus is transmitted by inhaling the dust of mouse urine and droppings. Don't stir up dust in areas where rodent droppings exist, such as in old cabins.

Zero Impact

The Aldo Leopold Wilderness is beautiful and primeval. Human visitors need to keep it that way. Travel lightly, leaving only footprints in your path.

Plan ahead. Have the appropriate maps, food, and equipment. Desperate hikers are usually not concerned with protecting natural resources. If possible, avoid high-use areas and peak seasons. Keep your group small and your pack light. Overburdened hikers are less considerate about what they leave behind.

Prepare. Repackage food to reduce your trash load. You will be carrying out what you don't consume, along with all the packaging material.

Toileting. Carry a trowel to bury human waste 6 to 8 inches deep. Toileting must be done 200 feet away from any body of water. If you are traveling in a canyon, try to get above the floodplain for your communion with nature. Pack out your used toilet paper and feminine hygiene products in resealable bags. Burning toilet paper is discouraged in the Aldo due to fire danger.

Tread lightly. Stay on existing trails whenever possible, and avoid cutting switchbacks. There are grazing allotments in the Aldo, so don't be startled if you encounter cattle, and be sure to leave all gates as you find them after you pass through.

Camp lightly. If possible, stay at an established campsite. Don't leave any traces of your stay on your site: no initials on trees, no cut or broken limbs, no trenches around tents, no debris. Do not attempt to burn your garbage; you'll just leave scorched trash tidbits behind.

Campfires. Open campfires are sometimes prohibited in the Aldo due to fire danger. Notices will be posted at trailheads if there is a fire restriction in effect. Use gas stoves to reduce impact on the campsite. If you have a campfire, keep it small. Use only small, already downed branches. Do not cut down trees, even dead ones. Never leave a fire untended, as the pesky Black Range winds surge to life in the afternoon. When you leave camp, douse your fire thoroughly and spread the dead embers. Finally, cover the cold embers with earth and naturalize the site. Remove any rock ring construction.

Protect the water. Water is a precious commodity for both humans and wildlife. Treat it accordingly. Never bathe or wash dishes directly in a water source. Move at least 100 feet away from springs and streams to do your washing. Food scraps and even biodegradable soaps pollute streams. Never throw garbage in streams.

Food. Carry all food and garbage out with you. Skunks, raccoons, and bears will dig up buried trash and learn to associate food with campsites, not a pleasant experience for later parties. Hang your food at night and whenever you are away from camp—10 feet off the ground and 4 feet away from the tree trunk. Always keep a clean camp.

Wildlife. Do not disturb or harass wildlife. If you hike with your dog, keep it under control at all times.

Pack out trash. If you packed it in, pack it out! All of it: cigarette butts, pop bottles, chewing gum, dental floss, fishing line, beer cans, candy and gum wrappers. Don't be a slob hiker.

Artifacts. Leave all historic and prehistoric artifacts in place. The federal Antiquities Act prohibits removal from federal land of any item more than 50 years old. Common courtesy also requires you to leave these treasures so your successors can enjoy the thrill of discovering them.

The bottom line is to make your passage through wild country wholly invisible to future hikers. Savor the beauty of the Aldo, and leave it for others to enjoy. Wildness is a precious resource, in short supply, that will endure only with your stewardship. Honor the memory of Leopold.

HOW TO USE THIS GUIDEBOOK

The vast Aldo Leopold Wilderness is a 202,016-acre wonderland of canyons, stream valleys, mesas, long ridges, and lofty peaks. Potential hikes are virtually unlimited, but we have put together trips in this book that are surely among the best. The descriptions of the fifty-three hikes presented in this guide will prepare you for your exploration of the Aldo. Following is some additional information to help you get the most out of this book.

All of the hikes presented here are complete, self-contained trips with essential information needed for the suggested route. Every hike begins and ends at one of nineteen national forest trailheads that can be driven to. The hikes are numbered in sequence, starting from the Circle Seven Trailhead and going clockwise around the Aldo Leopold Wilderness, ending at the Caledonia Trailhead. If you're basing your hikes from a single trailhead, this book offers several good trip ideas for you to choose from or to combine in various ways as options.

From a geographic standpoint, the Aldo Leopold Wilderness may be logically viewed as having two major components separated by the unbroken backbone of the Great Divide. Thirty-three miles of the Continental Divide National Scenic Trail (CDT) wind through the remote heart of the wilderness. Hikes 1 through 32 originate east of the Continental Divide; hikes 33 through 53 begin on or west of the divide.

You'll find in the following pages many, but not all, of the best hikes in the Aldo Leopold Wilderness. We wanted to save a few for you to find, although, every hike in this book will present unforeseen wilderness discoveries.

Types of Hikes
There are three basic types of hikes:

Out-and-back. These hikes travel to a specific destination or into a general region, then retrace the route back to the same trailhead.

Loop. In general, loop trips explore new country throughout all or most of the route by starting from and then circling back to the trailhead. All but one of the loops are "lollipops." A few of the hikes end with a short walk on a road to get back to the trailhead. This type of hike may also have a base camp at one location for a long day-hike loop.

Shuttle. A point-to-point hike that begins from one trailhead and ends at another requires shuttling a vehicle to the exit trailhead, having two vehicles (one left at the other end of the hike), or prearranging a pickup at a designated time and place. Logistics can sometimes be simplified with a midtrip key exchange between two groups starting at different trailheads. When the trip is completed, the two parties drive each other's vehicles home. The driving distance between trailheads is included for shuttle hikes.

Distances
Distances in the Aldo Leopold Wilderness tend to be underestimated on Forest Service trail signs, but this is not always the case. We used Forest Service distance estimates whenever we determined that they were accurate. In all cases, the total distance and key point mileage are our best field estimates based on timing a predetermined pace. Distances are often less important than difficulty.

Difficulty Ratings
To help you select and plan your trip, the difficulty of hikes is rated. By necessity, these ratings are subjective and are only a general guide. The variables that determine actual difficulty at a given time on the ground are numerous and, well, variable. Here are some general definitions.

Easy. Anyone in reasonable condition can do easy hikes given enough time. These hikes generally have gentle grades, but there may be short rocky sections and a few shallow stream crossings.

Moderate. These hikes are challenging to inexperienced wilderness travelers. The hike may have several stream crossings, steep pitches, and short sections where the trail is hard to follow. These hikes are suitable for hikers who have some experience and at least an average fitness level.

Strenuous. These hikes are suitable for experienced hikers with above-average fitness. Frequent river crossings and unmaintained trails are likely, along with steep grades, loose rock, and lots of elevation gain and loss. Some parts of the hike may be hard to follow, requiring route finding with a USGS quad map and compass.

Best Months

The "best" time for a particular hike, from the standpoint of comfortable hiking conditions, is as variable as Black Range weather. Typically, the beginning and ending months are marginal transition periods in terms of weather. Be sure to check local conditions prior to your trip.

Maps

Please keep in mind that the maps in this book are general schematics designed to get you to the trailhead and give you a good visual impression of the route. You need to take along more detailed maps for the actual hike, as indicated in the map information block. See Appendix A for more information.

Special Considerations

These are "red flags" that could be troublesome, but are not necessarily hazardous. The information presented is important to consider before embarking on the hike.

Key Points

Trail junctions or key natural features that will confirm your location and serve as an indicator of your progress during the hike are listed. Continue straight to the next key point unless a turn is indicated.

Elevation Profiles

Elevation profile graphs are provided for each hike. The graphs approximate the vertical ups and downs in relation to the distance between key points. They show major elevation changes along the route. Because of scale limitations, small changes, especially those less than 200 feet, might not be shown on the graphs. In general, the only elevation information presented for a given hike is that contained in the profile.

Hike Finder

	EASY	MODERATE	STRENUOUS
Short day hikes, up to 7 miles total distance	16 Lower Gallinas Canyon 45 South Diamond Creek 46 Diamond Creek	1 Circle Seven Creek 3 Morgan Creek 22 Sids Prong Saddle 25 McKnight Mountain 30 South Fork Powderhorn Canyon 32 Signboard Saddle	8 Cave Canyon
Long day hikes or two-day backpacks, more than 7 miles total distance		4 Morgan–North Seco Creek 7 North Seco–Morgan Creek 21 Crest–Gallinas Canyon 26 Mimbres Lake 33 Lower Mimbres River 39 Black Canyon 48 Upper Caledonia Trail	2 Circle Seven–Diamond Peak 3 Morgan Creek 6 North Seco Box 9 Las Animas Creek 10 Ladrone–Hillsboro Peak 11 Ladrone–Gallinas 12 Hillsboro Peak 13 Emory Pass–Gallinas Canyon 17 Railroad and East Railroad Canyons 18 Gallinas and Railroad Canyons 20 Crest–Emory Pass 23 Pretty Canyon–Crest Trail 24 Flower and Water Canyons 31 Powderhorn–McKnight Mountain 34 Mimbres River Forks 38 Rocky Point 44 Meown Hill 47 CDT–Diamond Creek

	EASY	MODERATE	STRENUOUS
Long backpacks, three-day trips and longer		40 Black Canyon Box	5 Spud Patch–North Seco Creek
			14 Emory Pass–Holden Prong
			15 Emory Pass–Prongs
			19 Sids and Holden Prongs
			24 Flower and Water Canyons
			27 McKnight–Mimbres
			28 McKnight–Mimbres Forks
			29 McKnight–North Seco
			35 Mimbres–Black Range Crest
			36 Mimbres–CDT
			37 CDT–Black Canyon
			41 Black Canyon–CDT
			42 Black Canyon–Mimbres
			43 Black and Morgan Canyons
			49 Diamond Peak
			50 Diamond Peak–Diamond Creek
			51 Diamond Peak–South Diamond
			52 CDT
			53 Caledonia–Emory Pass

Circle Seven Trailhead

"By 'wilderness' I mean a continuous stretch
of country preserved in its natural state,
open to lawful hunting and fishing,
big enough to absorb a two weeks' pack trip,
and kept devoid of roads, artificial trails, cottages,
or other works of man."

—Aldo Leopold, *Journal of Forestry*, 1921

1 Circle Seven Creek

Highlights: Riparian forest and meadows; seasonal stream
Type of hike: Out-and-back day hike
Total distance: 7.2 miles round-trip
Difficulty: Moderate
Best months: March through October
Maps: Forest Service Aldo Leopold Wilderness Map; Reeds Peak USGS quad
Special considerations: Expect wet foot stream crossings in the spring.

Finding the trailhead: From Interstate 25, 5 miles north of Truth or Consequences, New Mexico, take NM 52 west 31 miles to Winston. Turn left (south) at Winston through the tiny town toward Chloride. A half mile beyond Winston, turn left (south) on the signed road to the St. Cloud Mine, Forest Road 157. This road is graded gravel. Continue southwest for 5 miles. Here the wide, graded county-maintained road continues west to the St. Cloud Mine, and a narrow rough road on the left is signed FR 157. Turn left (south) on FR 157.

Following the contour of the land, FR 157 is rough when it follows canyons or drainages; when on the mesas its quality improves. Travel on FR 157 is slow, averaging about 10 miles an hour. Drive south on FR 157 another 12 miles to the Circle Seven Creek road (FR 730) on the right (west). A windmill, a tank, and a forest trail sign are at the junction. Turn right (west) on FR 730. Drive west on the high-center ungraded rough road, which frequently crosses the creek. At 2 miles there is a small sloping meadow that allows for vehicle parking and turning. The road is impassable beyond this spot (elevation 6,600 feet). To avoid the final 0.5 mile on the rough road with steeply pitched stream crossings, you can also park where there are flat campsites and old fire rings before the canyon narrows, and commence your hike from there.

Parking and trailhead facilities: Parking and limited campsites can be found in the sloping meadow. There is no reliable water.

Circle Seven Creek

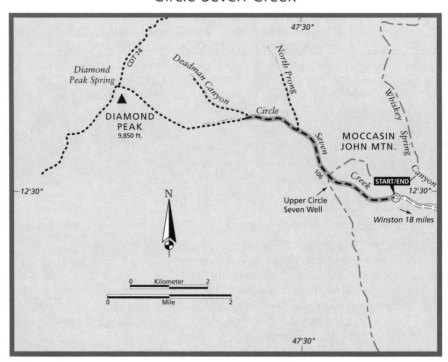

Key points:

- 0.0 Trail begins at stream crossing, on old road.
- 0.2 Old roadbed becomes more of a trail.
- 0.5 Dike gateway to broad valley.
- 1.2 Upper Circle Seven Well and wilderness boundary.
- 2.6 Mouth of North Prong.
- 3.6 Mouth of Deadman Canyon

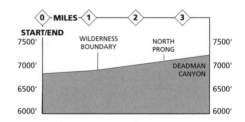

The hike: The unsigned trailhead for Circle Seven Creek is clearly marked by Mother Nature instead of the Forest Service. There are no trail signs, but an immense sandstone fin protrudes from Moccasin John Mountain north of the trailhead, rising 600 feet above the valley floor. Start your day hike to Deadman Canyon by following the old road across the stream. The crossings are about ankle deep even in a year with average snowpack, so wear suitable footgear.

As Trail 106 winds up the canyon, sometimes it's a footpath and sometimes it's an old roadway. There's a dense riparian mix of willow, cottonwood, and gambel oak, as well as ponderosa pine and juniper. Fallen trees periodically force you to make additional stream crossings to bypass the jumble. This is a rustic trail that requires some initiative. Lots of wildlife sign—elk, coyote, bear, turkey, cat—is evidence of light human use.

At 0.5 mile, the path and stream cut through a narrow dike, and you enter a broader valley. Fire-scarred ponderosa pines tower over the meadow. A pair of huge old alligator junipers bracket the trail, and the dramatic spires of Moccasin John Mountain continue to punctuate the northern skyline. At 1.0 mile, burned slopes above the creek bottom are a reminder of the significance of fire in molding the ecosystem. When the canyon opens wider, the increasing blowdown also illustrates the power of wind, especially when the canyon funnels its force into this narrow alley.

At 1.2 mile, you arrive in a meadow at Upper Circle Seven Well, as indicated on the topo map, with its windmill, tank, and ancient corral. The wilderness boundary is marked with a subtle sign on a stump as the trail goes through the old corral gate. For the next 1.4 miles, ancient blazes on fire-scarred trunks are your guide as the trail weaves back and forth across the creek, or up and over low ridges, never straying far from the streambed. The narrow earthen trail has a pleasant cushion of pine needles and oak litter. Intermittent meadows up to North Prong provide campsite options if you're planning on an extended stay.

At 2.6 miles, at the mouth of North Prong, the main trail takes a hairpin turn to the left (south), while a light use trail goes on up North Prong. Unless you're exploring North Prong as an option, stay on the main trail, which is marked with fresh blazes.

The next 0.5 mile above North Prong is a series of grassy benches with a gentle trail gradient, winding through clumps of gambel oak and ponderosa pine, which all carry the scars of fire. For the next 0.5 mile to the mouth of Deadman Canyon, the canyon narrows, stream crossings become even more frequent, and the trail all but disappears in places. At one such place, several rock cairns and a single tree blaze lead to a more distinct needle-covered trail. Evidence of past lightning fires is frequent. This stretch of trail passes by several dry gulches before reaching Deadman Canyon, which usually has a small stream in the spring. Deadman is guarded by two cone-shaped mountains, rising to 1,600 feet above the streambed.

When you have finished your explorations of lower Circle Seven Creek, return to the trailhead by the same route.

Options: One possibility is to explore North Prong Canyon. The slopes of this canyon are very rugged, but there is a use trail in the bottom that goes for about 0.5 mile. The crusty rock formations of the canyon walls are spectacular.

Another option is to hike about a mile up Deadman Canyon, to where it dramatically narrows between great walls that descend from the two dominant peaks. The lower benches of Deadman are graced with ponderosa pine parks, and they're open enough for easy going. Elk rubs and tracks are abundant, as are turkey tracks. The quiet of the secluded canyon provides an intense feeling of remoteness.

Rock spires above the North Prong of Circle Seven Creek.

2 Circle Seven–Diamond Peak

Highlights:	Riparian forest and meadows, seasonal stream, rugged canyon, along with spectacular vistas of cliff formations and the Continental Divide
Type of hike:	Out-and-back day hike or overnighter
Total distance:	14 miles round-trip
Difficulty:	Strenuous
Best months:	Late April through October
Maps:	Forest Service Aldo Leopold Wilderness Map; Reeds Peak USGS quad
Special considerations:	Expect wet foot stream crossings in the spring. The upper portion of the trail is dry and extremely steep, brushy and hard to find in places.

Finding the trailhead: From Interstate 25, 5 miles north of Truth or Consequences, New Mexico, take NM 52 west 31 miles to Winston. Turn left (south) at Winston through the tiny town toward Chloride. A half mile beyond Winston, turn left (south) on the signed road to the St. Cloud Mine, Forest Road 157. This road is graded gravel. Continue southwest for 5 miles. Here the wide, graded county-maintained road continues west to the St. Cloud Mine, and a narrow rough road on the left is signed FR 157. Turn left (south) on FR 157.

Following the contour of the land, FR 157 is rough when it follows canyons or drainages; when on the mesas its quality improves. Travel on FR 157 is slow, averaging about 10 miles an hour. Drive south on FR 157 another 12 miles to the Circle Seven Creek road (FR 730) on the right (west). A windmill, a tank, and a forest trail sign are at the junction. Turn right (west) on FR 730, a high-center ungraded rough road, that frequently crosses the creek. At 2 miles there is a small sloping meadow that allows for vehicle parking and turning. The road is impassable beyond this spot (elevation 6,600 feet). To avoid the final 0.5 mile on the rough road with steeply pitched stream crossings, park where there are flat campsites and old fire rings before the canyon narrows, and commence your hike from there.

Parking and trailhead facilities: Parking and limited campsites can be found in the sloping meadow. There is no reliable water.

Key points:
0.0	Trail begins at stream crossing, on old road.
0.2	Old roadbed becomes more of a trail.
0.5	Dike gateway to broad valley.
1.2	Upper Circle Seven Well and wilderness boundary.
2.6	Mouth of North Prong.
3.6	Mouth of Deadman Canyon.
4.9	Trail climbs out of canyon on north side.

Circle Seven–Diamond Peak

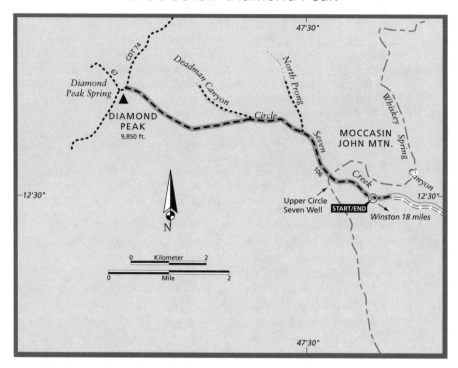

6.5 Signed junction of Circle Seven Trail 106 and CDT Trail 74.
6.7 Diamond Peak sign, fence, and spring.
7.0 Diamond Peak.

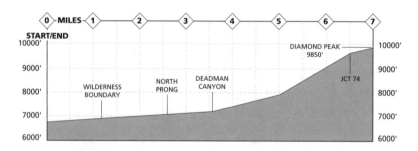

The hike: The 7-mile up-and-down route along the CDT from the north (see Hike 49) might be an easier way to reach Diamond Peak, but if you hike up Circle Seven Creek instead, you won't lose any of your hard-earned elevation until you're ready to head back down from the peak.

From the trailhead travel upstream. The trail becomes faint at times but never leaves the canyon. Watch for blazes and cairns along the way. At 2.6 miles you reach the mouth of North Prong on your right; here the main Circle Seven Trail bends in a hairpin turn to the left (south). In another 0.5 mile

Cliffs rise high above Circle Seven Canyon 1 mile below the wilderness boundary.

you reach Deadman Canyon, also on the right. See Hike 1 for details on this section of the hike.

Continue up the left (south) branch of Circle Seven on the main trail. The rocky trail stays in or close to the streambed for more than a mile before climbing out of the drainage on the north side. The steep, brushy trail gains an average of 1,000 feet per mile and is blocked by frequent downfall in its upper reaches. Despite lack of maintenance, the trail is usually easy to follow. After crossing an opening in a stock fence at 6.5 miles, the trail meets the Continental Divide National Scenic Trail (CDT) on the narrow crest.

From the divide, continue on the CDT to the left and uphill, where more blowdown from the fire might be encountered. At 6.7 miles the trail reaches a fence and a sign for the Diamond Creek Trail to the right. Despite the sign, the upper end of Diamond Creek Trail 40 no longer exists. The unsigned Trail 67 does head right (northwest) from just below the spring.

Diamond Spring sits just above the sign to the left of the trail. The spring is a shallow 4-foot-wide pool fed slowly by seepage from above. The tiny spring is a reliable water source early in the season, but would be questionable by early summer. The Forest Service trail crew wisely stockpiles jugs of water along the trail. As the CDT climbs above the spring, it passes along the lower edge of a large, grassy alpine meadow. The meadow slopes toward the spring and is ringed by aspen and a mix of both dead and live Douglas fir. Only 0.3 mile northwest of Diamond Peak, this high meadow is campable, especially if the spring is flowing.

The 9,850-foot peak is reached at 7.0 miles. This northern sentinel of the Aldo presents commanding views in every direction. The narrow ridge-top summit is encircled by locust and a few pine and fir trees, but opens enough for panoramas south to Hillsboro Peak and eastward all the way down Circle Seven Creek. Almost all of the Aldo can be seen from this prominent peak. Especially impressive is the extent of burnt forest across a maze of rough-hewn canyons all the way to Hillsboro Peak. The CDT climbs just west of the Diamond Peak summit to a CDT trail sign pointing south to Reeds Peak (9 miles).

When you've completed your climb of Diamond Peak, drop back down Circle Seven Creek for the steep return to the trailhead far below in the lower canyon.

Options: One possibility is to explore North Prong Canyon. The slopes of this canyon are very rugged, but there is a use trail in the bottom that goes for about 0.5 mile. The crusty rock formations of the canyon walls are spectacular.

Another side hike is up Deadman Canyon about a mile, to where the canyon dramatically narrows between great walls that descend from the two dominant peaks. The lower benches of Deadman are graced with ponderosa pine parks, and they're open enough for easy going. Elk rubs and tracks are abundant, as are turkey tracks. The quiet of the canyon provides an intense feeling of remoteness.

Morgan Creek Trailhead

*"It will be much easier to keep wilderness
areas than to create them."*

—Aldo Leopold, *Journal of Forestry,* 1921

3 Morgan Creek

Highlights:	Stream, riparian woodland, views of rugged mountainsides, historical artifacts
Type of hike:	Out-and-back day hike or short backpack
Total distance:	5.6 miles or 10 miles round-trip
Difficulty:	Moderate (5.6 miles) or strenuous (10 miles)
Best months:	March to November
Maps:	Forest Service Aldo Leopold Wilderness Map; Reeds Peak and Sugarloaf Peak USGS quads
Special considerations:	There are frequent stream crossings. Some route finding is necessary on the longer trip.

Finding the trailhead: From Interstate 25, 5 miles north of Truth or Consequences, New Mexico, take NM 52 west 31 miles to Winston. Turn left (south) at Winston through the tiny town toward Chloride. A half mile beyond Winston, turn left (south) on the signed road to the St. Cloud Mine, Forest Road 157. This road is graded gravel. Continue southwest for 5 miles. Here the wide, graded county-maintained road continues west to the St. Cloud Mine, and a narrow rough road on the left is signed FR 157. Turn left (south) on FR 157.

Following the contour of the land, FR 157 is rough when it follows canyons or drainages; when on the mesas its quality improves. Travel on FR 157 is slow, averaging about 10 miles an hour. Drive south on FR 157 for another 17 miles. In the middle of a broad valley, some remnant buildings of the defunct town of Hermosa stand on the hillside in front of you. A sign stating PRIVATE PROPERTY. PLEASE STAY ON ROADWAY also indicates this is a private inholding, further reinforced with a steel cable and I-beam post barricade indicating the boundary.

Located obscurely about 50 yards east of FR 157 is a tiny sign for FR 732. The main road, FR 157, continues south through the former Hermosa. Turn right (northeast) on FR 732, following Morgan Creek up the great bowl valley. The newly constructed trailhead is 0.5 mile west of Hermosa in a large flat area beneath towering cottonwoods and ponderosa pines. This short section of road is softer and kinder than FR 157 is. There is one shallow ford across Morgan Creek just before the trailhead, which is on the left, marked with a big kiosk.

Parking and trailhead facilities: There is a kiosk at the trailhead, along with flat campsites. There's no reliable water, although a murky spring can be found against the hillside just southeast of the campsite.

Morgan Creek

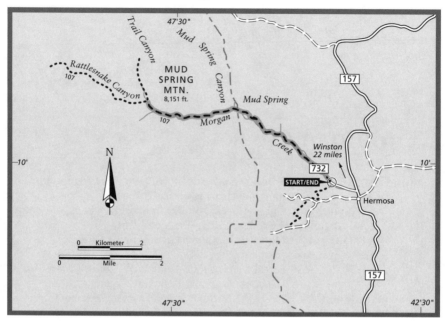

Key points:

0.0 Begin hike on road.
0.3 Stream crossings begin.
1.0 Valley narrows.
1.7 Trail follows streambed.
2.3 Trail in dry streambed.
2.8 Mud Spring, corral, wilderness boundary; turnaround point for shorter hike.
5.0 Corral; mouth of Rattlesnake Canyon.

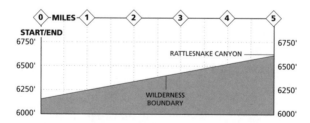

The hike: From the new trailhead, start your outing by hiking west on the old roadway. Immediately you'll have a muddy crossing where the old road has cut deep ruts, but it's not until 0.3 mile that wet foot crossings begin to be frequent. The old jeep road goes up the wide valley floor west of Hermosa, now the home of elk and turkey instead of cattle. At 1.0 mile the valley narrows as the sheer cliffs close in from the north. Groves of cottonwood and juniper increase on the trip upstream. The crossings are usually no more than ankle deep in the spring, but the creek is too wide to jump, so wear appropriate footgear.

At times the trail and the streambed are the same. This is no surprise: This used to be an extension of FR 732, and the cobblestones of Morgan Creek made a dandy roadbed. They make for a lumpy trail, but fortunately most of the route stays on earth, further softened with pine needles and oak debris.

The rugged cliffs of Mud Spring Mountain (8,151 feet) rise directly ahead when you emerge from the narrow valley and reach the first corral. Here, at the old corral gate, is the wilderness boundary, marked with a small metal sign. This is the turnaround spot for the 5.6-mile out-and-back hike.

Before you retrace your steps to the trailhead, you might explore the mouth of Mud Spring Canyon, just north of the corral, and try to locate the old spring along the east canyon wall. Odd pieces of old plumbing will help lead you to the appropriately named spring.

For the longer hike, follow the path through the corral and turn left (south) along the fence to cross the creek. On the opposite bank, the faint path resumes, going between two towering ponderosa pines. This lightly used trail beyond the wilderness boundary is often hard to locate. Although the terrain is not difficult, the 10-mile outing requires more alertness and route finding and thus is rated strenuous for its cerebral requirements.

The footpath winds upstream, sometimes through springs and seeps. The sharp rock face of Mud Spring Mountain provides a contrast to the soft greenery of the riparian woodland where the trail wanders. In addition to the natural wonders, you'll encounter the remains of a mining enterprise: The welded body of a boiler is embedded in a seepy area next to the trail at 4.5 miles. How on earth did it get here? This huge iron artifact seems so incongruous in the remote valley.

At 5.0 miles, you will reach the corral at the mouth of Rattlesnake Canyon. There are many campsites along Morgan Creek. Taking two days for this outing will give you time to explore the lightly used canyons at the head of Morgan Creek (see Options). Otherwise, this upper corral is the turnaround spot for the longer day hike. Retrace your pathway to the trailhead.

Options: Rattlesnake Canyon is a seldom used route to the Continental Divide, the top of which is burned out and hard to find. The V-shaped canyon at the lower end leaves no room for a trail, so the faint path zigzags through the ravine as it climbs. Frequent blowdown obstructs the trail, and pesky shrubs armed with prickers are constant companions. It's easy to see why even the Forest Service has avoided this one! But you are assured of solitude, except for wildlife, and the views of the surrounding ridges are breathtaking. It would be a brutal bushwhack to get to the divide by this route, so an out-and-back day hike should satiate your curiosity.

Another option is to continue up Morgan Canyon beyond the corral on an old faint trail used mostly by elk and other wildlife. The canyon is rough-hewn and rocky, with side slopes that angle immediately upward. About 0.8 mile above the corral, Trail Canyon comes in from the north. It appears to be misnamed. Although there's a faint trail in the bottom at the lower end,

Majestic volcanic rock cliffs overlook Morgan Creek Canyon.

it quickly disappears in the narrow rocky ravine. Save for a few stagnant pools, the canyon is dry even in a good rain year. Above Trail Canyon, Morgan Canyon narrows to a natural wind tunnel with wind-snapped tree trunks strewn about. A trail is reasonably distinct in places, but about 0.5 mile beyond Trail Canyon it becomes too brushy to use. At that point, sidehill up the left side of Morgan Creek for magnificent views of this rugged country. Abundant bear scat in this area demonstrates how remote it is.

4 Morgan–North Seco Creeks

Highlights:	Perennial streams with high canyon walls and distant rock rims, scenic rock formations on slopes of Lake Mountain along with vistas westward to the Black Range crest
Type of hike:	Out-and-back day hike
Total distance:	8.8 miles round-trip
Difficulty:	Moderate
Best months:	April, May, September, and October
Maps:	Forest Service Aldo Leopold Wilderness Map; Sugarloaf Peak, Reeds Peak, and Victoria Peak USGS quads
Special considerations:	There are several steep, dry sections. Water must be treated, but is generally available in South Fork Palomas and North Seco Creeks.

Morgan–North Seco Creeks

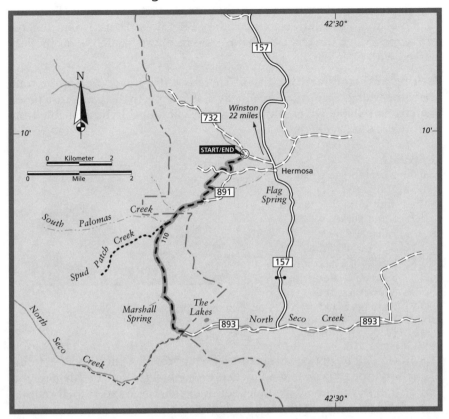

Finding the trailhead: From Interstate 25, 5 miles north of Truth or Consequences, New Mexico, take NM 52 west 31 miles to Winston. Turn left (south) at Winston through the tiny town toward Chloride. A half mile beyond Winston, turn left (south) on the signed road to the St. Cloud Mine, Forest Road 157. This road is graded gravel. Continue southwest for 5 miles. Here the wide, graded county-maintained road continues west to the St. Cloud Mine, and a narrow rough road on the left is signed FR 157. Turn left (south) on FR 157.

Following the contour of the land, FR 157 is rough when it follows canyons or drainages; when on the mesas its quality improves. Travel on FR 157 is slow, averaging about 10 miles an hour. Drive south on FR 157 for another 17 miles. In the middle of a broad valley, some remnant buildings of the defunct town of Hermosa stand on the hillside in front of you. A sign stating PRIVATE PROPERTY. PLEASE STAY ON ROADWAY also indicates this is a private inholding, further reinforced with a steel cable and I-beam post barricade indicating the boundary.

Located obscurely about 50 yards east of FR 157 is a tiny sign for FR 732. The main road, FR 157, continues south through the former Hermosa.

31

Turn right (northeast) on FR 732, following Morgan Creek up the great bowl valley. The newly constructed trailhead is 0.5 mile west of Hermosa in a large flat area beneath towering cottonwoods and ponderosa pines. This short section of road is softer and kinder than FR 157 is. There is one shallow ford across Morgan Creek just before the trailhead, which is on the left, marked with a big kiosk.

Parking and trailhead facilities: There is a flat grassy area at the trailhead for parking. Campsites are also available beneath the ponderosa pines. There is no reliable water, although water will probably be available from nearby Morgan Creek.

Key points:

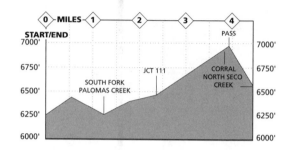

- 0.0 New Morgan Creek Trailhead for Lake Trail 110.
- 1.2 South Fork Palomas Creek.
- 1.7 Sign for old FR 891.
- 1.8 Sign for Lake Trail.
- 2.3 Signed junction with Spud Patch Trail 111.
- 3.7 Remains of old corral below Marshall Spring.
- 3.9 Pass between Marshall Creek and North Seco Creek.
- 4.4 Windmill and corral on North Seco Creek.

The hike: The newly constructed trailhead provides public access to the wilderness around private land owned by the Ladder Ranch. The new section of trail begins about 100 feet south of the kiosk and is well marked with abundant cairns. After 100 yards the trail reaches a gated fence with a grand view of Morgan Canyon to the west. The trail heads southwest across rolling pinyon-juniper foothills that were purchased from the Ladder Ranch by the Forest Service in 1993. The clear, soft dirt path contours around gullies with good views of the old townsite of Hermosa located 0.5 mile to the east. At 0.6 mile, a second ungated fence is crossed near the head of a small rocky canyon.

At 1.2 mile the trail drops gently to Palomas Creek, a bubbling live stream with more evidence of elk and turkeys than of hikers. Nonetheless, a tiny hiker sign points the way as the trail veers right (west) up the canyon. Here the new trail ends by joining an old two-track that is well marked with cairns at the many stream crossings. Canyon walls soar on the south side. At mile 1.7 the trail reaches a sign for FR 891. Across the creek at mile 1.8, another sign announces the Lake Trail, along with distances to Reeds Peak (8.25 miles) and Road No. 893 (2.75 miles). Just beyond is yet another sign for the wilderness boundary along with an outdated wooden sign that states WILDERNESS PERMIT REQUIRED. The Aldo is so lightly visited that we wondered if the sign was someone's idea of a joke.

The soft needle-cushioned path heads up Marshall Creek through a pine forest with juniper and gambel oak. You'll find early-season intermittent water

The only accurate sign here is the one proclaiming the wilderness boundary on South Fork Palomas Creek.

during a wet year, but otherwise, expect the stream to be dry. At mile 2.3 an old wooden trail junction sign points right to Spud Patch Creek Trail 111 and straight (left) to North Seco Creek (1.5 miles).

Continue to the left up Marshall Creek. The trail winds in and out of a narrowing creek bottom lined by red rock sandstone with impressive rock spires overhead on the left side. In a few spots the trail tread is hard to find, so look ahead for rock cairns, which are fairly abundant. The trail improves as it climbs moderately on the west slope dotted with pinyon-juniper, opening to scenic views across to the midslope rocky rims of Lake Mountain. With the aid of tree blazes, the trail stays left of an old two-track.

At 3.5 miles, follow the bed of an almost recovered jeep trail to a canyon overlook framed by stately ponderosa pines, then descend to the creek bottom. Pass by the charred remnants of an old corral just below Marshall Spring, then cross to the left side of the stream bottom. After a short steep climb to a pass at 3.9 miles, the trail drops to North Seco Creek over the next 0.5 mile. At first the trail drops steeply on an old jeep track to a narrow gully, where it weaves in and out of the bottom.

A faded wilderness sign is just west of an old windmill and corral with a large water tank in a grassy meadow at 4.4 miles. North Seco Creek flows just south of the meadow. Return to the trailhead by the same route.

Options: Explore farther up South Fork Palomas Creek by continuing to the right at the Road 891 sign (mile 1.7). The old washed-out road ends at the remains of a corral after about 0.6 mile.

For a great view of rock formations on Lake Mountain, hike up the Spud Patch Ridge Trail about 0.5 mile from the trail junction at mile 2.3.

Marshall Spring is about 0.3 mile up Marshall Creek from the old corral at mile 3.7. The spring and the creek below will probably be flowing into late spring.

5 Spud Patch–North Seco Creek

Highlights:	Perennial streams with high canyon walls and distant rock formations, panoramas from the Black Range crest
Type of hike:	Four- to five-day backpack loop
Total distance:	25.3 miles
Difficulty:	Strenuous
Best months:	May, September, and October
Maps:	Forest Service Aldo Leopold Wilderness Map; Sugarloaf Peak, Reeds Peak, and Victoria Park USGS quads
Special considerations:	There are several steep, dry sections, especially on Spud Patch Ridge. Water must be treated but is generally available in South Fork Palomas and North Seco Creeks, as well as Mimbres Lake.

Spud Patch–North Seco Creek

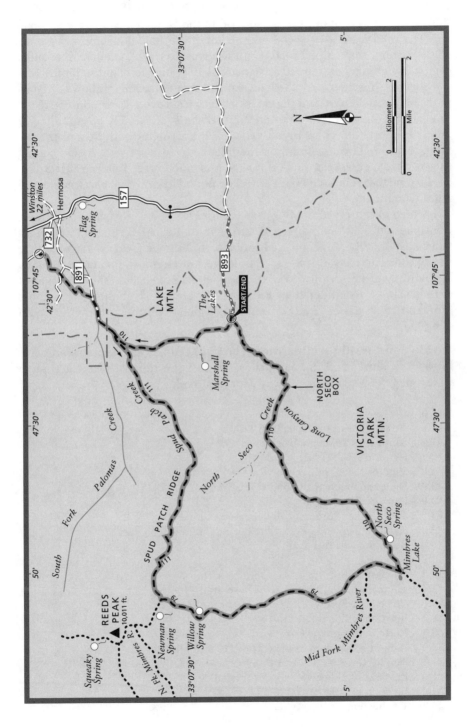

Finding the trailhead: From Interstate 25, 5 miles north of Truth or Consequences, New Mexico, take NM 52 west 31 miles to Winston. Turn left (south) at Winston through the tiny town toward Chloride. A half mile beyond Winston, turn left (south) on the signed road to the St. Cloud Mine, Forest Road 157. This road is graded gravel. Continue southwest for 5 miles. Here the wide, graded county-maintained road continues west to the St. Cloud Mine, and a narrow rough road on the left is signed FR 157. Turn left (south) on FR 157.

Following the contour of the land, FR 157 is rough when it follows canyons or drainages; when on the mesas its quality improves. Travel on FR 157 is slow, averaging about 10 miles an hour. Drive south on FR 157 another 17 miles. In the middle of a broad valley, some remnant buildings of the defunct town of Hermosa stand on the hillside in front of you. A sign stating PRIVATE PROPERTY. PLEASE STAY ON ROADWAY also indicates this is a private inholding, further reinforced with a steel cable and I-beam post barricade marking the boundary.

Located obscurely about 50 yards east of FR 157 is a tiny sign for FR 732. Continue south on the main road, through the former Hermosa. Turn right (northeast) on FR 732, following Morgan Creek up the great bowl valley. The newly constructed trailhead is 0.5 mile west of Hermosa in a large flat area beneath towering cottonwoods and ponderosa pines. This short section of road is softer and kinder than FR 157 is. There is one shallow ford across Morgan Creek just before the trailhead, which is on the left, marked with a big kiosk.

Parking and trailhead facilities: The trailhead has a large unpaved parking area, a kiosk, and flat campsites. There is no reliable water, although water may be available in nearby Morgan Creek.

Key points:

0.0	New trailhead for Lake Trail 110.
1.2	South Fork Palomas Creek.
1.7	Sign for old FR 891.
1.8	Sign for Lake Trail.
2.3	Signed junction with Spud Patch Trail 111.
2.9	First creek crossing.
3.5	Trail steepens dramatically above streambed.
5.0	Saddle above and beyond the head of Spud Patch Creek.
8.0	Black Range Crest Trail 79.
8.9	Willow Spring.
12.8	Junction with Middle Fork Mimbres Trail 78.
13.4	Mimbres Lake, junction with Lake Trail 110; turn left.
13.9	North Seco Spring.
18.6	Junction with cutover trail 87.
18.8	North Seco Canyon box.
20.9	Windmill, junction of Lake Trail 110 and FR 893.
21.4	Pass between North Seco Creek and Marshall Creek.
21.6	Remains of old corral below Marshall Spring.
23.0	Junction of Lake Trail 110 and Spud Patch Trail 111.
25.3	Trailhead on Morgan Creek.

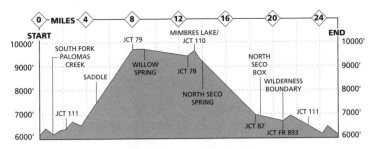

The hike: This backpack loop takes you from rolling terrain east of the Black Range Divide, through dramatic canyons via a steepening ridge to the Crest Trail, along the crest, then down another canyon, wrapping back to the starting trailhead. From the trailhead, take the new trail up the hillside 100 feet south of the kiosk, following it into Palomas Creek. Follow the trail, which becomes an old two-track roadway, upstream. Bear left at 1.8 miles into Marshall Creek at a sign for Lake Trail 111. The junction with Spud Patch is at mile 2.3, marked by an old wooden sign. See Hike 4 for details on this segment of the hike.

At the trail junction, turn right (west) and cross the gully to where a good trail sidehills up the right (north) side of narrow, rocky Spud Patch Creek. The trail (known as "the Spud") climbs steadily to the first crossing, where picturesque rock shelves form the streambed. After another 0.3 mile the trail steepens dramatically for about 0.2 mile, then contours around several side branches that are marked by monumental rock faces. The slopes are densely vegetated with pinyon-juniper and mountain mahogany, rendering this good trail all the better.

As the trail continues to gain elevation, it enters a forest of pine and Douglas fir. After climbing above the head of Spud Patch Creek, the Spud drops into a shallow saddle that is difficult to distinguish from its surroundings. A hard-to-find trail veers left (south) into North Seco Creek. For the next 3 miles, the trail steadily gains elevation, with two modest descents followed by steep pitches ever upward.

Although brushy in most places, there are occasional views both north and south into wild, remote east-side canyon country. A very steep climb just below the Crest Trail junction leads to a rocky overlook with spectacular vistas into North Seco, Massacre Canyon, and Animas Ridge all the way to Hillsboro Peak—virtually the entire southeast quarter of the Aldo! This upper stretch of the Spud is adorned with a mix of Douglas fir, subalpine fir, ponderosa pine, Southwest white pine, and lots of thorny mountain locust. At 8.0 miles (9,660 feet) the trail intersects with the Black Range Trail, where a sign proclaims that it's only 8.5 miles back to the Hermosa townsite. Along the crest, Reeds Peak rises only 1 mile to the north, and Mimbres Lake is nestled 5.5 miles southward.

When you reach the crest, you may consider investigating Newman Spring, 0.2 mile to the north, to get water before continuing your trip to Mimbres Lake. The sloping meadow of Newman Spring opens to an expansive view westward, providing a pleasant break in the otherwise dense forest.

The spring may be little more than a wet meadow seep, but it is usually a reliable water source, except later in the summer during a particularly dry year.

Head south on Black Range Crest Trail 79, one of the better-maintained routes in the Aldo, receiving attention from trail crews every two years. Don't have high hopes about locating water at Willow Spring. Its flow is only a seep, 0.9 mile south of the Spud Patch junction. You'll find some sporadic fire damage, blowdown, and mountain locust, but for the most part the well-defined trail remains in good condition. Most of the high Crest Trail is closed in with old growth, a "hall of trees" with towering monarchs lining the trail. But every so often this Gothic cathedral of nature opens to clear views in both directions that show the amazing contrast between rugged canyons and rock formations to the east and the softer wooded slopes on the west side. When you come across one of these "windows," whether due to a rock outcrop or lightning-caused fire, drop your pack and soak up the scenery. Or pause in the deep woods and sit awhile. Only the singing wind, the rustle of squirrels, and the calls of the birds break the stillness. This is an ancient forest. Try counting growth rings on one of the immense fallen giants that has been cut to clear the trail.

The trail maintains an overall moderate grade south of Willow Spring, with only a few short, steep ups and downs. Dropping into saddles and contouring around steep side slopes keeps the trail between 9,400 and 9,700 feet for most of the distance. At mile 12.8 the trail makes a gradual descent in a mature old-growth forest to the signed junction with Mid Fork Mimbres River Trail 78. The trail winds on to the south for another 0.6 mile, rising to 9,620 feet at Mimbres Lake, a swampy stock pond bounded on three sides by a forest of aspen. The lake looks lovely from the trail, reflecting the sky and the forest, glistening in the sun. A disintegrating fence surrounds the pond but no longer creates much of a barrier. The stagnant waters are enjoyed now by wildlife. Look for a variety of tracks in the soft earth near the pond. Mimbres Lake is a scenic spot for camping, but getting water, which requires treatment, is challenging. Wading in to the proper depth inevitably stirs up silt from the bottom. Stand still and wait for the silt to settle.

From the lake, your route continues east down Lake Trail 110. There is a trail sign at the junction. It's a little more than 5 miles from here to North Seco Creek, despite what the sign says. The trail descends gently through a stately stand of open old-growth aspen, spruce, and gigantic Douglas fir more than 4 feet in diameter. A steep drop brings you to the shallow seep of North Seco Spring. The spring is on the north slope of a steep gully draining to a tiny pool, next to an old broken-down fence shaded by a dark spruce-fir forest. Past the spring, the trail continues its downward gradient. This trail is lightly used, primitive, and obstructed by brush, downfall, and rocks in many places, thereby providing its own brand of isolation and wilderness adventure. The valley widens below the juncture of the North and South Forks of Seco Creek. After passing the remains of an old corral, Long Canyon enters from the south and is apt to carry water in a good snow year.

In the tight gorge below Long Canyon, the stream and the trail are one.

In times of high water, you will have to get wet. There are no bypass routes to avoid the box. This is a dramatic stretch of North Seco and an appropriate place to linger and appreciate the wonders of the wilderness. The box brings to mind two key characteristics needed in this incredibly rough wildland: respect and humility. The 0.5 mile of trail below the box is particularly rugged, brushy, and hard to find, with constant stream crossings, so your reverie will end quickly when you get back to the business of hiking through this country.

Continuing down the valley, you will encounter remnants of past ranching and mining. Above it all, ragged cliffs tower in a striking archway formation. The ruggedness of the land preserves its wildness. The trail is at times rough and brushy, sidehilling and frequently crossing the stream. Entering a wide mountain valley, you may hear an incongruous clanking noise that sounds loud after the cloak of silence in the wilderness. Adjacent to a welded 4-foot-tall water storage tank, an energetic eternal windmill continues to pump merrily even though no cows are coming to drink. Aermotor of Chicago built its windmills to last!

Lake Trail turns left (north) at the windmill. Cross the grassy meadow and pick up the trail in the gully where it weaves in and out of the bottom. Climb to the pass between North Seco and Marshall Creeks, and then descend into the Marshall drainage. You will pass the charred remains of an old corral just below Marshall Spring. The trail seesaws in and out of the bottom. In a few spots the trail tread is hard to find, so look ahead for rock cairns, which are fairly abundant.

At 23 miles, you will reach the intersection at the mouth of Spud Patch Creek that you passed on day one of your journey. Continue right (east) and retrace your route back to the trailhead on Morgan Creek to complete your central east-side loop in the Aldo.

Option: From the upper end of the Spud trail on the crest (mile 8.0) a round-trip hike of about 3 additional miles will get you up and back from Reeds Peak (10,011 feet), the central sentinel of the Aldo. Squeaky Spring is located just to the northwest of the summit and is a reliable water source. See Hike 42 for details.

Seco Creek Trailhead

"If preserved in its semi-virgin state,
the [headwaters of the Gila River]
could absorb a hundred pack trains
each year without overcrowding.
It is the last typical wilderness in the
southwestern mountains.
Highest use demands its preservation."

—Aldo Leopold, *Journal of Forestry,* 1921

---

6 North Seco Box

Highlights:	Riparian recovery zone, mountain stream, and wilderness solitude complete with scenic rugged canyon marked with varied rock formations and a deep canyon wall box
Type of hike:	Out-and-back day hike
Total distance:	11 miles round-trip
Difficulty:	Strenuous
Best months:	April to November
Maps:	Forest Service Aldo Leopold Wilderness Map; Apache Peak and Victoria Park USGS quads
Special considerations:	Expect wet foot crossings. The trail is rough and brushy below the box.

Finding the trailhead: From Interstate 25, 5 miles north of Truth or Consequences, New Mexico, take NM 52 west 31 miles to Winston. Turn left (south) at Winston through the tiny town toward Chloride. A half mile beyond Winston, turn left (south) on the signed road to the St. Cloud Mine, Forest Road 157. This road is graded gravel. Continue southwest for 5 miles. Here the wide, graded county-maintained road continues west to the St. Cloud Mine, and a narrow rough road on the left is signed FR 157. Turn left (south) on FR 157.

Following the contour of the land, FR 157 is rough when it follows a canyon or drainage; when on the mesas its quality improves. Travel on FR 157 is slow, averaging about 10 miles an hour. Drive south on FR 157 for another 17 miles. In the middle of a broad valley, some remnant buildings of the defunct town of Hermosa stand on the hillside in front of you. A sign stating PRIVATE PROPERTY. PLEASE STAY ON ROADWAY also indicates this is a private inholding, further reinforced with a steel cable and I-beam post barricade indicating the boundary.

Located obscurely about 50 yards east of FR 157 is a tiny sign for FR 732. Continue south on the main road, through former Hermosa. This unmaintained stretch of FR 157 ends 2.5 miles south of the townsite at a locked gate.

North Seco Box

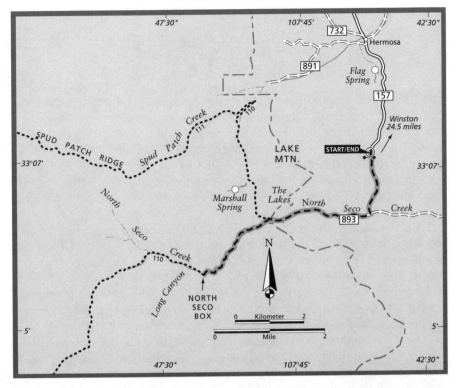

This is a rough, four-wheel-drive high-center road, with steep pitches and deep ruts. Flag Spring has eroded the road severely 1.2 miles south of Hermosa. A small parking slot permits one vehicle to pull off there, and you can hike the next 1.3 miles to the end of the road and the trailhead. Otherwise, continue driving south on the tortuous road 1.3 miles to the locked gate atop the mesa north of North Seco Creek. Here there is room to turn around and park.

Parking and trailhead facilities: There is a large, flat, unpaved parking area at the Seco Creek trailhead, with no protection from sun or wind. The Morgan Creek trailhead is better for camping. There is no water at the trailhead.

Key points:

0.0	Locked gate at end of road. Commence hiking on former road south.
0.8	View of valley of North Seco Creek.
1.1	Cross stream and turn right (west).
1.7	Stream crossing (one of many).
1.9	Road ends, trail continues; canyon narrows.
3.3	Springs appear in widening valley.
3.4	Windmill, stock tank, wilderness boundary.
4.3	Trail joins an old rocky jeep track.
5.1	Old stock fence.
5.5	North Seco Canyon box.

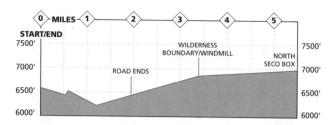

MILES 0 1 2 3 4 5

START/END
7500'

6000'

WILDERNESS
BOUNDARY/WINDMILL

NORTH
SECO BOX

7500'

ROAD ENDS

7000'

6500'

6000'

The hike: From the trailhead high on the dry mesa to a lush stream valley, through a narrow rocky canyon to a grassy mountain meadow, and then into a mountain gorge, this hike covers a variety of ecosystems within only a few miles. Since the former private inholding along North Seco Creek was acquired by the Forest Service and cattle grazing was terminated, the riparian zone has been nursed back to health. Now the footprints are those of elk, deer, turkey, bear, coyote, and cat. The Forest Service is justifiably proud of this demonstration recovery area.

From the locked gate at the end of FR 157, commence your hike by heading south down the old roadbed. There is no sign at the gate, but there are no other choices anyway. After several ups and downs on the road (mostly steeply down as you go south), you arrive at an overlook with a view of North Seco opening below. The stripe of pines and cottonwoods with a grassy carpet beneath are a startling break from the dusty pastels of the dry pinyon-juniper mesa and the south-facing slope. In the spring, the glistening water in the creek also stands out like a neon advertisement in the valley.

At 1.1 mile you arrive at the stream, where a wet-foot crossing is likely in the spring. A windmill and muddy stock pond are located on the south of the road next to the junction of FR 157 and an old two-track roadway still identified as Forest Road 893 on the wilderness map. This latter pathway becomes your trail as you turn right and head west upstream.

The broad, grassy stream valley, bracketed with gently sloping hillsides, makes for easy walking. The earthen trail winds along with the pines and the cottonwoods. Several old campsites exist along the way, usually near stream crossings, which begin 0.6 mile up the valley from the windmill, and increase in frequency after that. At the south edge of the meadow, about 0.7 mile from the windmill junction, you may spot a metal bed frame, which lies amid crushed and rusted old tin cans. There's no trace of a dwelling, which must have burned down during the frequent fires that sweep down the creek valley and keep the grasslands open. The Apache Creek quad shows a nearby gravesite, north of the creek. Perhaps there's some connection with the bed frame.

Shortly afterward, the valley begins to narrow. Large fallen boulders have blocked the old roadway, and your two-track pathway becomes a forest trail. For the next 1.5 miles, the narrow canyon forces the stream into a rocky channel, resulting in noisy stairstep falls and deep pools in early spring runoff.

Continuing west, the tight valley again widens, and squishy springs erupt from the earth along the trail. Just beyond the swampy zone, a welded 4-foot-tall water storage tank appears, still filled by the energetic action of the eternal windmill that continues to pump merrily even though no cows are

Looking down the bubbling brook of North Seco Creek.

coming to drink. A sign indicates the end of Forest Road 893 and the beginning of Lake Trail 110.

After pausing in the shade at the edge of the meadow near the clanking Aermotor Company windmill, continue your hike southwest on Trail 110. One hundred yards west of the windmill and corral on North Seco Creek, a forest trail sign points upstream next to an old hitching rail. The path leads up the right side of the delightfully babbling brook. The trail is faint after crossing the stream, but quickly becomes more distinct as the valley narrows, with the trail sidehilling through a dense ponderosa pine–Douglas fir forest. After crossing the creek at 4.3 miles, the trail joins an old, mostly recovered two-track as the forest changes to pinyon-juniper. The following 0.7-mile stretch is rugged and brushy, with frequent crossings adjacent to flat grassy benches. Ragged cliffs tower above the north side in a striking archway formation. Scattered mining debris includes a rusted boiler from long ago.

At 5.1 miles the trail passes through an old stock fence and then becomes more primitive in a narrow brushy canyon. A canyon box is reached at 5.5 miles. The 0.5 mile below the box is particularly rugged, brushy, and hard to find, with constant stream crossings. If the creek is running high, you'll have two choices: Turn around or slog and wade through the water for about 100 yards. A short steep climb to the right (north) yields a spectacular view into the box from a rock ledge. The box and this tortuous terrain bring to mind two key attributes needed in this incredibly rough wildland: respect and humility.

After exploring the box on North Seco Creek, return to the mesa-top trailhead by the same route.

Option: During periods of low water, you can wade the streambed in the box another 0.3 mile to the mouth of Long Canyon, or beyond, depending on time and energy.

7 North Seco–Morgan Creek

Highlights:	Riparian recovery zone, mountain stream, scenic rock formation on slopes of Lake Mountain along with vistas westward of the Black Range crest, perennial streams with high canyon walls and distant rock formations
Type of hike:	Shuttle day hike
Total distance:	7.8 miles
Difficulty:	Moderate
Best months:	April, May, and September to November
Maps:	Forest Service Aldo Leopold Wilderness Map; Apache Peak, Reeds Peak, Sugarloaf Peak, and Victoria Park USGS quads
Special considerations:	Expect wet foot crossings.

North Seco–Morgan Creek

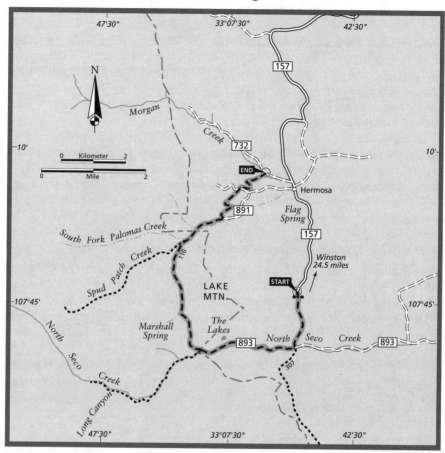

Finding the trailheads: *Beginning trailhead*: From Interstate 25, 5 miles north of Truth or Consequences, New Mexico, take NM 52 west 31 miles to Winston. Turn left (south) at Winston through the tiny town toward Chloride. A half mile beyond Winston, turn left (south) on the signed road to the St. Cloud Mine, Forest Road 157. This road is graded gravel. Continue southwest for 5 miles. Here the wide, graded county-maintained road continues west to the St. Cloud Mine, and a narrow rough road on the left is signed FR 157. Turn left (south) on FR 157.

Following the contour of the land, FR 157 is rough when it follows a canyon or drainage; when on the mesas its quality improves. Travel on FR 157 is slow, averaging about 10 miles an hour. Drive south on FR 157 for another 17 miles. In the middle of a broad valley, some remnant buildings of the defunct town of Hermosa stand on the hillside in front of you. A sign stating PRIVATE PROPERTY. PLEASE STAY ON ROADWAY also indicates this is a private inholding, further reinforced with a steel cable and I-beam post barricade marking the boundary.

Located obscurely about 50 yards east of FR 157 is a tiny sign for FR 732. Continue south on the main road, through the former Hermosa. This unmaintained stretch of road ends 2.5 miles south of the townsite at a locked gate. This is a rough, four-wheel-drive high-center road, with steep pitches and deep ruts. Flag Spring has eroded the road severely about 1.2 miles south of Hermosa. A small parking slot permits one vehicle to pull off there, and you can hike the next 1.3 miles to the end of the road and the trailhead. Otherwise, continue driving south on the tortuous road 1.3 miles to the locked gate atop the mesa north of North Seco Creek, where there is room to turn around and park.

Ending trailhead: At the northern boundary of the Hermosa private inholding, turn right (west) on FR 732, following Morgan Creek up the great bowl valley. The newly constructed trailhead is 0.5 mile west of Hermosa in a large flat area beneath towering cottonwoods and ponderosa pines. This short section of road is softer and kinder than FR 157 is. There is one shallow ford across Morgan Creek just before the trailhead, which is on the left, marked with a big kiosk.

The driving distance between trailheads is 3.1 miles.

Parking and trailhead facilities: *Beginning trailhead:* There is large, flat, unpaved parking area, with no protection from sun or wind. The Morgan Creek trailhead is better for camping. There is no water at this trailhead.

Ending trailhead: A large grassy area is suitable for parking and camping beneath ponderosa pines. Water is not reliable, although there may be a spring just southwest of the kiosk.

Key points:
0.0   Locked gate at end of road. Commence hiking on former road south.
1.1   Cross stream and turn right (west).
1.7   Stream crossing (one of many).
1.9   Road ends, trail continues; canyon narrows.
3.3   Springs appear in widening valley.
3.4   Windmill, stock tank, wilderness boundary.
3.9   Pass between Marshall Creek and North Seco Creek.
4.1   Remains of old corral below Marshall Spring.
5.5   Signed junction of Seco Creek Trail 110 and Spud Patch Creek Trail 111.
6.0   Wilderness boundary, sign for Lake Trail.
6.1   Sign for old FR 891.
6.6   Trail leaves South Fork Palomas Creek.
7.8   Morgan Creek trailhead.

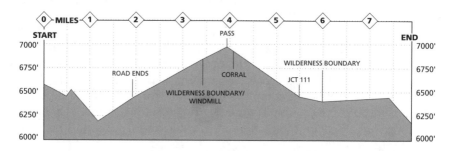

The hike: At the trailhead, follow the old roadbed south, descending to North Seco Creek at 1.1 miles. Cross the creek and turn right (west), following the creek upstream. After several wet foot crossings the roadway becomes a trail, which continues up the narrowing valley. At 3.4 miles, you will arrive at a windmill and stock tank at the end of the defunct Forest Road 893, and the intersection with Lake Trail 110. (See Hike 6 for details.)

After pausing in the shade at the edge of the meadow near the clanking Aermotor Company windmill, bear right (north) on Lake Trail 110. From North Seco Creek, the trail climbs for the next 0.5 mile. After weaving in and out of the bottom of a narrow gully, the trail ascends steeply on an old jeep track to a pass at 3.9 miles. Beyond the pass, the trail drops quickly to Marshall Creek, and at 4.1 miles passes by the charred remnants of an old corral just below Marshall Spring (6,800 feet). As you follow Marshall Creek northward, the trail tread is hard to find in a few spots. Look ahead for rock cairns, which are fairly abundant. Blazes are also helpful. At mile 5.5 (6,440 feet) an old wooden trail junction sign points left to Spud Patch Creek Trail 111.

Turn right (north) at the sign, onto the soft needle-cushioned path that drops gently down Marshall Creek. After 0.5 mile the trail exits the wilderness and passes by a Lake Trail sign, followed quickly by a sign for Road 891 next to the bubbling South Fork Palomas Creek. Here the trail coincides with the old two-track of Road 891 and is well marked with rock cairns at each of many stream crossings. Canyon walls soar on the south side.

At mile 6.6 a tiny hiker sign points left to the section of trail that leads north from South Fork Palomas Creek to Morgan Creek. This is a newly constructed trail that provides public access to and from the wilderness around private land owned by the Ladder Ranch. The soft dirt trail crosses an ungated fence near the rocky head of Curtis Canyon. Soon after leaving the canyon, good views open eastward to the old townsite of Hermosa. The trail contours around side gullies and across rolling pinyon-juniper foothills that were purchased from the Ladder Ranch by the Forest Service in 1993. The new trail reaches a ridge and a second gated fence, overlooking Morgan Creek Canyon, with a short 100-yard descent to the new trailhead and kiosk at mile 7.8 on Morgan Creek.

Option: To hike this loop without the car shuttle, walk the 3.1 miles of road from the Morgan Creek Trailhead to the North Seco Trailhead. The road section will be hot later in the day, so you would want to do that portion of the hike first thing in the morning.

Bald Hill Trailhead

". . . for in this precious remnant of the old frontier
[The Creator] piled up the hills 'high, wide, and handsome.'
In every point where roads might enter is set a rugged mountain.
Wherever a foaming trout-stream has cut its way thru
the mountain wall a jagged box
canyon says, 'They shall not pass.'"

—Aldo Leopold, *Outdoor Life,* 1925

8 Cave Canyon

Highlights:	A huge cave alcove with a chance to observe raptors and other wildlife, broad vistas of brushy canyons and hillsides
Type of hike:	Out-and-back day hike
Total distance:	5.6 miles round-trip
Difficulty:	Strenuous
Best months:	April, May, September, and October
Maps:	Forest Service Aldo Leopold Wilderness Map; Apache Peak USGS quad
Special considerations:	Small streams may be dry by late spring or early summer; carry ample water.

Finding the trailhead: From Interstate 25, 12 miles south of Truth or Consequences, New Mexico, take NM 152 (the Geronimo Trail Scenic Byway) west 24 miles. After a narrow bridge, and after milepost 43, turn right (north) at a small sign for Forest Road 157. Drive north 11.5 miles on the slow, rocky, lightly maintained road. After you pass through a signed private inholding along Percha Creek at 8 miles from the highway, there is a junction where FR 157 bends sharply to the right (north) and a rough jeep track continues west. Turn right and continue north on FR 157. The road becomes considerably rougher for the final 3.5 miles, requiring four-wheel drive to reach the Bald Hill trailhead. A small parking and camping area is on the crest of the road beside Bald Hill. The deeply rutted road becomes hazardous thereafter as it drops into McCann Gulch, indicated by scattered jeep parts along the road.

Parking and trailhead facilities: There is parking space for two or three vehicles, limited camping space, and no water or other facilities.

Key points:
- 0.0 Unsigned trailhead.
- 0.2 McCann Gulch.
- 1.1 Cave Creek.
- 2.0 Large cave above Cave Creek.
- 2.8 Wilderness boundary, junction with trail to East Curtis Canyon.

48

Cave Canyon

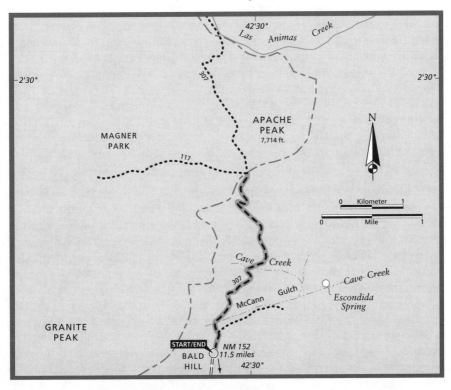

The hike: After chugging up the rough four-wheel-drive road (FR 157), park in the narrow notch immediately east of
Bald Hill. This unsigned trailhead is where
the Forest Service wilderness map shows
FR 157 ending and Trail 307 beginning.
The trail follows a rutted jeep track down
to McCann Gulch and then climbs to a
divide above Cave Creek with panoramic
vistas of rugged brushy hills on all sides,
a land of pinyon-juniper and beavertail
cactus.

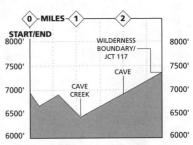

The deeply rutted jeep track plunges
steeply downhill, parallels Cave Creek, and then crosses the rocky bottom
at 1.1 miles. Posts without signs, campsites, and fire rings are found at this
junction. After crossing the creek, the trail changes to a narrow single-track
that is primitive and rocky but well defined. The country has a rough-hewn
flavor with a high desert community of beavertail, cholla, and yucca cactus
along with pinyon-juniper and mountain mahogany. After a steady climb,
the trail arrives at a switchback at 2.0 miles, opposite the huge alcove of a
dark cave entrance overlooking the head of Cave Canyon. From the switch-

back, a use trail cuts left on down to Cave Canyon but disappears in the brush before reaching back up to the cave. The temptation is to take a 0.3-mile round-trip hike to the cave, but during our visit we observed a pair of raptors nesting on the rock face cliff of the cave. Not wanting to disturb these magnificent birds, we backed off. The other side of the canyon leading to the cave is extremely brushy, so it's best to observe from a respectful distance. We noticed, for example, how swarms of swallows suddenly disappeared as soon as the hawks showed up.

The trail climbs steadily in a series of long switchbacks to a signed trail junction on a prominent narrow ridge at mile 2.8. This is also the wilderness boundary, but the sign is missing. There must be a good story behind a rusty old wheelbarrow leaning up against a sign that points straight ahead to Animas Creek (2.5 miles) and left (west) to East Curtis Canyon (3.5 miles).

Options: A side trip from the Cave Canyon Trail is a rugged outing toward Magner Park and East Curtis Spring. Trail 117 barely exists on the ground, although it's still on the wilderness map. At the spring at the western end, it can't be found at all, but from the 7,350-foot pass below Apache Peak, at least it's slightly visible. The faint pathway heads west, sidehilling along the ridge and eventually curling over the top at 0.5 mile to a viewpoint down into Animas Creek. After the viewpoint, the trail is thick with every species of prickly shrub common in the mountains, as well as beavertail and cholla cactus. The ridge-top trail is further encumbered with blowdown. Weaving around the obstacles makes it difficult to locate the trail, which is thoroughly overgrown and brushy. Only the most masochistic hiker would enjoy this "trail"!

Apache Peak (7,714 feet) is about 0.75 mile north of the trail junction. To

A large alcove cave entrance overlooks the head of aptly named Cave Canyon.

make the strenuous ascent of this seldom visited summit, drop down the trail toward Las Animas Creek for about 0.4 mile to an elevation of about 7,080 feet. From an open sandy slope on the southwest flank of Apache Peak, scramble up a brushy chute between rock outcrops to the top, gaining about 630 vertical feet along with a sweeping view of this rugged southeast corner of the Aldo.

9 Las Animas Creek

Highlights:	A huge cave alcove with a chance to observe raptors and other wildlife; broad vistas of brushy canyons, hillsides, and colorful canyon rims; a high desert stream with deep pools and grottoes
Type of hike:	Out-and-back day hike, overnighter, or two- to three-day backpack
Total distance:	11.6 miles
Difficulty:	Strenuous
Best months:	April, May, June, September, and October
Maps:	Forest Service Aldo Leopold Wilderness Map; Victoria Park and Apache Peak USGS quads
Special considerations:	All or most of the hike to Las Animas Creek could be dry by late spring or early summer; carry ample water. There is no public access to Las Animas Creek below the forest boundary from the east; use the route described in this hike.

Finding the trailhead: From Interstate 25, 12 miles south of Truth or Consequences, New Mexico, take NM 152 (the Geronimo Trail Scenic Byway) west 24 miles. After a narrow bridge, and after milepost 43, turn right (north) at a small sign for Forest Road 157. Drive north 11.5 miles on the slow, rocky, lightly maintained road. After you pass through a signed private inholding along Percha Creek at 8 miles from the highway, There is a junction where FR 157 bends sharply to the right (north) and a rough jeep track continues west. Turn right and continue north on FR 157. The road becomes considerably rougher for the final 3.5 miles, requiring four-wheel drive to reach the Bald Hill trailhead. A small parking and camping area is on the crest of the road beside Bald Hill. The deeply rutted road becomes hazardous thereafter as it drops into McCann Gulch, indicated by scattered jeep parts along the road.

Parking and trailhead facilities: There is parking space for two or three vehicles, limited camping space, and no water or other facilities.

Key points:
- 0.0 Unsigned trailhead.
- 0.2 McCann Gulch.
- 1.1 Cave Creek.

Las Animas Creek

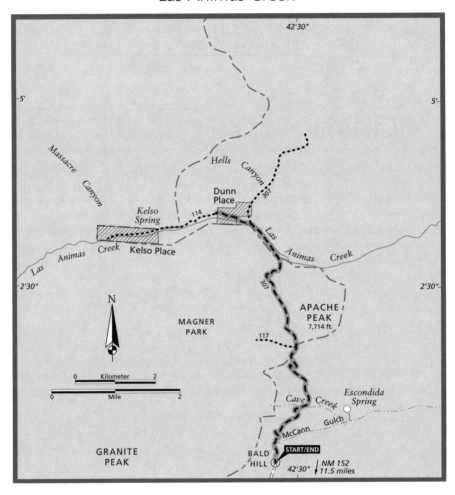

2.0   Large cave above Cave Creek.
2.8   Wilderness boundary, junction with trail to East Curtis Canyon.
2.9   Old stock fence.
5.0   Trail joins jeep road along Las Animas Creek.

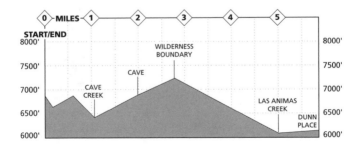

5.5   Trail 307 continues north (right).

5.8   Dunn Place (cabin ruins) on Las Animas Creek.

The hike: From the parking area, continue on foot along FR 157, now a deeply rutted track, dropping into McCann Gulch. The track crosses Cave Creek at 1.1 miles, in the bottom, and becomes a trail (Trail 307), climbing toward the cave at 2.0 miles. Beyond the cave, the trail switchbacks on up to a ridge below Apache Peak at 2.8 miles. The ridge marks the wilderness boundary. See Hike 8 for details on this section of the hike.

From the wilderness boundary on the saddle, the trail passes through an old stock fence, opening to a grand view of the rugged south buttress of Apache Peak. The trail then sidehills and drops through a pine forest on an open sandy slope below the peak. As the trail continues its descent, it remains well defined but is sometimes sloughed in. Steep grades with loose sand and gravel alternate with contour stretches and a few rock talus chutes. For a while the trail follows a dry gully, then follows a low center ridge near the bottom. A short canyon lined with colorful white and buff formations is on the left. At mile 5 a primitive road is reached in the cottonwood bottom of Las Animas Creek, next to a barbed wire fence. This junction is marked only with a small rock cairn; there is no sign. Memorize this spot for the return trip.

There is no public access to the national forest boundary below here. Anyone with a key to the locked gate can drive a four-wheel-drive vehicle up, but Las Animas Creek gets only light vehicular use and the two-track makes a great hiking trail. From this point, turn left (west) and hike up the wide scenic valley. Undulating ribs and bands of red volcanics line this stretch of the Las Animas, with faces of white sandstone exposed by erosion. Las Animas is a lovely desert stream with pools deep enough for trout and a healthy riparian bottom.

After another 0.4 mile, the jeep road and creek become one and the same for about 100 yards, passing by a low-slung grotto. The trail leaves the stream and climbs a low rise on the north side for about 0.1 mile to the hard-to-find trail junction for the continuation of Trail 307. Pieces of an old wooden sign lie on a cut stump in a grove of oak and juniper, and ponderosa pines stand tall on the left. The sign points right to Hermosa Trail 307 and left to Animas Creek Trail 114.

After several more creek crossings, the dirt road passes by the Dunn Place at mile 5.8. All that remains are the ruins of two north-side cabins on a large grassy bench studded with oak, juniper, and pine. Striking views unfold to distant rock rims at the mid and top levels of adjacent hillsides. After enjoying this wonderful stream and bottomland with its colorful canyon rims, retrace your route to the Bald Hill trailhead.

Options: Although not recommended if this hike is done as a long day trip, you might want to consider climbing Apache Peak as a side hike if you're planning to camp along Las Animas Creek for a night or two. Apache Peak (7,714 feet) is about 0.75 mile north of the East Curtis Spring trail junction. To make the strenuous ascent of this summit, drop down the trail toward

Las Animas Creek forms deep pools just below the Dunn Place.

Las Animas Creek for about 0.4 mile to an elevation of about 7,080 feet. From an open sandy slope on the southwest flank of Apache Peak, scramble up a brushy chute between rock outcrops to the top, gaining about 630 vertical feet along with a sweeping view of this rugged southeast corner of the Aldo.

A much easier 1.2-mile round-trip side hike is to take the good Trail 307 north of Las Animas Creek to the abandoned Hells Canyon windmill with its dry tank. Stunning red rock cliffs tower to the northwest. This trail eventually becomes a jeep road before reaching North Seco Canyon 6 miles farther north.

If you're camping overnight along the Las Animas, you might want to day hike another 2 miles above the Dunn Place to the Kelso Place, which reveals an interesting chapter in regional history. Just north of the old ranch, on a grassy flat north of the river, are fifteen rock-mounded graves and an impressive granite monument with a brass plaque. The graves date from September 1879, when a band of Apaches, led by Chief Victorio, lured a 9th Cavalry regiment into a trap in the narrow canyon, which is located immediately to the northwest of the gravesites. The battle in Massacre Canyon was won by the Apaches. The monument dates from 1990; it was established by the Medal of Honor Society and is dedicated to the three officers who led the regiment into the canyon.

Of the fifteen men buried here, only three are identified with first and last names. Two of the graves belong to the Navajo scouts who were killed; these men are identified only as Sam and Baraja. The other ten don't even have first names; they are unknown soldiers. Apparently the army record-keeping was imprecise in the 1870s. The 9th Cavalry was a unit of the famed buffalo soldiers, made up of Black Americans.

The Medals of Honor were awarded to the three officers who led the 9th Cavalry into the trap to be massacred. A glance at the topo map reveals what an ideal spot this canyon was for the wily Apaches. Once in the canyon, the army troops had no chance for escape. The three heroic officers are not buried here, so clearly all of them survived the massacre. None of the enlisted men received a medal.

This is a thought-provoking stop on your wilderness trek in Apache country.

Ladrone Trailhead

"This is the last stand—these hills are meant to play in, not stay in."

—Aldo Leopold, *Outdoor Life,* 1925

10 Ladrone–Hillsboro Peak

Highlights:	Access to the popular Hillsboro Peak area by way of a wild, lightly used trail with scenic views of rocky rims in the upper reaches
Type of hike:	Out-and-back day hike
Total distance:	8.8 miles round-trip
Difficulty:	Strenuous
Best months:	May to early October
Maps:	Forest Service Aldo Leopold Wilderness Map; Kingston and Hillsboro Peak USGS quads
Special considerations:	The trail is steep, rough, and brushy, so make the climb to Hillsboro early in the day. Carry lots of water. Except during early spring, don't count on finding any water between Middle Percha Creek and Hillsboro Peak. Because the road along Middle Percha is primitive, add at least 2 miles round-trip to the hike if you're accessing the trailhead in a passenger car.

Finding the trailhead: To reach the unsigned lower Ladrone trailhead from Interstate 25, 12 miles south of Truth or Consequences, New Mexico, take NM 152 (the Geronimo Trail Scenic Byway) west 26 miles to Kingston. Turn right (northwest) onto Kingston's main thoroughfare, continuing west 0.3 mile through town to the junction with Forest Road 40E (signed) at the outskirts of the tiny settlement. Remnants of an ominous sign warn of PRIMITIVE ROAD AND DANGEROUS CONDITIONS, but the steep, rocky, and rough four-wheel-drive road is passable for 3 miles up Middle Percha Creek. The best place to park and hike is at an elevation of about 6,940 feet just before a creek crossing. After this crossing, the narrowing two-track becomes even rougher, and within 0.6 mile becomes too deeply rutted for even a four-wheel drive. The creek crossing, 3 miles above Kingston, is the logical place to start hiking the Ladrone Trail.

Parking and trailhead facilities: Numerous wooded campsites line the road along the creek. Middle Percha Creek is intermittent but contains some year-round water along steeper upper sections. The trailhead is unsigned, but there are flat spaces every so often for parking.

56

Ladrone–Hillsboro Peak

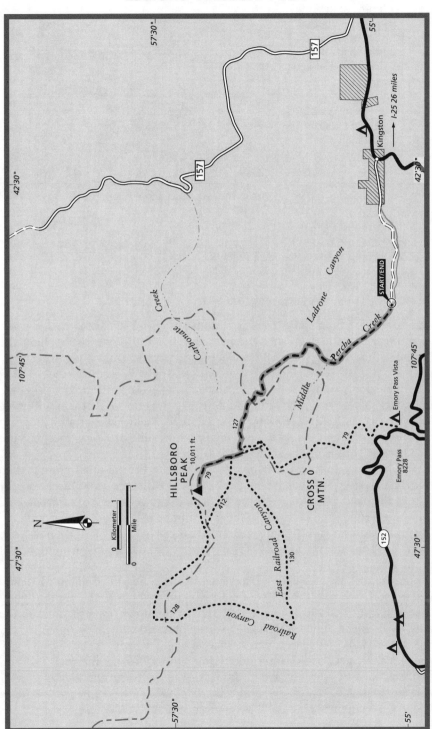

Key points:

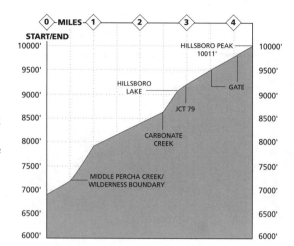

- 0.0   Unsigned trailhead/parking space just before stream crossing.
- 0.4   Road becomes deeply rutted and turns to single-track trail.
- 0.5   Trail crosses Middle Percha Creek at the unsigned wilderness boundary.
- 1.0   Ridge above Ladrone Gulch.
- 2.5   Head of Carbonate Creek.
- 2.8   Hillsboro Lake.
- 3.0   Signed trail junction with Black Range Crest Trail 79.
- 3.6   Trail passes through gate/fence.
- 4.1   Second stock gate crosses trail.
- 4.4   Hillsboro Peak lookout (10,011 feet).

The hike: The rough jeep track continues above the suggested parking area for another 0.4 mile up Middle Percha Creek, but you'll be a lot happier walking here than trying to drive the deeply rutted two-track. In mixed pine–Douglas fir–oak woodland, the two-track changes to a single-track trail at 0.5 mile, soon reaching Middle Percha Creek and the unsigned wilderness boundary. There is an old campsite at this point, but the stream will most likely be dry here. After crossing the streambed, the trail heads straight north up a side gully. Old blazes appear regularly on pine and oak trees, but the tread of the trail is hard to find in places.

You're likely to find water below the Middle Percha crossing, but then this steep, rugged trail will be dry all the way to Hillsboro Peak! After a steady climb, the trail reaches the dividing ridge between Middle Percha and Ladrone Gulch, drops into the gulch, and climbs steeply at times around the heads of Ladrone and Carbonate Creek. Although brushy for the most part, the trail opens to occasional vistas of rugged rims and canyons fanning off to the east.

After some very steep pitches and contour stretches, the trail improves and widens somewhat. Although well marked with tree blazes the path is lightly used and apt to be blocked with downfall in the upper mile. Just below the crest of the Black Range at mile 2.8, the trail passes by the tiny mountain pond of Hillsboro Lake. Lined by aspen, spruce, and fir and overseen by rugged rocky rims, this is a very scenic interlude in the dense old-growth forest. The trail then steepens for a rapid ascent to the crest at 3.0 miles and a gain thus far of 2,300 feet. A sign commemorates the one hundredth anniversary of Aldo Leopold's birth in 1887, as well as reentrance to the wilderness. Various signs identify this 9,250-foot-high saddle as a four-way junction between the north-south Black Range Crest Trail 79 and Hillsboro Peak Bypass Trail 412.

After taking a well-deserved break at this shady, relaxing spot, continue right (north) on Crest Trail 79 for another 1.4 miles to Hillsboro Peak. From the junction, the trail makes a series of long, easy switchbacks in the pine-fir forest, and passes through a gate. After continuing through aspen groves, a second gate is reached at mile 4.1. The trail is wide and well graded for the final 200-foot climb over a distance of 0.3 mile to the long, open ridge-top summit of 10,011-foot-high Hillsboro Peak, complete with cabins, lookout, and heliport.

A friendly Forest Service sign welcomes you to the top, as will a friendly lookout ranger if you visit during the fire season when the lookout is manned. The ranger lives in the west cabin, but the east cabin is left open for the public to use, both for safety purposes and as a practical way to prevent break-ins. The east cabin was built in 1925 and remains in good condition, thanks to responsible people who are careful to clean up after they leave. In addition to providing refuge from an almost constant wind, the cabin has a sheltered front porch with a fabulous view eastward. The logbook is entertaining to read, with many entries extolling the beauty and solitude of the Aldo. You can feel the exuberance of people when they write about "a lovely walk in the high country, so happy to be here!"

The lookout and ranger cabin were constructed in 1934, replacing the previous wooden lookout. For an incredible 360-degree view of the entire Black Range and surrounding valleys and mountains, climb to the lookout cabin. The metal stairway is sturdy and guarded by railings, but those with a fear of heights would probably be happier on the ground. With permission from the ranger, you can fill up your water bottles from an otherwise locked rain

Backpacking to the 10,011-foot summit of Hillsboro Peak.

cistern near the cabin. You might also be able to obtain water from a spring some 600 feet below and to the north of the lookout.

To complete this out-and-back hike to Hillsboro Peak, retrace your route back down to Middle Percha Creek, more than 4 miles and 3,000 feet below.

Option: If you drop down to the spring, you might want to climb back to Black Range Crest Trail 79 on the west side of the peak and continue down to Hillsboro Bypass Trail 412. Turn left onto the bypass trail and follow it back to the four-way trail junction in the saddle south of Hillsboro Peak. This option adds about 1.5 miles to the hike, as well as scenic views into East Railroad Canyon, while eliminating a considerable amount of up-and-down hiking.

11 Ladrone–Gallinas

Highlights:	Wide variety on both sides of a popular stretch of the Black Range crest by way of a wild, lightly used east-side trail, along with scenic views of rocky canyons, rims, and formations on the west side of the crest; a babbling brook with bedrock pools and grassy benches
Type of hike:	Shuttle day hike or overnighter
Total distance:	7.9 miles
Difficulty:	Strenuous
Best months:	April through October
Maps:	Forest Service Aldo Leopold Wilderness Map; Kingston and Hillsboro Peak USGS quads
Special considerations:	The Ladrone trail is steep, rough, and brushy, so make the climb early in the day. Carry lots of water. Except during early spring, don't count on finding any water between Middle Percha Creek and Hillsboro Peak. Because the road along Middle Percha is primitive, add at least 1 mile to the hike if you're accessing the Ladrone Trailhead in a passenger car. There are numerous crossings of the small stream in Railroad and Gallinas Canyons.

Finding the trailheads: *Beginning trailhead:* To reach the unsigned lower Ladrone Trailhead from Interstate 25, 12 miles south of Truth or Consequences, New Mexico, take NM 152 (the Geronimo Trail Scenic Byway) west 26 miles to Kingston. Turn right (northwest) onto Kingston's main thoroughfare, continuing west 0.3 mile through town to the junction with Forest Road 40E (signed) at the outskirts of the tiny settlement. Remnants of an ominous sign warn of PRIMITIVE ROAD AND DANGEROUS CONDITIONS, but the steep, rocky, and rough four-wheel-drive road is passable for 3 miles up Middle Percha Creek. The best place to park and hike is at an elevation of about 6,940 feet just before a creek crossing. After this crossing, the narrowing two-track becomes even

60

Ladrone–Gallinas

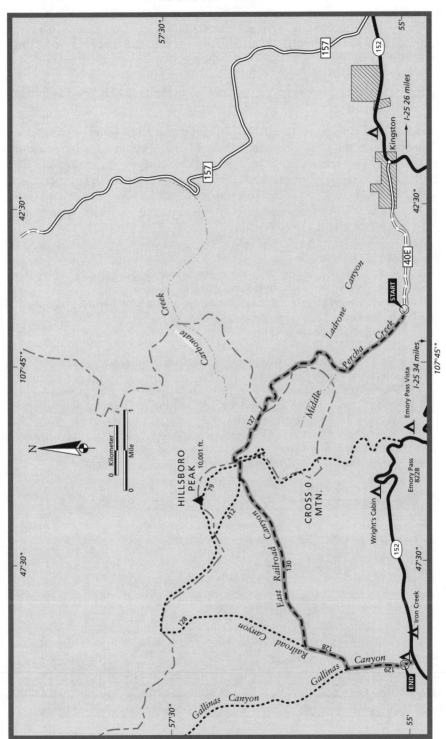

rougher, and within 0.6 mile becomes too deeply rutted for even a four-wheel drive. The creek crossing, 3 miles above Kingston, is the logical place to start hiking the Ladrone Trail.

Ending trailhead: From Kingston, go west on NM 152 for 12 miles to a small "129" sign on the highway. Turn right (north) into the undeveloped campground. The trailhead is at the north end of the unpaved camping area, 0.3 mile north of the highway.

The road mileage between the two trailheads is about 15 miles, 12 of which are paved.

Parking and trailhead facilities: *Beginning trailhead:* Numerous wooded campsites line the road along the creek. Middle Percha Creek is intermittent but contains some year-round water along steeper upper sections. The trailhead is unsigned, but there are flat spaces every so often for parking.

Ending trailhead: The trailhead is unsigned but has ample space for parking, a pit toilet, garbage cans, a picnic table, and flat campsites along Gallinas Creek. There is no reliable water.

Key points:
0.0   Unsigned trailhead/parking space just before stream crossing.
0.4   Road becomes deeply rutted and turns to single-track trail.
0.5   Trail crosses Middle Percha Creek at the unsigned wilderness boundary.
1.0   Ridge above Ladrone Gulch.
2.5   Head of Carbonate Creek.
2.8   Hillsboro Lake.
3.0   Signed trail junction with Black Range Crest Trail 79, optional side hike north on Trail 79 to Hillsboro Peak.
3.2   Signed trail junction with East Railroad Canyon Trail 130; turn left.
6.1   Signed trail junction of East Railroad Canyon Trail 130 and Railroad Canyon Trail 128; continue left.
6.7   Signed trail junction of Gallinas Canyon Trail 129 and Railroad Canyon Trail 128; continue left.
7.9   Unsigned trailhead on north side of primitive campground.

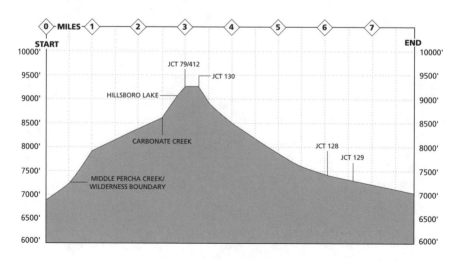

The hike: The hike begins on a rough road, which becomes a trail in 0.5 mile. This trail continues winding and rising for 3.0 miles to reach the Black Range Crest in a 9,250-foot-high saddle. Here you encounter the junction of the Crest Trail 79 and the Hillsboro By-Pass Trail 412.

After a steady climb, the trail reaches the dividing ridge between Middle Percha and Ladrone Gulch, drops into the gulch, and climbs steeply at times around the heads of Ladrone and Carbonate Creek. Although brushy for the most part, the trail opens to occasional vistas of rugged rims and canyons fanning off to the east. After some very steep pitches and contour stretches, the path improves and widens somewhat. Although well marked with tree blazes, the trail is lightly used and apt to be blocked with downfall in the upper mile.

Just below the crest of the Black Range at mile 2.8, the trail passes by the tiny mountain pond of Hillsboro Lake. Lined by aspen, spruce, and fir and overseen by rugged rocky rims, this is a very scenic interlude in the dense old-growth forest. The trail steepens for a rapid ascent to the crest at 3.0 miles and a gain thus far of 2,300 feet. A sign commemorates the one hundredth anniversary of Aldo Leopold's birth in 1887, as well as reentrance to the wilderness. This 9,250-foot-high saddle is a four-way junction between the north-south Black Range Crest Trail 79 and Hillsboro Peak Bypass Trail 412.

From the saddle, follow Trail 412 to the left (west). It angles slightly downhill and contours through a pine-fir forest to another trail junction in only 0.2 mile. At this second junction there is a sign for the Black Range Crest Trail and Hillsboro Bypass Trail 412. The sign for the trail to the left dropping into East Railroad Canyon points the way to the Gallinas Canyon Trail 129 (3.5 miles). Turn left here.

Trail 130 drops steeply into East Railroad Canyon in a pine-fir forest. After

Tiny Hillsboro Lake is nestled in an aspen grove just below the crest of the Black Range.

only 0.1 mile the trail has already lost 200 feet of elevation as it descends the right side of the gully above an old upside-down stock tank. It then does a bit of up and down to mile 3.6 before plunging to a side ravine that may carry early season water at 3.9 miles. Although steep, the trail is well blazed and easy to follow.

The trail climbs out of the ravine, sidehills, and then drops steeply across bedrock to the bottom, meeting the main canyon at 4.1 miles. Cross the streambed a few times, drop along the right side of the canyon, and cross again below a distinctive rock column with a human-shaped profile. The canyon is narrow, rocky, and brushy down to mile 5.0. The trail winds in and out of several side gullies, then drops pleasantly along the right side of the stream with several flat benches of Douglas fir and gambel oak. After passing by a brushy spring at 5.5 miles, the canyon closes in and becomes rockier. At 5.9 miles a picturesque stream spills over a 10-foot waterfall to a huge circular pool. The trail climbs 40 feet along a rocky sidehill, and at 6.1 miles reaches a signed junction with Railroad Canyon Trail 128 in a ponderosa pine park.

The pleasant, gentle gradient trail continues left down the canyon, winding in and out of the creek bottom, with a forest of ponderosa pine, Douglas fir, and gambel oak. The signed junction with Gallinas Canyon Trail 129 is reached after another 0.6 mile.

Continuing downstream to the left, the trail soon passes through a gap in the bedrock, with cliffs and walls rising high overhead. Pools scoured out of rock bowls offer a pleasant interlude along the stream. The trail climbs 50 feet above and then back to the creek, reaching an old corral at 7.5 miles. The delightful path winds through an open mix of pine, Douglas fir, and oak, with grassy flats along the canyon floor. The trail ends along a primitive two-track road and campsite, 7.9 trail miles from the Ladrone Trailhead.

Option: Consider climbing Hillsboro Peak (10,011 feet) from the saddle/trail junction south of the peak, 3.0 miles from the starting point. The summit is 1.4 miles and 760 feet higher by way of a good trail, and is well worth a side trip for the view alone. During the fire season you can visit with the Forest Service lookout person and duck out of the wind in a cabin left open for the public. If the lookout ranger is there, you might be able to fetch water from the locked cistern. Otherwise, Hillsboro Spring is a steep 600 vertical feet below the north side of the peak.

Emory Pass Trailhead

*"I say no reason is good enough to justify opening up the Gila.
I say that to open up the Gila wilderness is not development,
but blindness. The very fact that it is the last wilderness is in
itself proof that its highest use is to remain so."*

—Aldo Leopold, *Outdoor Life,* 1925

12 Hillsboro Peak

          Highlights: High crest of Black Range with fabulous views; lofty Hillsboro Peak (southern sentinel of the Aldo) with historic cabin and manned lookout
          Type of hike: Out-and-back day hike or overnight backpack
          Total distance: 10 miles round-trip
          Difficulty: Strenuous
          Best months: April to November
          Maps: Forest Service Aldo Leopold Wilderness Map; Hillsboro Peak USGS quad
Special considerations: In early spring you might encounter snowbanks in shady spots. The trail is dry all the way to the peak. Carry plenty of water.

Finding the trailhead: From Interstate 25, 12 miles south of Truth or Consequences, New Mexico, take NM 152 (the Geronimo Trail Scenic Byway) west 34 miles to Emory Pass. Turn right (north) at the pass to the vista parking lot. The faded sign for Trail 79 is located immediately south of the pit toilet on the west side of the 0.2-mile paved road to the parking area.

Parking and trailhead facilities: A paved parking area, picnic table, pit toilet, and interpretive display of area's history and geology are at the trailhead. There is no water.

Key points:
  0.0   Overlook trailhead.
  0.4   Heliport and communications tower.
  1.9   Signed wilderness boundary.
  2.1   Trail reenters wilderness.
  3.6   Another entrance to the wilderness, along with a signed four-way trail junction between the Crest Trail 79, Ladrone Trail 127 east to Kingston, and Hillsboro Peak Bypass Trail 412.
  4.2   Trail passes through a gate/fence.
  4.7   Second stock gate crosses trail.
  5.0   Hillsboro Peak lookout (10,011 feet).

Hillsboro Peak

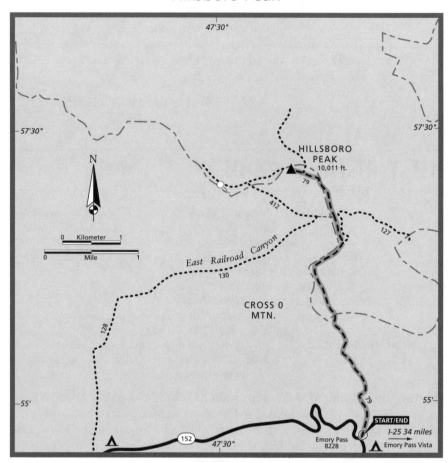

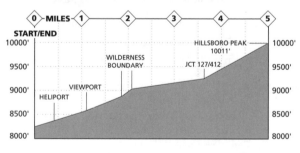

The hike: Hillsboro Peak is perhaps the most popular hike in the Aldo Leopold Wilderness, and one of the most popular in the entire Gila National Forest. It is still a long way from being crowded, and unless you're there on a summer weekend, you might have the entire hike to yourself. Beginning at Emory Pass, the trail stays high on the crest of the Black Range all the way to 10,011-foot Hillsboro Peak. Unlike hikes from canyon mouth trailheads lower down, you'll gain much of the elevation on the drive to the trailhead.

At the scenic overlook and parking area, a small sign points to Trail 79 just south of the rest room. At first the trail climbs steeply to the north and then contours on an old roadbed to a heliport and communications tower at 0.4 mile. The trail passes a gate and hiker's maze at 0.5 mile, and curves to the west side of the ridge, where it becomes a good single-track trail. After climbing gently, the first good viewpoint is reached at mile 1.1, opening to a rocky cliff face to the north.

The trail continues on a moderate grade with grand vistas of a densely forested mountainscape to the south and west. The trail weaves in and out of the wilderness boundary, reaching the first signed entrance at 1.9 miles, and then switchbacks to a ridge top where it meets the boundary again at 2.1 miles. From here the trail sidehills on the east side of the crest through a spruce-fir forest. This pleasant stretch of trail continues for another mile to a rocky viewpoint toward the southeast. The crest narrows, becoming rocky in places, with grand views into the rugged rocky reaches of upper East Railroad Canyon.

At 3.6 miles the trail reaches a small open saddle on the ridge with a sign commemorating the one hundredth anniversary of Aldo Leopold's birth in 1887. This is also a well-signed junction of the Crest Trail going straight, Ladrone Trail 127 turning right (east) down to Kingston, and Hillsboro Peak Bypass Trail 412 heading west around the head of East Railroad Canyon. People have made a dry camp in this saddle, but if it's late in the day and you need to set up camp, drop down 0.2 mile on Trail 127 to tiny Hillsboro Lake where you'll find water, potable once its treated.

After taking a well-deserved break at this shady, relaxing spot, continue north on Crest Trail 79 for another 1.4 miles to Hillsboro Peak. The trail makes a series of long, easy switchbacks in the pine-fir forest, and passes through a gate. After continuing through aspen groves, a second gate is reached at mile 4.7. The trail is wide and well graded for the final 200-foot climb over a distance of 0.3 mile to the long, open ridge-top summit of 10,011-foot-high Hillsboro Peak, complete with cabins, lookout, and heliport.

A friendly Forest Service sign welcomes you to the top, as will a friendly lookout ranger if you visit during the fire season when the lookout is manned. The ranger lives in the west cabin, but the east cabin is left open for the public to use, both for safety purposes and as a practical way to avoid break-ins. The east cabin was built in 1925 and remains in good condition, thanks to responsible people who are careful to clean up after they leave. In addition to providing refuge from an almost constant wind, the cabin has a sheltered front porch with a fabulous view eastward. The logbook is entertaining to read, with many entries extolling the beauty and solitude of the Aldo. You can feel the exuberance of people when they write about "a lovely walk in the high country, so happy to be here!"

The lookout and ranger cabin were constructed in 1934, replacing the previous wooden lookout. For an incredible 360-degree view of the entire Black Range and surrounding valleys and mountains, climb to the lookout cabin. The metal stairway is sturdy and guarded by railings, but those with a fear

View to north from the Hillsboro Peak portion of Trail 79 (1.6 miles north of Emory Pass).

of heights would probably be happier on the ground. With permission from the ranger, you can fill up your water bottles from an otherwise locked rain cistern near the cabin. You might also be able to obtain water from a spring some 600 feet below and to the north of the lookout.

To complete this out-and-back hike to Hillsboro Peak, retrace your route back down to Emory Pass.

Option: If you drop down to the spring, you might want to take the trail on the west side of the peak back to Black Range Crest Trail 79 and continue down to Hillsboro Bypass Trail 412. Turn left onto the bypass trail and follow it back to the four-way trail junction in the saddle south of Hillsboro Peak. This option adds about 1.5 miles to the hike, as well as scenic views into East Railroad Canyon, while eliminating a considerable amount of up-and-down hiking.

13 Emory Pass–Gallinas Canyon

Highlights:	High crest of Black Range with fabulous views, rugged canyons, and a pleasant stream with picturesque rock formations
Type of hike:	Shuttle day hike or overnighter
Total distance:	8.5 miles
Difficulty:	Strenuous
Best months:	April to November
Maps:	Forest Service Aldo Leopold Wilderness Map; Hillsboro Peak USGS quad
Special considerations:	In early spring you might encounter snowbanks in shady spots. The trail is dry all the way to the peak; carry plenty of water. There are numerous small stream crossings.

Finding the trailheads: *Beginning trailhead:* From Interstate 25, 12 miles south of Truth or Consequences, New Mexico, take NM 152 (the Geronimo Trail Scenic Byway) west 34 miles to Emory Pass. Turn right (north) at the pass to the vista parking lot. The faded sign for Trail 79 is located immediately south of the pit toilet on the west side of the 0.2-mile paved road to the parking area.

Ending trailhead: From Emory Pass, drive 4 miles west on NM 152 to a small "129" sign on the highway. Turn right (north) into the undeveloped campground. The trailhead is at the north end of the unpaved camping area, 0.3 mile north of the highway.

The driving distance between the two trailheads is about 4 paved miles.

Parking and trailhead facilities: *Beginning trailhead:* A paved parking area, picnic table, pit toilet, and interpretive display of area's history and geology are at the trailhead. There is no water.

Emory Pass–Gallinas Canyon

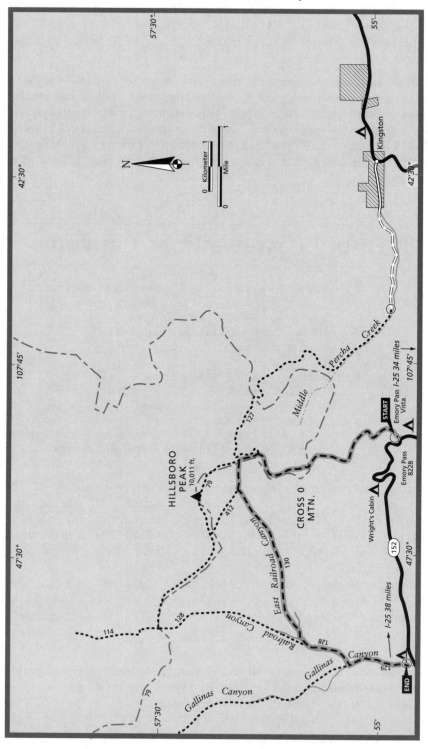

Ending trailhead: Unsigned trailhead has ample space for parking, a pit toilet, garbage cans, a picnic table, and flat campsites along Gallinas Creek. There is no reliable water.

Key points:
- 0.0   Emory Pass trailhead.
- 0.4   Heliport and communications tower.
- 1.9   Signed wilderness boundary.
- 3.6   Wilderness boundary; signed four-way trail junction of Crest Trail 79, Ladrone Trail 127, and Hillsboro Peak Bypass Trail 412; go left on Bypass Trail.
- 3.8   Signed trail junction with East Railroad Canyon Trail 130; turn left.
- 6.7   Signed trail junction of East Railroad Canyon Trail 130 and Railroad Canyon Trail 128; continue left.
- 7.3   Signed trail junction of Gallinas Canyon Trail 129 and Railroad Canyon Trail 128; continue left.
- 8.5   Unsigned trailhead on north side of primitive campground.

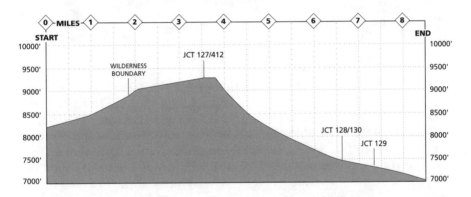

The hike: This hike takes you along the Black Range crest for 3 miles, then descends swiftly onto the west side of the divide, via rocky forested canyons.

At the scenic overlook and parking area, a small sign points to Trail 79 just south of the rest room. At first the trail climbs steeply to the north and then contours on an old roadbed to a heliport and communications tower at 0.4 mile. The trail passes a gate and hiker's maze at 0.5 mile, and curves to the west side of the ridge, where it becomes a good single-track trail. After climbing gently, the first good viewpoint is reached at mile 1.1, opening to a rocky cliff face to the north.

The trail weaves in and out of the wilderness, reaching the first signed entrance at 1.9 miles, and then switchbacks to a ridge top where it meets the boundary again at 2.1 miles. From here the trail sidehills on the east side of the crest through a spruce-fir forest. This pleasant stretch of trail continues for another mile to a rocky viewpoint toward the southeast. The crest narrows, becoming rocky in places, with grand views into the rugged rocky reaches of upper East Railroad Canyon.

At 3.6 miles the trail reaches a small open saddle on the ridge with a sign commemorating the one hundredth anniversary of Aldo Leopold's birth in

A hiker pauses to take in the view from the Hillsboro Peak Trail.

1887. This is also a well-signed junction of the Crest Trail going straight, Ladrone Trail 127 turning right (east) down to Kingston, and Hillsboro Peak Bypass Trail 412 heading west around the head of East Railroad Canyon.

Turn left on the Bypass Trail, which angles slightly downhill and contours through a pine-fir forest to a trail junction and sign for the Black Range Crest Trail and Hillsboro Bypass Trail 412 only 0.2 mile from the saddle. Turn left on Trail 130, which drops steeply into East Railroad Canyon in a pine-fir forest. After only 0.1 mile the trail has already lost 200 feet of elevation as it descends the right side of the gully. It then does a bit of up and down to mile 4.2 before plunging to a side ravine that may carry early season water at 4.5 miles. Although steep, the trail is well blazed and easy to follow.

The trail climbs out of the ravine, sidehills, and then drops steeply across bedrock to the bottom, meeting the main canyon at 4.7 miles. Cross the streambed a few times, drop along the right side of the canyon, and cross again below a distinctive rock column with a human-shaped profile. After passing by a brushy spring at 6.1 miles, the canyon closes in and becomes rockier. At 6.5 miles the stream spills over a 10-foot waterfall to a huge circular pool. The trail climbs 40 feet along a rocky sidehill, and at 6.7 miles reaches a signed junction with Railroad Canyon Trail 128 in a ponderosa pine park. Turn left again.

The pleasant gentle gradient trail continues down the canyon, winding in and out of the creek bottom, with a forest of ponderosa pine, Douglas fir, and gambel oak. The signed junction with Gallinas Canyon Trail 129 is reached after another 0.6 mile. Continue downstream.

The trail soon passes through a gap in the bedrock, with cliffs and walls rising high overhead. Pools scoured out of rock bowls offer a pleasant interlude along the stream. The trail climbs 50 feet above and then back to the creek, reaching an old corral at 8.1 miles. The delightful path winds through an open mix of pine, Douglas fir, and oak, with grassy flats along the canyon floor. The trail ends along a primitive two-track road and campsite, 8.5 trail miles from the Emory Pass trailhead.

Option: Consider climbing Hillsboro Peak (10,011 feet) from the saddle/trail junction south of the peak, 3.6 miles from the starting point. The summit is 1.4 miles and 760 feet higher by way of the good Crest Trail, and is well worth a side trip for the view alone. During the fire season you can visit with the Forest Service lookout ranger and duck out of the wind in a cabin left open for the public. If the lookout ranger is there, you might be able to fetch water from the locked cistern. Otherwise, the closest water is at Hillsboro Spring, a steep 600 vertical feet below the north side of the peak.

14 Emory Pass–Holden Prong

Highlights:	Vistas from the Crest Trail to a rugged narrow canyon with a stream
Type of hike:	Three- to four-day out-and-back backpack
Total distance:	27.8 miles round-trip
Difficulty:	Strenuous
Best months:	April through October
Maps:	Forest Service Aldo Leopold Wilderness Map; Hillsboro Peak and Victoria Park USGS quads
Special considerations:	Campsites are infrequent down Holden Prong. There are many stream crossings; some may be deep during spring.

Finding the trailhead: From Interstate 25, 12 miles south of Truth or Consequences, New Mexico, take NM 152 (the Geronimo Trail Scenic Byway) west 34 miles to Emory Pass. Turn right (north) at the pass to the vista parking lot. The faded sign for Trail 79 is located immediately south of the pit toilet on the west side of the 0.2-mile paved road to the parking area.

Parking and trailhead facilities: A paved parking area, picnic table, pit toilet, and interpretive display of area's history and geology are at the trailhead. There is no water.

Key points:
- 0.0 Emory Pass trailhead.
- 0.4 Heliport and communications tower.
- 1.9 Signed wilderness boundary.
- 2.1 Trail reenters wilderness.
- 3.6 Wilderness boundary; signed four-way trail junction of Crest Trail 79, Ladrone Trail 127 east to Kingston, and Hillsboro Peak Bypass Trail 412; continue left on Bypass Trail.

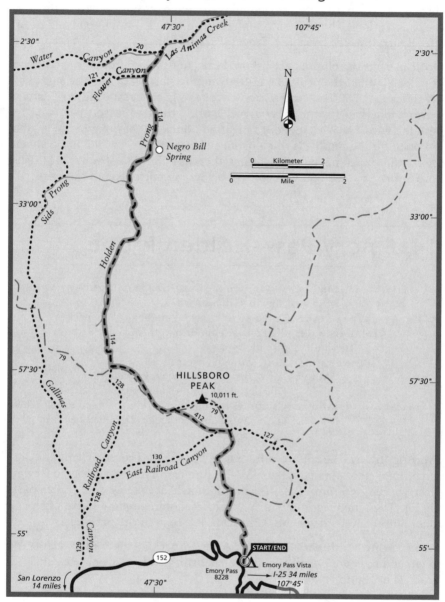

3.8	Signed trail junction with East Railroad Canyon Trail 130; continue right.
4.9	Signed trail junction with Black Range Crest Trail 79; continue left.
6.5	Holden Prong Saddle, junction of Trails 79, 128, and 114; turn right.
10.7	Mouth of Sids Prong.
12.1	Side path to Negro Bill Spring.
13.4	Mouth of Flower Canyon, junction with Trail 121; stay right.
13.9	Mouth of Water Canyon, junction with Trail 20.

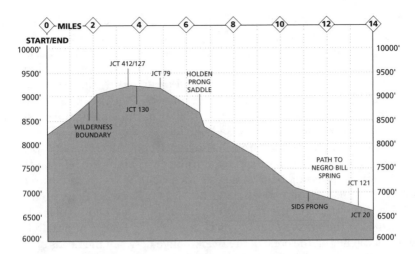

The hike: From the broad vistas along the Black Range Crest to the narrow canyon of Holden Prong, this backpack outing provides variety. At the scenic overlook and parking area, a small sign points to Trail 79 just south of the rest room. At first the trail climbs steeply to the north, then contours on an old roadbed to a heliport and communications tower at 0.4 mile. The trail passes a gate and hiker's maze at 0.5 mile, and curves to the west side of the ridge, where it becomes a good single-track trail.

After climbing gently, the first good viewpoint is reached at mile 1.1, opening to a rocky cliff face to the north. The trail continues on a moderate grade with grand vistas of a densely forested mountainscape to the south and west. The trail weaves in and out of the wilderness, reaching the first signed entrance at 1.9 miles, and then switchbacks to a ridge top where it meets the boundary again at 2.1 miles. From here the trail sidehills on the east side of the crest through a spruce-fir forest. This pleasant stretch of trail continues for another mile to a rocky viewpoint toward the southeast. The crest narrows, becoming rocky in places, with grand views into the rugged rocky reaches of upper East Railroad Canyon.

At 3.6 miles the trail reaches a small open saddle on the ridge, where a sign commemorates the one hundredth anniversary of Aldo Leopold's birth in 1887. This is also a well-signed trail junction of the Crest Trail going straight, Ladrone Trail 127 turning right (east) down to Kingston, and the Hillsboro Peak Bypass Trail 412 heading west around the head of East Railroad Canyon. People have made a dry camp in this saddle, but if it's late in the day and you need to set up camp, drop down 0.2 mile on Trail 127 to tiny Hillsboro Lake where you'll find water, potable once it's treated.

The route to Holden Prong follows Trail 412, the peak bypass. From the junction in the saddle, Trail 412 goes to the left (west). It angles slightly downhill and contours through a pine-fir forest to a trail junction and sign for the Black Range Crest Trail and Hillsboro Bypass Trail 412. The sign for the trail to the left dropping into East Railroad Canyon points the way to the Gallinas Canyon Trail 129 (3.5 miles). Continue straight ahead and to the right on the bypass trail.

The good, well-constructed trail contours around the scenic head of East Railroad Canyon, winding through a pine-fir forest with cliffs rising overhead. Shortly after passing a stock fence, there is a signed junction in a pleasant pine-studded saddle. This is the intersection of the Bypass Trail and the Black Range Crest Trail. Don't be confused by an old WILDERNESS PERMIT REQUIRED sign on the trail to the lookout. Permits have not been required since the Aldo was designated wilderness in 1980. Continue along the crest ridge westward, toward Holden Prong Saddle.

The Crest Trail descends through a lovely aspen-oak woodland sprinkled with a few gigantic Douglas fir trees. Climb gently along the left (south) side of the ridgeline, passing below massive rock outcrops with a fractured rock chimney. There are some good views down into Railroad Canyon, then the trail drops through a dense thicket of gambel oak, favored by black bear in the spring, to the grassy opening of Holden Prong Saddle at mile 6.5. This scenic saddle lies on the crest of the Black Range between the heads of Holden Prong to the north and Railroad Canyon to the south.

The Holden Prong trail sign suggests it's 6.5 miles to Animas Creek. Although it's about a mile farther than that, the journey down the prong is scenic as it travels along the stream through dense forest. The stream crossings, especially in early spring, can be challenging; it might be above your knees at some crossings. As a result, it is slow going, but this is beautiful country, so why rush it?

Turn right (north) on Holden Prong Trail 114. The trail drops quickly in the first 0.2 mile, descending 300 feet through dense aspen and subalpine fir. The narrow valley cut by the stream does not have many campsites, especially in the first 3.5 miles, so don't put off your selection until late in the day. There are long stretches of the trail with no clear level spots at all. The narrow, rocky canyon is cluttered with downfall, although the trail is clear and well maintained. The dampness of the shady canyon has protected it from the fires that are common elsewhere in the Aldo, so the old-growth forest is reminiscent of the Germanic forests described by the Brothers Grimm.

You will no doubt notice the blazes on the route: They've been painted on the tree trunks and boulders along the trail with white paint and a 4-inch brush. Perhaps this technique of trail marking is kinder than the traditional gouges in the bark, and they sure stand out, but they are sort of garish in this dark, woodsy canyon. Because we didn't see them elsewhere in the Aldo, apparently it was only an experiment not repeated.

At 10.7 miles, the rocky mouth of Sids Prong is on the left. You may spot its stream joining Holden Prong, but there is no trail there. At 12.1 miles, watch for a stream or a trickle on the east bank of the prong, indicating the location of Negro Bill Spring. At this point, the trail cuts through a lumpy grass meadow west of the creek, so you could easily miss it. Another hint of the spring is a defunct signpost standing on the right side of the trail. Only the rusty bolts remain; the sign to this politically incorrect spring is gone, as is the trail. Trail 309, although still on the wilderness map, is unmaintained and has been erased by the wilderness. To visit the spring, cross

Holden Prong is a sizable stream 2 miles below the saddle.

the prong on the barely visible pathway and climb about 100 feet above the stream on the east bank into the rolling ponderosa pine park. Follow the little stream to its source at the spring, about 0.1 mile from the prong. There is no trail beyond the spring, just a few stray old blazes, done the traditional way.

Continue down the prong to the north if you want to go all the way to Animas Creek. The valley floor broadens as you descend, so there are more possibilities for campsites. Towering stone obelisks stand starkly against the sky before you reach the mouth of Flower Canyon 6.9 miles from the saddle. The junction with Trail 121 up Flower Canyon is marked with a downed old sign propped on a ponderosa pine on the west side of the trail. The trail up Flower Canyon is faint. Another 0.5 mile brings you to the mouth of Water Canyon and another junction. Trail 20 goes left, while the Prong Trail bends eastward, continuing along Animas Creek. There is a flat grassy area at the junction, which is the destination of this hike. Return to Emory Pass by the same route.

Option: On your return to the trailhead, you might want to hike up and over Hillsboro Peak, skipping the bypass route on Trail 412. Stay on the Crest Trail (79) to the peak, and continue on it down to the south all the way back to Emory Pass.

Note: If you are looking for a loop trip instead of an out-and-back, Trail 116 up East Curtis Canyon, continuing as Trail 117 along the Animas Divide to Hillsboro Peak, might look like a decent route on the Forest Service wilderness map. Even the more detailed USGS quads (Victoria Park and Apache Peak) don't indicate the true brutality of this trail. So it's time for a reality check. First of all, it's about 14 long, slow, dry miles to the junction below Hillsboro Peak, not the 8 miles on the sign at the Animas junction. Second, both water and campsites are rare. It's at least 4 arduous miles, gaining more than 1,800 feet, to reach even marginal campsites, which may be waterless. Also be aware that Trail 117 beyond East Curtis Spring through Magner Park no longer exists; likewise the cutover Trail 309 to Negro Bill Spring has been erased by the wilderness.

About a mile south of East Curtis Spring, Trail 117 leaves the dry streambed and climbs toward Granite Peak. Things only get worse in this second half. Not only is it dry and devoid of campsites, it is extremely brushy, with catclaw, mountain locust, and gambel oak clustered on the trail in great profusion. Burned areas in which the trail completely vanishes add to the challenge, as does the subsequent downfall. The East Curtis Canyon–Animas Divide trail is no longer maintained by the Forest Service, even though it is still on the map. The New Mexico Department of Game and Fish, capitalizing on the difficulties of the East Curtis route, has established peregrine falcons in the canyon and would prefer that hiker traffic remain nonexistent. It's a perfect place for raptors, not backpackers.

15 Emory Pass–Prongs

Highlights:	Vistas from the Black Range Crest, deep mountain canyons with perennial streams
Type of hike:	Four- to five-day backpack loop
Total distance:	33.2 miles
Difficulty:	Strenuous
Best months:	April through October
Maps:	Forest Service Aldo Leopold Wilderness map; Hillsboro Peak and Victoria Park USGS quads
Special considerations:	The trail is dry to the head of Sids Prong. Carry ample water. The nearly abandoned trail into Flower Canyon is extremely rough, steep, and brushy. It is recommended only for seasoned hikers. Holden Prong has numerous stream crossings that may be deep during the spring. There are very few campsites along Holden Prong.

Finding the trailhead: From Interstate 25, 12 miles south of Truth or Consequences, New Mexico, take NM 152 (the Geronimo Trail Scenic Byway) west 34 miles to Emory Pass. Turn right (north) at the pass to the vista parking lot. The faded sign for Trail 79 is located immediately south of the pit toilet on the west side of the 0.2-mile paved road to the parking area.

Parking and trailhead facilities: A large paved parking area, picnic table, pit toilet, and interpretive display of area's history and geology are at the trailhead. There is no water.

Key points:

0.0	Emory Pass trailhead.
0.4	Heliport and communications tower.
1.9	Signed wilderness boundary.
2.1	Trail reenters wilderness.
3.6	Wilderness boundary; signed four-way trail junction of Crest Trail 79, Ladrone Trail 127 east to Kingston, and Hillsboro Peak Bypass Trail 412.
3.8	Signed trail junction with East Railroad Canyon Trail 130; continue right.
4.9	Signed trail junction with Black Range Crest Trail 79; continue left.
6.5	Saddle, junction with Trails 79, 128, and 114; continue straight ahead.
9.0	Saddle, junction of Sids Prong and Gallinas Canyon Trails; turn right.
11.9	Corral in Sids Prong.
15.3	Leave Prong; trail follows tributary north.
16.8	Drop to Pretty Creek.
17.0	Junction of Flower Canyon Trail 121 and Pretty Canyon Trail 812; continue right.
18.8	Dividing ridge between Water and Flower Canyons.
19.8	Signed junction with Holden Prong Trail 114; turn right.
21.1	Side path to Negro Bill Spring.
22.5	Mouth of Sids Prong.
26.7	Black Range Crest, junction of Trails 79 and 128; turn left.

Emory Pass–Prongs

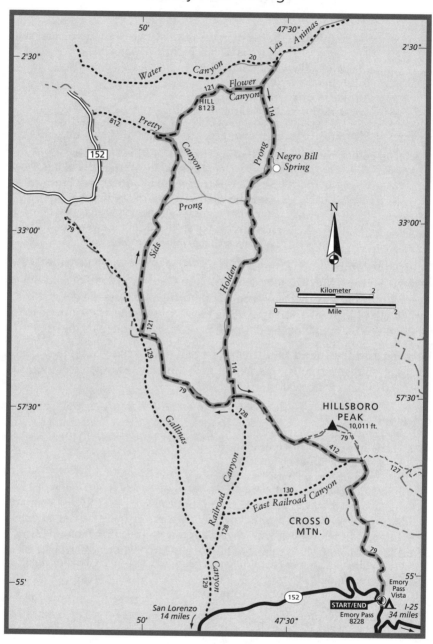

28.3   Junction with Hillsboro Peak Bypass Trail 412; turn right.
29.4   Junction with East Railroad Canyon Trail 130; continue left.
29.6   Junction with Crest Trail 79; turn right.
33.2   Emory Pass trailhead.

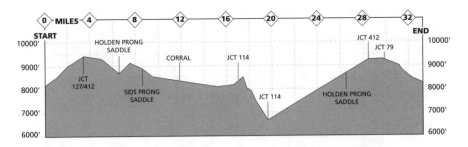

The hike: From the broad vistas along the Black Range Crest to the narrow canyons of Sids and Holden Prongs, this backpack provides incredible variety. At the scenic overlook and parking area, a small sign points to Trail 79 just south of the rest room. At first the trail climbs steeply to the north, then contours on an old roadbed to a heliport and communications tower at 0.4 mile. The trail passes a gate and hiker's maze at 0.5 mile, and curves to the west side of the ridge, where it becomes a good single-track trail. After climbing gently, the first good viewpoint is reached at mile 1.1, opening to a rocky cliff face to the north.

The trail continues on a moderate grade with grand vistas of a densely forested mountainscape to the south and west. The trail weaves in and out of the wilderness, reaching the first signed entrance at 1.9 miles, and then switchbacks to a ridge top where it meets the boundary again at 2.1 miles. From here the trail sidehills on the east side of the crest through a spruce-fir forest. This pleasant stretch of trail continues for another mile to a rocky viewpoint toward the southeast. The crest narrows, becoming rocky in places, with grand views into the rugged rocky reaches of upper East Railroad Canyon.

At 3.6 miles the trail reaches a small open saddle on the ridge with a sign commemorating the one hundredth anniversary of Aldo Leopold's birth in 1887. This is also a well-signed trail junction of the Crest Trail going straight, Ladrone Trail 127 turning right (east) down to Kingston, and Hillsboro Peak Bypass Trail 412 heading west around the head of East Railroad Canyon. People have made a dry camp in this saddle, but if it's late in the day and you need to set up camp, drop down 0.2 mile on Trail 127 to tiny Hillsboro Lake where you'll find water, potable once it's treated.

The route to Holden Prong follows Trail 412, the peak bypass to the left (west). It angles slightly downhill and contours through a pine-fir forest to a trail junction in only 0.2 mile. The bypass trail continues straight ahead to the right. The good, well-constructed trail contours around the scenic head of East Railroad Canyon, winding through a pine-fir forest with cliffs rising overhead. Shortly after passing a stock fence, a signed junction is reached in a pleasant pine-studded saddle. This is the intersection of the Bypass Trail and the Black Range Crest Trail. Don't be confused by an old WILDERNESS PERMIT REQUIRED sign on the trail to the lookout. Permits have not been required since the Aldo was designated wilderness back in 1980. Continue westward along the ridge toward Holden Prong Saddle.

The Crest Trail descends through a lovely aspen-oak woodland sprinkled with a few gigantic Douglas fir trees. Climb gently along the left (south) side of the ridgeline, passing below massive rock outcrops with a slotted, fractured rock chimney. There are some good views down into Railroad Canyon, then the trail drops through a dense thicket of gambel oak, favored by black bear in the spring, to the grassy opening of Holden Prong Saddle at mile 6.5. This scenic saddle lies on the crest of the Black Range between the heads of Holden Prong to the north and Railroad Canyon to the south.

Continue west on the Crest Trail, which climbs steadily up a gambel oak slope with scenic views back to the east side of upper Railroad Canyon. The trail passes by an old stock fence that runs parallel to the downhill side of the trail, then gradually climbs to a forest of aspen and southwestern white pine, reaching the dividing ridge between West Railroad Canyon and Gallinas Canyon at 7.5 miles. For the most part, the trail is good, but in this section it narrows and is somewhat overgrown with thorny mountain locust. A gradual descent over the next 1.5 miles brings you to Sids Prong saddle and the four-way signed trail junction of the Crest Trail, Gallinas Canyon Trail 129, and Sids Prong Trail 121.

After pausing at the saddle, continue north (right) into Sids Prong. The wide valley of the prong features grassy benches framed by old-growth pine and fir. These meadows are nearly continuous for the next 3 miles down the prong, like descending stairsteps along the stream. These lush grasslands are home to thousands of busy rodents whose earthen runs are most noticeable in early spring after the melting of the snow. The presence of this subterranean population brings various predators to the valley: red-tailed hawks, bears, and coyotes. The lumpy earth resulting from all this activity makes it difficult to find a suitable tent site, although small campsites are dotted along the lower stream edge.

The trail slopes gradually but steadily down the valley. The meadows become broader with decreasing elevation. There's an old corral about midway down the valley, which grows narrow at the lower end before the trail cuts off on its winding route to Pretty Canyon. If you plan to camp soon, you should select a site here in lower Sids Prong.

The route out of the prong over to Pretty Canyon is clear and easy to follow, with blazes and a conspicuous track on the ground. This is fortunate, because the lower trail location is shown incorrectly on the wilderness map and it does not appear at all on the 1963 Victoria Park quad. At 17.0 miles, you arrive at the junction with the Flower Canyon Trail, which you are going to take, heading right (east) and the Pretty Canyon Trail going uphill to your left (west).

The Flower Canyon segment down to Holden Prong is for the well-conditioned adventurer. For all practical purposes, the trail is no longer maintained. In places the trail is so steep, rough, and brushy that you'll wonder if you've lost it. These disadvantages are offset to some extent by the spellbinding beauty and solitude of surrounding canyons and formations and by the opportunities for excellent loop hikes that this trail provides.

At first the trail climbs along a grassy hillside and enters a pine forest, reaching the ridge directly above the head of Flower Canyon at 17.4 miles. The ridge top is well marked with rock cairns. Pause here for a spectacular view. For the next 0.5 mile, the brushy trail (white oak and locust) is hard

Backpacking on the crest of the Black Range southwest of Hillsboro Peak.

to find as it plunges down a rocky, sandy ridgeline gully. The brush makes this a tricky section of trail, but if you angle left (north) to the ridge between Water and Flower Canyons, you'll pick up a much more distinct trail by mile 18.1. The trail sidehills up and then around the north slope of hill 8123 (shown on the quad map). Varying between pure route finding and following the occasional rock cairn, the trail offers astounding views of raw, exposed rock formations—great twisted slabs and monumental pillars. A stunning viewpoint (an excuse to take a break) is reached at 18.2 miles. The narrow trail then becomes more distinct with a few blazed trees, but drops steeply on a loose gravelly surface along the left side of the ridge, crossing a saddle into Flower Canyon at mile 18.8.

From the dividing ridge, the trail follows the steep left side of a gully down to Flower Canyon at 19.3 miles. Appropriately, the canyon treated us to a lovely display of lupine and yellow aster during our early spring hike. The trail crosses the tiny stream and descends gently along the right side before climbing 50 feet above canyon walls. Red rock forms the streambed, with high red rock rims beyond and above Holden Prong. At mile 19.6 the trail climbs high on the left side above a chasm with waterfalls when the stream is running.

This is a confusing spot. Contour straight to a rock cairn and you'll quickly find the trail as it drops to the stream bottom. After crossing to the right, the trail climbs and contours above the narrow drainage down to its junction with the Holden Prong Trail in a ponderosa pine flat. You'll appreciate this lovely park next to the delightful pools and rushing water of Holden Prong after your rugged descent from Pretty Canyon. There are several campsites near this junction, and farther downstream at the Water Canyon Trail junction as well. Your camping choices will be limited farther up this prong.

To complete the loop trip, head south up Holden Prong on Trail 114. Towering stone obelisks stand starkly against the sky upstream from the junction. One mile from the beginning of the Holden Prong Trail, there is a rare 0.15-mile stretch of straight, flat trail on the west side of the prong. Watch for a stream or a trickle on the east bank of the prong, which will indicate the location of Negro Bill Spring. At this point, the trail cuts through a lumpy grass meadow west of the creek, so you could easily miss it. Another hint of the spring is a defunct signpost standing next to the trail. Only the rusty bolts remain; the sign to this politically incorrect spring is gone, as is the trail. Trail 309, although still on the wilderness map, is unmaintained and has been erased by the wilderness. To visit the spring, cross the prong on the barely visible pathway and climb about 100 feet above the stream on the east bank into the rolling ponderosa pine park. Follow the little stream to its source at the spring, about 0.1 mile from the prong. There is no trail beyond the spring, just a few stray old blazes.

Continuing upstream on the prong, the trail departs from streamside on two occasions when the valley becomes a rocky gorge with no space for a trail. During these short hillside interludes, the tumultuous sound of falls and rapids fills the narrow canyon. At 22.5 miles, the rocky mouth of Sids Prong is on the right. The journey up Holden Prong is scenic as it travels along the stream through the dense forest. The stream crossings, especially in early spring, can be challenging; the water might be above your knees at some crossings. As a result, it is slow going, but this is beautiful country, so why rush it?

You will no doubt notice the blazes on the route: They've been painted on the tree trunks and boulders along the trail with white paint and a 4-inch brush. Perhaps this technique of trail marking is kinder than the traditional gouges in the bark, and they sure stand out, but they are sort of garish in this dark, woodsy canyon. Because we didn't see them elsewhere in the Aldo, apparently it was only an experiment that was not repeated.

Campsites become less frequent as you ascend this narrow canyon. Don't put off your selection until late in the day. There are long stretches of the trail with no clear level spots at all. The narrow, rocky canyon is cluttered with downfall, although the trail is clear and well maintained. The dampness of the shady canyon has protected it from the fires that are common elsewhere in the Aldo; here the old-growth forest is reminiscent of the Germanic forests described by the Brothers Grimm.

After following the stream for 6.5 miles, the trail begins to switchback up the steep slope at the head of the valley, climbing through thickly bunched aspen to reach the Black Range Crest at 26.7 miles.

At this saddle, you have completed the loop portion of the backpack. Return to the Emory Pass trailhead by taking the Crest Trail left (east) to Hillsboro Peak Bypass Trail 412, then turning south on Trail 79.

Option: On your return to the trailhead, you might want to hike up and over Hillsboro Peak, skipping the bypass route on Trail 412. Stay on the Crest Trail to the peak, and continue on it to the south all the way back to Emory Pass.

Note: If you are tempted to take the East Curtis–Animas Divide trail on your loop trip, reconsider. Taking Trail 116 up East Curtis Canyon and Trail 117 along the Animas Divide to Hillsboro Peak looks like a decent route on the Forest Service wilderness map. Even the more detailed topo maps (Victoria Park and Apache Peak) don't indicate the true brutality of this trail. It's about 14 long, slow miles to the junction below Hillsboro Peak, not the 8 miles on the sign at the Animas junction, and both water and campsites are rare. It's at least 4 arduous miles, gaining more than 1,800 feet, to reach even marginal campsites, which may be waterless. Also, Trail 117 beyond East Curtis Spring through Magner Park no longer exists; likewise the cutover Trail 309 to Negro Bill Spring has been erased by the wilderness.

About a mile south of East Curtis Spring, Trail 117 leaves the dry streambed and climbs toward Granite Peak. Things only get worse in this second half. Not only is it dry and devoid of campsites, it is extremely brushy, with catclaw, mountain locust, and gambel oak clustered on the trail in great profusion. Burned areas in which the trail completely vanishes add to the challenge, as does the subsequent downfall. The East Curtis Canyon–Animas Divide trail is no longer maintained by the Forest Service even though it is still on the map. The New Mexico Department of Game and Fish, capitalizing on the difficulties of the East Curtis route, has established peregrine falcons in the canyon and would prefer that hiker traffic remain nonexistent. It's a perfect place for raptors, not backpackers.

Gallinas Canyon

"Now the question is this:
Why should not the Gila area . . .
be declared permanently roadless,
and dedicated to that particular form
of public recreation beloved by the wilderness hunter?"

—Aldo Leopold, *Outdoor Life,* 1925

16 Lower Gallinas Canyon

Highlights: Delightful trail, forest, stream, and canyon, all readily accessible throughout much of the year
Type of hike: Out-and-back day hike
Total distance: 2.4 miles round-trip
Difficulty: Easy
Best months: April through October
Maps: Forest Service Aldo Leopold Wilderness Map; Hillsboro Peak USGS quad
Special considerations: There are several crossings of the small creek, plus one short steep stretch.

Finding the trailhead: From Interstate 25, 12 miles south of Truth or Consequences, New Mexico, take NM 152 (the Geronimo Trail Scenic Byway) west 38 miles to a small "129" sign on the highway. Turn right (north) into the undeveloped campground. The trailhead is at the north end of the unpaved camping area, 0.3 mile north of the highway.

Parking and trailhead facilities: There is a primitive campground at trailhead, as well as a large unpaved parking area, pit toilet, garbage cans, a picnic table, and flat campsites along Gallinas Creek. There is no reliable water.

Key points:
0.0   Unsigned trailhead at north end of primitive campground.
0.4   Old corral.
1.2   Signed junction of Gallinas Canyon Trail 129 and Railroad Canyon Trail 128.

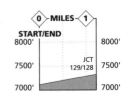

The hike: Unless you shorten some of the canyon hikes, you won't find many other short, easy hikes in this book. It's no coincidence that the hike also falls outside of the formal wilderness boundary. After all, much of the Aldo is far too rugged for any hike to be called "easy." But in terms of hiking quality, this compares favorably with any of the other wilderness canyon hikes. Gallinas Canyon drains a large roadless area that is contiguous

Lower Gallinas Canyon

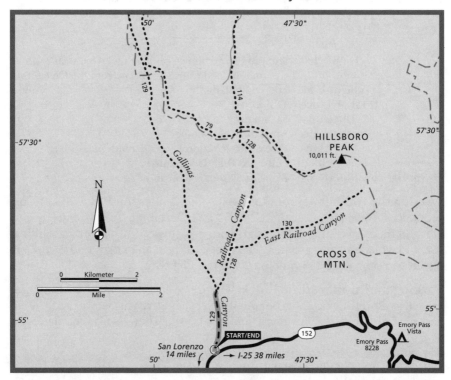

to the wilderness, and for all practical purposes is actually part of the Aldo.

The trail starts out as a primitive two-track, but quickly changes to a clear single-track trail after crossing the creek. The delightful path winds through an open mix of pine, Douglas fir, and oak, with flat campsites adjacent to several crossings. After 0.4 mile, the trail passes by an old corral, followed quickly by a 50-foot climb above and then back down to the stream. Pools scoured out of rock bowls offer a pleasant interlude along the creek at 0.9 mile. Ponderosa pine contrasts with dry slopes of cactus. At mile 1.1 the trail passes through a gap in the bedrock, with cliffs and rock walls rising high overhead. After crossing the stream to the left side, an old wooden sign marks the trail junction at mile 1.2. Gallinas Canyon Trail 129 climbs uphill to the left as the Railroad Canyon Trail 128 continues straight ahead to the right.

Retrace your route to complete this scenic round-trip in lower Gallinas Canyon.

Options: From the stream junction there are three options for longer hikes: Continue up Gallinas Canyon to the left or hike another 0.6 mile up Railroad Canyon and take either the East Railroad Canyon Trail to the right or the main Railroad Canyon trail to the left. For longer loop hikes that explore each of these upper canyons, refer to Hikes 17, 18, and 19. Also, Hike 11 ends up in Gallinas Canyon after descending East Railroad Canyon from the crest of the Black Range.

17 Railroad and East Railroad Canyons

Highlights:	Stunning mountain streams in rocky canyons with well-maintained trails and vistas from the Crest Trail
Type of hike:	Loop day hike
Total distance:	11.5 miles
Difficulty:	Strenuous
Best months:	April through October
Maps:	Forest Service Aldo Leopold Wilderness Map; Hillsboro Peak USGS quad
Special considerations:	Expect wet foot crossings.

Finding the trailhead: From Interstate 25, 12 miles south of Truth or Consequences, New Mexico, take NM 152 (the Geronimo Trail Scenic Byway) west 38 miles to a small "129" sign on the highway. Turn right (north) into the undeveloped campground. The trailhead is at the north end of the unpaved camping area, 0.3 mile north of the highway

Parking and trailhead facilities: There is a large unpaved parking area as well as a primitive campground with pit toilet, garbage cans, a picnic table, and several flat campsites along Gallinas Creek. There is no reliable water.

Key points:

0.0	Unsigned trailhead at north end of primitive campground.
0.4	Old corral.
1.2	Signed junction of Gallinas Canyon Trail 129 and Railroad Canyon Trail 128; stay right.
1.8	Signed junction of Railroad Canyon Trail 128 and East Railroad Canyon Trail 130; stay left.
2.1	Mouth of West Railroad Canyon.
4.1	Holden Prong Saddle; turn right.
5.7	Signed junction of Crest Trail 79 and Hillsboro Peak Bypass Trail 412; turn right.
6.8	Signed junction with East Railroad Canyon Trail 130; turn right.
9.7	Signed junction with Railroad Canyon Trail 128; continue left, downstream.
10.3	Signed junction with Gallinas Canyon Trail 129; continue downstream.
11.5	Trailhead at primitive campground.

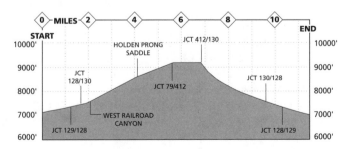

Railroad and East Railroad Canyons

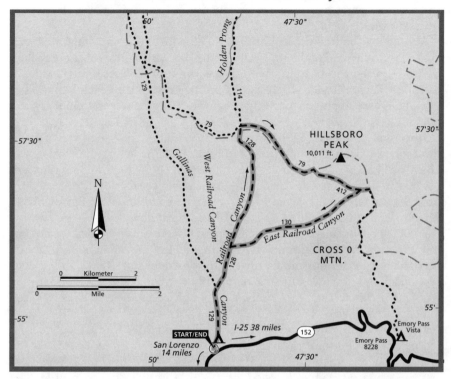

The hike: The trail starts out as a primitive two-track, but quickly changes to a clear single-track trail after crossing the creek. The delightful path winds through an open mix of pine, Douglas fir, and oak, with flat camp-sites adjacent to several crossings. After 0.4 mile the trail passes by an old corral, followed quickly by a 50-foot climb above and then back down to the stream. Pools scoured out of rock bowls offer a pleasant interlude along the creek at 0.9 mile. Ponderosa pine contrasts with dry slopes of cactus. At mile 1.1 the trail passes through a gap in the bedrock, with cliffs and rock walls rising high overhead. After crossing the stream to the left side, an old wooden sign marks a trail junction at mile 1.2. Disregard Gallinas Canyon Trail 129, which climbs uphill to the left. Stay on Railroad Canyon Trail 128, continuing straight ahead to the right.

The pleasant, gentle gradient continues up Railroad Canyon as the trail winds in and out of the creek bottom in a forest of ponderosa pine, Douglas fir, and gambel oak. After another 0.6 mile, a signed trail junction is reached in a small pine flat. The Railroad Canyon Trail continues straight up the main left branch. The East Railroad Canyon Trail, your return route, is on the right.

Heading up Railroad Canyon to the left (north), Trail 128 is well blazed and in good condition. At 2.1 miles a house-size boulder lies near the mouth of the West Fork of Railroad Creek. The trail climbs steadily up the right (east) side of the canyon above a narrow rock chasm containing deep green pools. At 2.7 miles, begin sidehilling and climbing steadily out of the canyon on the left side in a series of steep pitches and shallow switchbacks. The forest of stately pines and Douglas firs changes to an oak brush hillside over the next mile.

At mile 3.8 the trail passes through an old stock fence in a mature aspen grove. The upper end of the trail is steep and dry with a series of short switchbacks. With the gap in sight, the trail levels out to Holden Prong Saddle at 4.1 miles. This 8,716-foot-high saddle, on the crest of the Black Range, consists of a grassy opening ringed by aspen, southwestern white pine, spruce, and fir.

Turn right and head east on Crest Trail 79. You'll enjoy good views down into Railroad Canyon as the trail skirts the ridgeline above it. Bear right at Hillsboro Peak Bypass Trail 412, 1.6 miles from the Crest Trail junction, unless you've decided to take a side trip to the peak (see Option). After slightly more than a mile on the Bypass Trail, the signed junction with East Railroad Canyon Trail 130 is reached. Turn right and head downhill.

Trail 130 drops steeply into East Railroad Canyon in a pine-fir forest. After only 0.1 mile the trail has already lost 200 feet of elevation as it descends the right side of the gully above an old upside-down stock tank. It then does a bit of up and down to mile 7.2 before plunging to a side ravine that may carry early season water at 7.5 miles. Although steep, the trail is well blazed and easy to follow.

The trail climbs out of the ravine, sidehills, and then drops steeply across bedrock to the bottom, meeting the main canyon at 7.7 miles. Cross the streambed a few times, dropping along the right side of the canyon, and cross again below a distinctive rock column with a human-shaped profile. The canyon is narrow, rocky, and brushy down to mile 8.6. The trail winds in and out of several side gullies, then drops pleasantly along the right side of the stream with several flat benches of Douglas fir and gambel oak. After passing by a brushy spring at 9.1 miles, the canyon closes in and becomes rockier. At 9.5 miles a picturesque stream spills over a 10-foot waterfall to a huge circular pool. The trail climbs 40 feet along a rocky sidehill, and at 9.7 miles reaches a signed junction with Railroad Canyon Trail 128 in a ponderosa pine park.

Having completed the loop portion of the outing, turn left and retrace your route along the Railroad–Gallinas stream, downhill all the way, back to the trailhead on NM 152.

Option: For a slightly longer trip, you can continue on Trail 79 along the crest instead of taking the Bypass Trail, and visit the lookout atop Hillsboro Peak (10,111 feet). Continue past the lookout on Trail 79 to the east end of the Bypass Trail. There you will turn right (west) and hike 0.2 mile to the East Railroad Canyon Trail. This extension adds about 2 miles to the route and 1,600 feet of elevation gain and loss.

Junction of Railroad and East Railroad Canyon Trails.

18 Gallinas and Railroad Canyons

Highlights:	Woodsy steep-walled canyons, the Black Range Crest
Type of hike:	Loop day hike
Total distance:	11.8 miles
Difficulty:	Strenuous
Best months:	April through October
Maps:	Forest Service Aldo Leopold Wilderness Map (1984/revised 2000); Hillsboro Peak USGS quad
Special considerations:	Expect wet foot crossings when streams are running high.

Finding the trailhead: From Interstate 25, 12 miles south of Truth or Consequences, New Mexico, take NM 152 (the Geronimo Trail Scenic Byway) west 38 miles to a small "129" sign on the highway. Turn right (north) into the undeveloped campground. The trailhead is at the north end of the unpaved camping area, 0.3 mile north of the highway.

Parking and trailhead facilities: There is large unpaved parking area and a primitive campground with pit toilet, garbage cans, a picnic table, and several flat campsites along Gallinas Creek. There is no reliable water.

Key points:
- 0.0   Gallinas Canyon trailhead.
- 0.4   Old corral.
- 1.2   Signed junction of Gallinas Canyon Trail 129 and Railroad Canyon Trail 128; go left.
- 1.9   Pass through gate in stock fence.
- 5.2   Black Range crest, junction of Crest Trail 79 and Sids Prong Trail 121; turn right.
- 7.7   Junction of Railroad Canyon Trail 128 and Holden Prong Trail 114; turn right.
- 9.7   Mouth of West Railroad Canyon.
- 10.0 Junction with East Railroad Canyon Trail 130; continue downstream.
- 10.6 Junction with Gallinas Canyon Trail 129; continue downstream.
- 11.8 Trailhead at primitive campground.

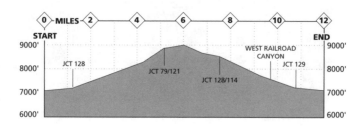

The hike: This "lollipop loop" day hike is more easily done in a clockwise direction. The "stem" up Railroad Canyon is a delightful forested trail along the stream, so repeating that segment is most pleasurable. The route takes

Gallinas and Railroad Canyons

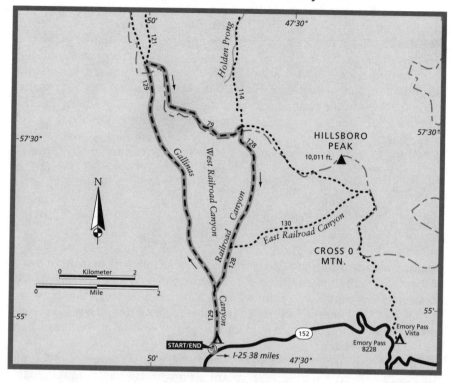

you to and from the Black Range Crest via two major canyons that lie outside of the Aldo Leopold Wilderness. These canyons are as scenic and primitive as any within the wilderness itself.

The trail starts out as a primitive two-track, but quickly changes to a clear single-track trail after crossing the creek. The delightful path winds through an open mix of pine, Douglas fir, and oak, with flat campsites adjacent to several crossings. After 0.4 mile the trail passes by an old corral, followed quickly by a 50-foot climb above and then back down to the stream. Pools scoured out of rock bowls offer a pleasant interlude along the creek at 0.9 mile. Ponderosa pine contrasts with dry slopes of cactus. At mile 1.1 the trail passes through a gap in the bedrock, with cliffs and rock walls rising high overhead. After crossing the stream to the left side, an old wooden sign marks the trail junction at mile 1.2.

Go left (northwest) on Gallinas Canyon Trail 129, steeply switchbacking up the dry, rocky hillside above the confluence of the two streams. At first glance you might have your doubts about taking this trail because Railroad Canyon continues its mellow streamside gradient, but the first mile of the Gallinas Trail is the hardest section. The first 0.7 mile is a brutal stretch of trail, climbing steeply and leaving the delightful brook behind. After gaining 300 feet in elevation, you pass through a gated stock fence and follow a side gully down to the main Gallinas Creek, which is reached after 1 mile.

From here the trail follows the gentle woodland streambed straight north to the saddle above Sids Prong on the Black Range crest. The Gallinas valley is dominated by towering ponderosa pines above the boulder-ridden stream, which can usually be stepped or hopped across. The shady south slope is coated with a dark fir forest, while the sunny north side is open ponderosa parkland. The enchanting cushioned forest path is narrow but easy to follow. Small campsites occur intermittently along the shaded creek. The tumbled boulders and woody debris in Gallinas Creek are evidence of powerful stream activity in times of heavy rains. The blowdown also shows that this is a windy corridor below the Black Range divide. After following the creek for more than a mile, the trail climbs gradually and eventually begins to switchback through a solid forest of aspen in the last 0.7 mile before the crest.

At the crest, you will meet Black Range Crest Trail 79 and Sids Prong Trail 121, which continues north. The Black Range crest is the southern boundary of the Aldo Leopold Wilderness; you might see a wilderness boundary sign at the saddle. Turn right and head east-southeast on the broad Crest Trail. Originally built as a fire road, the Crest Trail is rather wide. It also doesn't fool around with switchbacks, since vehicles don't mind elevation changes as much as hikers do. The Crest Trail does, however, weave from one side of the divide to the other, often avoiding the top points of the ridge route. Seesaw on this route for 2.5 miles to the next junction, enjoying the views as you catch the panoramas through the forest cover. The valleys and ravines on either side of the crest are wild and rugged, the home of wildlife, where few humans venture.

Railroad Canyon Trail 128 and Holden Prong Trail 114 are reached at another saddle. Here you turn right (south) leaving the Crest Trail to begin the downhill portion of the hike. You'll be glad to be doing this route clockwise: There is a series of steep dry switchbacks and a sloping sidehill descent before you arrive in the stream bottom almost 1.5 miles below the saddle. You'll spot the mouth of the West Fork of Railroad Creek on your right; a house-sized boulder lies near its mouth.

At the junction with East Railroad Canyon Trail 130 on your left, continue downstream another 0.6 mile to reach the confluence of Gallinas and Railroad Canyons where you turned on the first leg of your hike. Retrace your route down to the trailhead at the primitive campground.

Option: The loop can be lengthened 3.3 miles by continuing southeast along the crest from Holden Prong Saddle, and then descending East Railroad Canyon (see Hike 17).

Huge Douglas fir log cut on Railroad Canyon Trail 128.

19 Sids and Holden Prongs

Highlights:	Delightful trails, forests, streams, and canyons
Type of hike:	Three- to four-day backpack loop
Total distance:	24.1 miles
Difficulty:	Strenuous
Best months:	April through October
Maps:	Forest Service Aldo Leopold Wilderness Map; Hillsboro Peak and Victoria Park USGS quads
Special considerations:	The nearly abandoned trail into Flower Canyon is extremely rough, steep, and brushy. It is recommended only for seasonal hikers. Holden Prong has numerous stream crossings that may be deep during the spring. There are few campsites along Holden Prong.

Finding the trailhead: From Interstate 25, 12 miles south of Truth or Consequences, New Mexico, take NM 152 (the Geronimo Trail Scenic Byway) west 38 miles to a small "129" sign on the highway. Turn right (north) into the undeveloped campground. The trailhead is at the north end of the unpaved camping area, 0.3 mile north of the highway.

Parking and trailhead facilities: The unsigned trailhead has ample space for parking, as well as a pit toilet, garbage cans, a picnic table, and flat campsites along Gallinas Creek. There is no reliable water.

Key points:

0.0	Gallinas Canyon trailhead.
0.4	Old corral.
1.2	Signed junction of Gallinas Canyon Trail 129 and Railroad Canyon Trail 128; go left.
1.9	Pass through gate in stock fence.
2.2	Drop to Gallinas Creek.
5.2	Black Range crest, junction of Crest Trail 79 and Sids Prong Trail 121; go north on Sids Prong.
8.1	Corral in Sids Prong.
8.6	Leave prong; trail follows tributary south.
10.1	Drop to Pretty Creek.
10.3	Junction with Pretty Canyon Trail 812 and Flower Canyon Trail 121; turn right.
13.1	Signed junction with Holden Prong Trail 114; turn right up Holden Prong.
14.1	Side path to Negro Bill Spring.
15.8	Mouth of Sids Prong.
20.0	Black Range crest, junction of Crest Trail 79 and Railroad Canyon 128; go south.
22.0	Mouth of West Railroad Canyon.
22.3	Junction of Railroad and East Railroad Canyons; continue downstream
22.9	Junction of Railroad and Gallinas Canyons; continue downstream.
24.1	Gallinas Canyon trailhead.

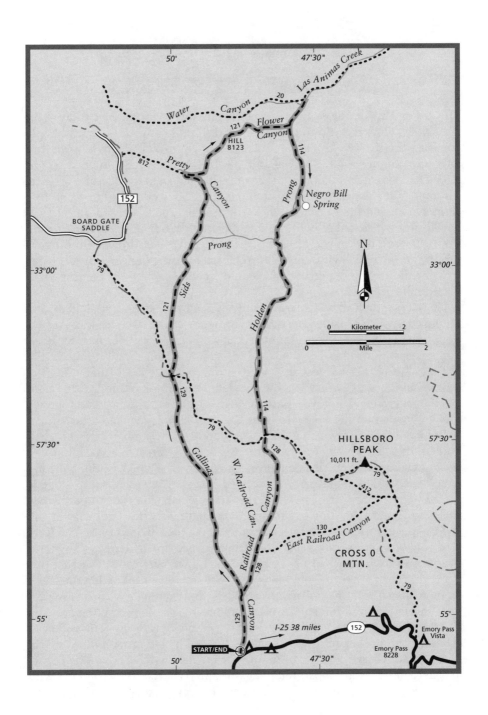

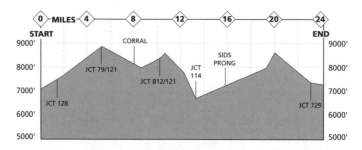

The hike: This outing in the prongs goes up and over the Black Range divide twice, allowing you to explore four different canyons. The trail starts out as a primitive two-track, but quickly changes to a clear single-track trail after crossing the creek. The delightful path winds through an open mix of pine, Douglas fir, and oak, with flat campsites adjacent to several crossings. After 0.4 mile the trail passes by an old corral, followed quickly by a 50-foot climb above and then back down to the stream. Pools scoured out of rock bowls offer a pleasant interlude along the creek at 0.9 mile. Ponderosa pine contrasts with dry slopes of cactus. At mile 1.1 the trail passes through a gap in the bedrock, with cliffs and rock walls rising high overhead. After crossing the stream to the left side, an old wooden sign marks the trail junction at mile 1.2.

Go left (northwest) on Gallinas Canyons Trail 129, steeply switchbacking up the dry, rocky hillside above the confluence of the two streams. At first glance you might have your doubts about taking this trail because Railroad Canyon continues its mellow streamside gradient, but the first mile of the Gallinas Trail is the hardest section. The first 0.7 mile is a brutal stretch of trail, climbing steeply and leaving the delightful brook behind. After gaining 300 feet in elevation, you pass through a gated stock fence and follow a side gully down to the main Gallinas Creek, which is reached after 1 mile.

From here the trail follows the gentle woodland streambed straight north to the saddle above Sids Prong on the Black Range crest. The Gallinas valley is dominated by towering ponderosa pines above the boulder-ridden stream, which can usually be stepped or hopped across. The shady south slope is coated with a dark fir forest, while the sunny north side is open ponderosa parkland. The enchanting cushioned forest path is narrow but easy to follow. Small campsites occur intermittently along the shaded creek. The tumbled boulders and woody debris in Gallinas Creek are evidence of powerful stream activity in times of heavy rains. The blowdown also shows that this is a windy corridor below the Black Range divide. After following the creek for more than a mile, the trail climbs gradually and eventually begins to switchback through a solid forest of aspen in the last 0.7 mile before the crest.

After pausing at the saddle, continue north into Sids Prong. The wide valley of the prong features grassy benches framed by old-growth pine and fir. These meadows are nearly continuous for the next 3 miles down the prong, like descending stairsteps along the stream. What a contrast with wild Holden Prong in the next valley to the east. Holden's narrow wooded canyon barely allows the sun to enter, while the gentle hillsides of Sids allow for an open valley floor. These lush grasslands are home to thousands of busy rodents whose earthen runs are most noticeable in early spring after the melting of the snow. The presence of this subterranean population brings various predators to the valley: red-tailed hawks, bears, and coyotes. The lumpy earth resulting from all this activity makes it difficult to find a suitable tent site, although small campsites are dotted along the lower stream edge.

The trail descends gradually but steadily down the valley. The meadows become broader with decreasing elevation. There's an old corral about midway down the valley, which grows narrow at the lower end before the trail cuts off on its winding route to Pretty Canyon. If you plan to camp soon, you should select a site here in lower Sids Prong.

The route out of the prong over to Pretty Canyon is clear and easy to follow, with blazes and an increasingly conspicuous track on the ground. This is fortunate, because the lower trail location is shown incorrectly on the wilderness map and it does not appear at all on the 1963 Victoria Park quad. At 10.3 miles, you arrive at the junction with the Flower Canyon Trail, which you are going to take, heading right (east) and the Pretty Canyon Trail going uphill to your left (west).

The Flower Canyon segment down to Holden Prong is for the well-conditioned adventurer. For all practical purposes, the trail is no longer maintained. In places the trail is so steep, rough, and brushy that you'll wonder if you've lost it. These disadvantages are offset to some extent by the spellbinding beauty and solitude of surrounding canyons and formations and by the opportunities for excellent loop hikes that this trail provides. Because of the difficulties, this Flower Canyon extension of Sid's Prong Trail 121 is recommended only as the downhill leg of a strenuous hiking or backpacking loop. Also, because the trail is hard to find in spots, don't forget to bring, and use, the Victoria Park USGS quad.

At first the trail climbs along a grassy hillside and enters a pine forest, reaching the ridge directly above the head of Flower Canyon at 10.7 miles. The ridge top is well marked with rock cairns; pause here for a spectacular view. For the next 0.5 mile, the brushy trail (white oak and locust) is hard to find as it plunges down a rocky, sandy ridgeline gully. The brush makes this a tricky section of trail, but if you angle left (north) to the ridge between Water and Flower Canyons, you'll quickly pick up a much more distinct trail. The trail sidehills up and then around the north slope of hill 8123 (shown on the quad map). Varying between pure route finding and following the occasional rock cairn, the trail offers astounding views of raw, exposed rock formations—great twisted slabs and monumental pillars. The narrow trail then becomes more distinct with a few blazed trees, but drops steeply on a loose gravelly surface along the left side of the ridge, crossing a saddle into Flower Canyon at mile 12.1.

From the dividing ridge, the trail follows the steep left side of a gully down to Flower Canyon at 12.6 miles. Appropriately, the canyon treated us to a lovely display of lupine and yellow aster during our early spring hike. The trail crosses the tiny stream and descends gently along the right side before

A steep gravelly stretch of the lower Flower Canyon Trail 121.

climbing 50 feet above canyon walls. Red rock forms the streambed, with high red rock rims beyond and above Holden Prong. At mile 12.9 the trail climbs high on the left side above a chasm with waterfalls when the stream is running.

This is a confusing spot. Contour straight to a rock cairn and you'll quickly find the trail as it drops to the stream bottom. After crossing to the right, the trail climbs and contours above the narrow drainage down to its junction with the Holden Prong Trail in a ponderosa pine flat at 13.1 miles. You'll appreciate this lovely park next to the delightful pools and rushing water of Holden Prong after your rugged descent from Pretty Canyon. There are several campsites near this junction, and farther downstream at the Water Canyon Trail junction as well. Your camping choices will be limited farther up this prong.

To complete the loop, turn right (south) up Holden Prong on Trail 114. Towering stone obelisks stand starkly against the sky upstream from the junction. One mile from the beginning of the Holden Prong Trail, there is a rare 0.15-mile stretch of straight, flat trail on the west side of the prong. Watch for a stream or a trickle on the east bank of the prong, indicating the location of Negro Bill Spring.

At this point, the trail cuts through a lumpy grass meadow west of the creek, so you could easily miss it. Another hint of the spring is a defunct signpost standing next to the trail. Only the rusty bolts remain; the sign to this politically incorrect spring is gone, as is the trail. Trail 309, although still on the wilderness map, is unmaintained and has been erased by the wilderness. To visit the spring, cross the prong on the barely visible pathway and climb about 100 feet above the stream on the east bank into the rolling ponderosa pine park. Follow the little stream to its source at the spring, about 0.1 mile from the prong. There is no trail beyond the spring, just a few stray old blazes.

Continuing upstream on the prong, the trail departs from streamside on two occasions when the valley becomes a rocky gorge with no space for a trail. During these short hillside interludes, the tumultuous sound of falls and rapids fills the narrow canyon. At 15.8 miles, the rocky mouth of Sids Prong is on the right. The journey up the prong is scenic as it travels along the stream through the dense forest. The stream crossings, especially in early spring, can be challenging; the water might be above your knees at some crossings. As a result, it is slow going, but this is beautiful country, so why rush it?

You will no doubt notice the blazes on the route: They've been painted on the tree trunks and boulders along the trail with white paint and a 4-inch brush. Perhaps this technique of trail marking is kinder than the traditional gouges in the bark, and they sure stand out, but they are sort of garish in this dark, woodsy canyon. Because we didn't see them elsewhere in the Aldo, apparently it was only an experiment that was not repeated.

Campsites become less frequent as you ascend this narrow canyon. Don't put off your selection until late in the day. There are long stretches of the trail with no clear level spots at all. The narrow, rocky canyon is cluttered with downfall, although the trail is clear and well maintained. The dampness of the shady canyon has protected it from the fires that are common elsewhere in the Aldo; here the old-growth forest is reminiscent of the Germanic forests described by the Brothers Grimm.

After following the stream for 6.5 miles, the trail begins to switchback up the steep slope at the head of the valley, climbing through thickly bunched aspen to reach the Black Range crest at 20.0 miles. The 8,716-foot-high saddle consists of a grassy opening ringed by aspen, southwestern white pine, spruce, and fir. A dry campsite sits symbolically on the edge of the saddle just above a recent burn in upper Railroad Canyon. Continue your hike over the saddle, dropping southward into Railroad Canyon on a steep, dry trail with a series of short switchbacks. The steep descent to the streambed continues for more than a mile before reaching the bottom near the mouth of the West Fork.

Continue on the clear, well-maintained trail downstream, passing the junction of East Railroad Canyon and the Gallinas Canyon Trail you took earlier. The stream crossings are a refreshing way to finish an outstanding wilderness outing.

Option: If your plans allow for a layover day at the foot of Holden Prong, you might wish to explore down Animas Creek on a day hike. It is 2.5 miles from the Holden Prong–Flower Canyon junction to East Curtis. If you explore that far, continue another 0.25 mile to the Kelso Place on Animas Creek just east of the Curtis junction.

For background information on the Kelso Place, see page 55.

Note: Before contemplating a return leg on the Curtis Canyon–Animas Divide route, read the information in Hike 15's Option section. Holden Prong is vastly more scenic and pleasant!

Crest Trailhead

*". . . the wilderness is the one thing on earth
which was furnished complete and perfect."*

—Aldo Leopold, *Outdoor Life,* 1925

20 Crest–Emory Pass

Highlights:	Magnificent views of the region from the crest of the Black Range
Type of hike:	Shuttle day hike
Total distance:	13.2 miles
Difficulty:	Strenuous
Best months:	May through October
Maps:	Forest Service Aldo Leopold Wilderness Map; Victoria Park and Hillsboro Peak USGS quads
Special considerations:	In the early spring, check with the Forest Service in Mimbres for road conditions; snowbanks may linger on FR 152 into May, making the road to the beginning trailhead impassable. The only water near the trail is at Hillsboro Spring, which may be under snow in the early spring.

Finding the trailheads: *Beginning trailhead:* On New Mexico 35, 1.5 miles north of the Forest Service Ranger Station in Mimbres, turn right (east) on McKnight Road (signed), also Forest Road 152. The road is maintained gravel for 8 miles, to the junction of FR 537; thereafter it becomes steep and rocky, with hairpin turns. A four-wheel-drive high-clearance vehicle is required. Drive 4 miles beyond the junction to the Black Range Crest trailhead, which is on the right where the road makes a wide turn to the north.

Ending trailhead: From Interstate 25, 12 miles south of Truth or Consequences, take NM 152 (the Geronimo Trail Scenic Byway) west 34 miles to Emory Pass. (From the junction of NM 152 and NM 61 in San Lorenzo, it is 25 miles east on NM 152 to Emory Pass.) Turn north at the pass to the vista parking lot. The faded sign for Trail 79 is located immediately south of the pit toilet on the west side of the 0.2-mile paved road to the parking area.

Parking and trailhead facilities: *Beginning trailhead:* There is room for two or three vehicles to park along the road, limited camping, and no water.

Ending trailhead: A paved parking area, picnic table, pit toilet, and interpretive display of area's history and geology are at the trailhead. There is no water.

The driving distance between trailheads is about 50 miles, of which 12 are unpaved.

Crest–Emory Pass

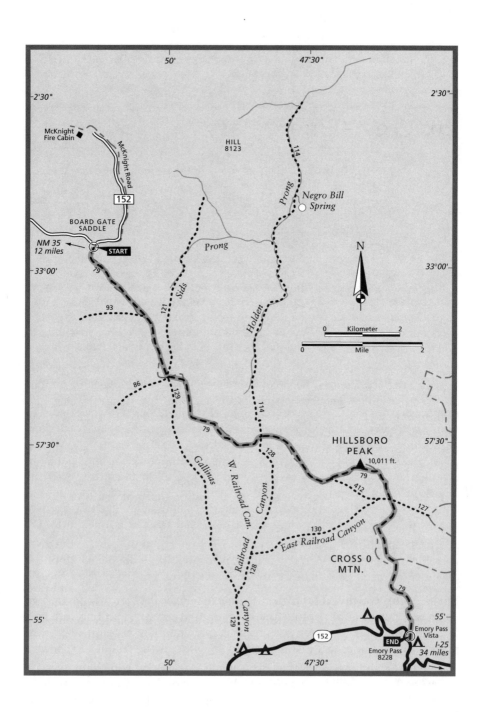

Key points:

0.0 Trailhead on McKnight Road (FR 152).
1.5 Junction with East Canyon Trail 93.
2.3 Junction with Quaking Aspen Trail 86.
2.75 Junction with Sids Prong Trail 121 and Gallinas Canyon Trail 129.
5.25 Junction with Holden Prong Trail 114 and Railroad Canyon Trail 128.
6.85 Junction with Hillsboro Bypass Trail 412.
8.2 Hillsboro Peak, lookout, and cabin.
9.6 Junction with Bypass Trail 412 and Ladrone Canyon Trail 127.
12.8 Pass through Forest Service heliport.
13.2 Emory Pass trailhead.

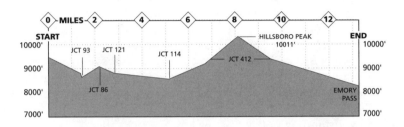

The hike: The Black Range Crest Trail is a typical up-and-down ridgeline trail. It was once an old jeep road, built in the 1930s as a fire road, which is good news and bad news. The good news is that the signed mileages are pretty accurate because they were based on odometer readings, but the bad news is that it was not engineered with hikers in mind. There are few switchbacks to soften the elevation changes, and the hauls upward or downward are often long, 0.5 mile or more. But there are frequent open saddles where it is inviting to pause and enjoy the scenery. There are also rock outcroppings from which to savor the views of southwestern New Mexico. The wind in the big old trees hums or roars, depending on its velocity, so there is soothing background music for your hike.

At the trailhead on McKnight Road, the trail is signed FOREST TRAIL only. There is no trail number sign. Twenty yards south of the road, the Crest Trail begins behind the buried steel I-beams that prohibit vehicles from using the trail. This is also the Aldo Leopold Wilderness boundary. The mileage sign suggests distances of 8.5 miles to Hillsboro Peak and 12.5 miles to Emory Pass. These numbers are slightly optimistic.

The wide trail begins by winding through an aspen grove to a saddle at 0.3 mile. From here it descends steadily on the west side of the ridge for more than 0.5 mile. Ironically, the Crest Trail avoids the crest itself, and sidehills along the east side or the west side of the Black Range summit mounds, providing good views in both directions. You might encounter some blowdown on the trail, particularly in the early spring, but generally the Crest Trail is open and clear.

The first trail junction is the East Canyon Trail 93, on your right (west) at 1.5 miles. It is in a saddle and signed, although it obviously doesn't get much traffic. The Quaking Aspen Trail 86 junction, also on the right (west) occurs

105

at 2.3 miles, also in a saddle, signed, and very lightly used. The virtue of a crest trail, of course, is that you remain on the crest, so making decisions at junctions is simplified.

The short Black Range Crest is a good test trail if you are contemplating a trek on one of America's famous through hikes. Crest travel greatly reduces the risk of getting lost. There are no streams to ford and no wrong turns to take. The undulating mountain crest, on the other hand, does have some variety. With each bend, new views open up, new foliage appears, or you might come upon a band of turkeys in an open saddle. The only drawback is lack of water. On this dry trail, it is necessary to carry all the water you'll need.

Shortly after the Quaking Aspen junction, you arrive at the Gallinas–Sids Prong saddle, a four-way junction. Beneath the towering pines is a disintegrating wooden stock fence. There's a small metal wilderness boundary sign near Sids Prong Trail 121, which heads north. In addition, there is a historic artifact: a wooden Black Range Primitive Area sign, left over from 1980 when the Aldo Leopold Wilderness was designated by Congress. The sign is carved on the back of an old Hermosa/Chloride road sign, probably originally from the 1920s when both of those towns existed. The Forest Service evidently has had a long-standing policy of recycling.

Continue along the crest for 2.5 miles to reach the junction with Holden Prong on the north and Railroad Canyon on the south. There's a portion of the trail that might be rather thorny, although the Forest Service trail crew tries to clear the trail at least every two years. Continue along the crest to the junction with the Hillsboro Peak Bypass Trail, another 1.6 miles. Taking the bypass route allows you to omit some elevation gain, but you'll also miss a potential water stop (although if there is snow, the Hillsboro Spring might be buried) and a wonderful view from the peak. It's a 1,300-foot elevation gain in 1.35 miles, slightly softened by switchbacks. And after all, if you're doing the Crest Trail, you need to include the peak. It's worth it!

A friendly Forest Service sign welcomes you to the top, as will a friendly lookout ranger if you visit during the fire season when the lookout is manned. The ranger lives in the west cabin, but the east cabin is left open for the public to use, both for safety purposes and as a practical way to avoid break-ins. The east cabin was built in 1925 and remains in good condition, thanks to responsible people who are careful to clean up after they leave. In addition to providing refuge from an almost constant wind, the cabin has a sheltered front porch with a fabulous view eastward. The logbook is entertaining to read, with many entries extolling the beauty and solitude of the Aldo. You can feel the exuberance of people when they write about "a lovely walk in the high country, so happy to be here!"

The lookout and ranger cabin were constructed in 1934, replacing the previous wooden lookout. For an incredible 360-degree view of the entire Black Range and surrounding valleys and mountains, climb to the lookout cabin. The metal stairway is sturdy and guarded by railings, but those with a fear of heights would probably be happier on the ground. With permission from the ranger, you can fill up your water bottles from an otherwise locked rain

The head of Gallinas Canyon is covered with impenetrable mountain locust and Gambel oak along with snags from an old fire.

cistern near the cabin. You might also be able to obtain water from the Hillsboro Spring, some 600 feet below and to the north of the lookout.

Trail 79 from the lookout drops steeply, with switchbacks, passing through a couple of stock fences and reaching a trail junction in a saddle at 9.6 miles. Here a sign announces the wilderness boundary and commemorates the one hundredth anniversary of Aldo Leopold's birth. Continue along the seesawing Crest Trail, heading south 3.6 miles to Emory Pass. The trail shifts from a narrow footpath to a wide old jeep trail, and eventually to a road when you get close to the heliport. Watch for a sign on your left after the heliport that will direct you down to your destination at the Emory Pass parking lot.

Option: To do the crest trip as a backpack, you would need to drop into Sids or Holden Prong if you wanted water at your campsite. Depending on the timing of your visit, this would require a drop of about 0.5 mile in order to reach water in either stream.

21 Crest–Gallinas Canyon

Highlights:	From the vistas of the crest to intimate canyons, a hike that's almost all downhill
Type of hike:	Shuttle day hike
Total distance:	8.0 miles
Difficulty:	Moderate
Best months:	May through October
Maps:	Forest Service Aldo Leopold Wilderness Map; Victoria Park and Hillsboro Peak USGS quads
Special considerations:	In the early spring, check with the Forest Service in Mimbres for road conditions; snowbanks may linger on FR 152 into May, making the road to the beginning trailhead impassable. Expect wet foot crossings in the canyon during times of high water.

Finding the trailheads: *Beginning trailhead:* On New Mexico 35, 1.5 miles north of the Forest Service Ranger Station in Mimbres, turn right (east) on McKnight Road (signed), also Forest Road 152. The road is maintained gravel for 8 miles, to the junction of FR 537; thereafter it becomes steep and rocky, with hairpin turns. A four-wheel-drive high-clearance vehicle is required. Drive 4 miles beyond the junction to the Black Range Crest trailhead, which is on the right where the road makes a wide turn to the north.

Ending trailhead: From Interstate 25, 12 miles south of Truth or Consequences, take NM 152 (the Geronimo Trail Scenic Byway) west 38 miles to a small "129" sign on the highway. (From the NM 152/NM 61 junction in San Lorenzo, drive east on NM 152 for 21 miles to the "129" sign.) Turn north into the undeveloped campground. The trailhead is at the north end of the unpaved camping area, 0.3 mile north of the highway.

The driving distance between trailheads is about 46 miles, of which 12 are unpaved.

Parking and trailhead facilities: *Beginning trailhead:* There is room for two or three vehicles to park along the road, limited camping, and no water.

Ending trailhead: A large unpaved parking area is at the trailhead, along with a primitive campground with pit toilet, garbage cans, a picnic table, and flat campsites along Gallinas Creek. There is no reliable water, although it is usually available from the stream.

Key points:
- 0.0   Trailhead on McKnight Road (FR 152).
- 1.5   Junction with East Canyon Trail 93.
- 2.3   Junction with Quaking Aspen Trail 86.
- 2.75 Junction with Sids Prong Trail 121 and Gallinas Canyon Trail 129; turn right.
- 5.75 Trail angles out of the Gallinas bottom.
- 6.75 Drop to stream. Junction with Railroad Canyon Trail 128; turn right.
- 8.0   Trailhead at Gallinas Canyon campground.

Crest–Gallinas Canyon

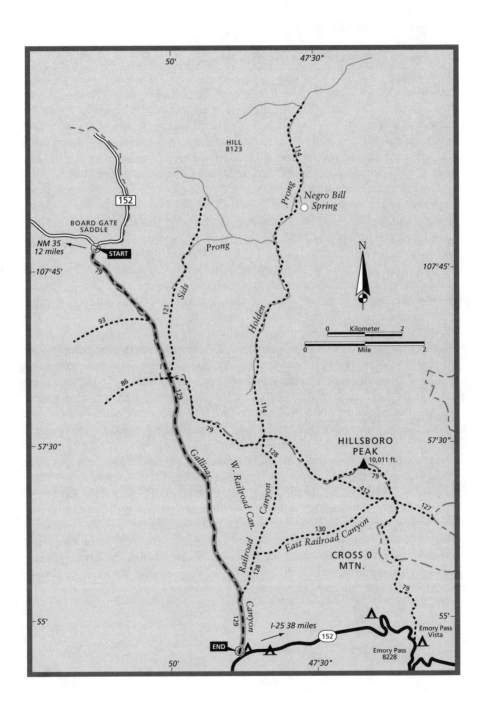

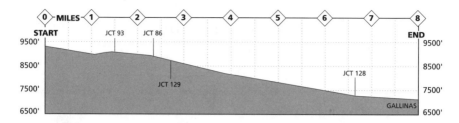

The hike: This shuttle day hike takes you from the crest of the mountains down Gallinas Canyon to the primitive campground on the highway. Although most of it lies outside of the Aldo Leopold Wilderness, this short hike provides solitude, quiet, and remoteness in primitive forest. Carry water with you; the first half of the trek will definitely be dry. Water may exist in Gallinas Creek, which you follow during most of the second half, but it must be treated before drinking.

From the trailhead, follow the wide Crest Trail as it winds along to the south. Disregard the first two trail junctions; both of these are on the right (west) and are lightly used. At 2.75 miles is a four-way junction in the saddle, where the Sids Prong Trail 121 goes to the left (north) and the Gallinas Canyon Trail 129 goes to the right (south). Here you leave the Crest Trail and head right (south), downhill, into Gallinas Canyon. See Hike 20 for details on this segment of the hike.

From the crest, the trail descends rapidly through an aspen forest at the top of the valley. Eventually you reach the spring and continue along the watercourse for a mile. Gallinas Canyon is a delightful route along the brook, through towering ponderosa pines. Rocky boulders in the stream and huge trunks of downfall attest to the power of both water and wind in the valley. Even at times of high water, the stream crossings can be hopped if you're nimble. The final mile of the Gallinas stretch is dry, however, as the trail climbs up a side slope to cross a ridge before switchbacking steeply down to the confluence of Gallinas and Railroad Canyons.

At the junction with Railroad Canyon, turn right and follow the now larger stream down to the campground. In this last leg of the hike, you might have to get your feet wet, depending on the water level. The 1.2-mile stretch of canyon to the trailhead is a pleasant stroll interspersed with stream crossings to keep you cool and to make sure you don't hurry this final section. The pools and riffles are surrounded by forest and boulders. Even this close to a major highway, you can enjoy the quiet and solitude of wilderness. You will reach the campground at the trailhead all too soon, and will probably be disappointed that the journey wasn't longer!

22 Sids Prong Saddle

Highlights:	Panoramic views from the Black Range crest
Type of hike:	Out-and-back day hike
Total distance:	5.5 miles round-trip
Difficulty:	Moderate
Best months:	May through October
Maps:	Forest Service Aldo Leopold Wilderness Map; Victoria Park and Hillsboro Peak USGS quads
Special considerations:	In the early spring, check with the Forest Service in Mimbres for road conditions; snowbanks may linger on FR 152 into May, making the road impassable. There is no water on the trail.

Finding the trailhead: On New Mexico 35, 1.5 miles north of the Forest Service Ranger Station in Mimbres, turn right (east) on McKnight Road (signed), also Forest Road 152. The road is maintained gravel for 8 miles, to the junction of FR 537; thereafter it becomes steep and rocky, with hairpin turns. A four-wheel-drive high-clearance vehicle is required. Drive 4 miles beyond the junction to the Black Range Crest trailhead, which is on the right where the road makes a wide turn to the north.

Parking and trailhead facilities: There is room for two or three vehicles to park along the road, limited camping, and no water.

Key points:

0.0   Trailhead on McKnight Road (FR 152).

1.5   Junction with East Canyon Trail 93.

2.3   Junction with Quaking Aspen Trail 86.

2.75 Junction with Sids Prong Trail 121 and Gallinas Canyon Trail 129.

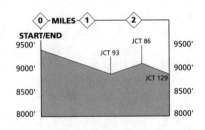

The hike: The Black Range Crest Trail is a typical up-and-down crest trail. It is an old jeep road, built in the 1930s as a fire road, which is good news and bad news. The good news is that the signed mileages are pretty accurate because they were based on odometer readings, but the bad news is that it was not engineered with hikers in mind. There are few switchbacks to soften the elevation changes, and the hauls upward or downward are often quite long, 0.5 mile or more. But there are frequent saddles where it is generally open and inviting to pause and enjoy the scenery. There are also rock outcroppings from which to savor the views of western New Mexico. The wind in the big old trees hums or roars, depending on its velocity, so there is soothing background music for your hike.

At the trailhead on McKnight Road, the trail is signed FOREST TRAIL only. There is no trail number sign. Twenty yards south of the road, the Crest Trail begins behind the buried steel I-beams that prohibit vehicles from using the

Sids Prong Saddle

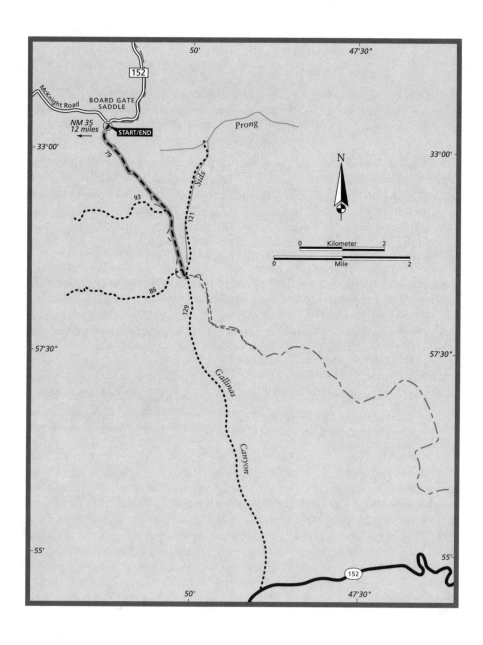

trail. This is also the Aldo Leopold Wilderness boundary. The mileage sign suggests distances of 8.5 miles to Hillsboro Peak and 12.5 miles to Emory Pass.

The wide trail begins by winding through an aspen grove to a saddle at 0.3 mile. From here it descends steadily on the west side of the ridge for more than 0.5 mile. Ironically, the Crest Trail avoids the crest itself, and side-hills along the east side or the west side of the Black Range summit mounds, providing good views in both directions. You might encounter some blow-down on the trail, particularly in the early spring, but generally the Crest Trail is open and clear.

The first trail junction is the East Canyon Trail 93, on your right (west) at 1.5 miles. It is in a saddle and signed, although it obviously doesn't get much traffic. The Quaking Aspen Trail 86 junction, also on the right (west) occurs at 2.3 miles, also in a saddle, signed, and very lightly used. The virtue of a crest trail, of course, is that you remain on the crest, so making decisions at junctions is simplified.

The short Black Range Crest is a good test trail if you are contemplating a trek on one of America's famous through hikes. Crest travel greatly reduces the risk of getting lost. There are no streams to ford and no wrong turns to take. The undulating mountain crest, on the other hand, does have some variety. With each bend, new views open up, new foliage appears, or you might come upon a band of turkeys in an open saddle. The only drawback is lack of water. On this dry trail, it is necessary to carry all the water you'll need.

Shortly after the Quaking Aspen junction, you arrive at the Gallinas–Sids Prong saddle, a four-way junction. Beneath the towering pines is a disintegrating wooden stock fence. There's a small metal wilderness boundary sign near Sids Prong Trail 121, which heads north. In addition, there is a historic artifact: a wooden Black Range Primitive Area sign, left over from 1980 when the area became the Aldo Leopold Wilderness. The sign is carved on the back of an old Hermosa/Chloride road sign, probably originally from the 1920s when both of those towns existed. The Forest Service evidently has had a long-standing policy of recycling. The saddle is the turnaround spot for the out-and-back day hike. Retrace your steps to the trailhead, enjoying the views from a different angle.

Pretty Canyon Trailhead

*"Wilderness areas are primarily a proposal to conserve
at least a sample of a certain kind of recreational environment,
of which game and hunting is an essential part,
but nevertheless only a part."*

—Aldo Leopold, *Outdoor Life,* 1925

23 Pretty Canyon–Crest Trail

Highlights: Two wilderness canyons for solitude, the Black
Range crest for magnificent views

Type of hike: Shuttle day hike or overnight backpack

Total distance: 9.3 miles

Difficulty: Strenuous

Best months: May through October

Maps: Forest Service Aldo Leopold Wilderness Map;
Victoria Park and Hillsboro Peak USGS quads

Special considerations: In the early spring, check with the Forest Service in
Mimbres for road conditions; snowbanks may linger
on FR 152 into May, making the road impassable.

Finding the trailheads: *Beginning trailhead:* On New Mexico 35, 1.5 miles
north of the Forest Service Ranger Station in Mimbres, turn right (east) on
McKnight Road (signed), also Forest Road 152. The road is maintained gravel
for 8 miles, to the junction of FR 537; thereafter it becomes steep and rocky,
with hairpin turns. A four-wheel-drive high-clearance vehicle is required.
Drive 6.5 miles beyond the junction, a total of 14.5 miles, to the sign for the
Pretty Canyon Trail on your right.

Ending trailhead: You will drive past the exit trailhead for the Black Range
Crest Trail 2.5 miles before you get to the Pretty Canyon trailhead. Its Forest Trail sign is not prominent, but it is 12 miles up the McKnight Road, where
the road has reached the crest and makes a wide turn to the north.

The driving distance between trailheads is 2.5 miles, unpaved.

Parking and trailhead facilities: Both trailheads have space for two or three
vehicles along the roadway. There is no camping at the trailheads. Camp nearby
at McKnight Cabin or the trailhead for the Crest Trail, 0.5 mile north of Pretty
Canyon on FR 152. There is no water at either trailhead.

Key points:

0.0 Signed trailhead on McKnight Road (FR 152).

1.9 Trail drops into upper Pretty Canyon.

2.4 Trail junction, Sids Prong Trail sign; bear right.

2.8 Aspen transition to ponderosa pine.

114

Pretty Canyon–Crest Trail

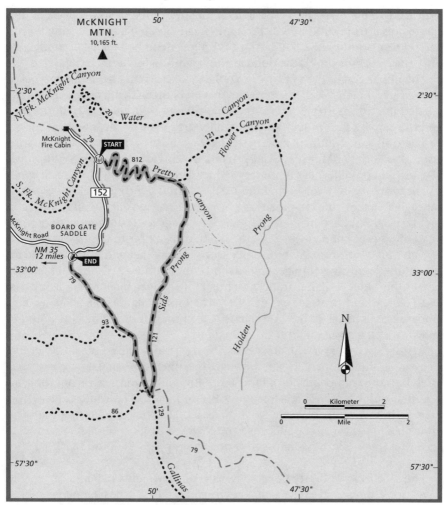

3.1   Climb bank to ponderosa pine park.
4.7   Corral.
6.4   Wallow at head of stream.
6.6   Junction with Crest Trail 79 and Gallinas Canyon Trail 129; turn right.
7.0   Junction with Quaking Aspen Trail 86.

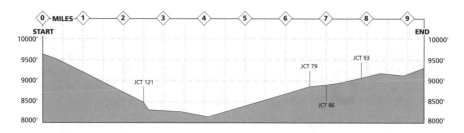

7.8   Junction with East Canyon Trail 93.

9.3   Trailhead on McKnight Road.

The hike: This hike can be done as a long day hike or as an overnighter. Campsites are plentiful in Sids Prong. Instead of using a shuttle vehicle, you can hike an additional 2.5 miles on McKnight Road between the trailheads. This road portion should be done at the beginning of your outing.

The upper end of Pretty Canyon Trail 812 has recently been reconstructed with a series of long, well-graded switchbacks. Someone with a sense of humor labeled the trail "Purty Canyon" on the trailhead sign. Indeed, both the trail and the canyon are "purty" and are well worth visiting for the views alone.

The trail starts out in aspen on the narrow crest of the Black Range, with grand views down McKnight Canyon and southwest to the Gila Wilderness. The unsigned wilderness boundary coincides with the top of this ridge, adjacent to the road. For the first 0.5 mile, the trail gently switchbacks down through an aspen thicket, passes the first good overlook at 0.6 mile, and then reenters oak and aspen thickets. Mile 1.4 brings an even better view from an open grassy knob all the way to Hillsboro Peak far to the southeast.

The trail continues down through more brushy oak and then drops to an aspen-lined gully, reaching early season water at mile 1.9. The trail has now joined the older, original trail, which is still distinct but brushy in places. Weave back and forth across the tiny stream, through aspen thickets, and along a grassy bench to the trail sign for Sids Prong Trail 121 at a little stream crossing (if it's spring, and if there's water).

At the sign, bear right. The Sids Prong Trail follows the little Pretty Canyon drainage downstream through the narrow V-shaped valley. This stretch of the trail begins as a faint footpath, going southeast from the trail sign and quickly stepping across tiny Pretty Creek. The route is clear and easy to follow, with blazes and an increasingly conspicuous track on the ground. This is fortunate, because the lower trail location is shown incorrectly on the wilderness map and it does not appear at all on the 1963 Victoria Park quad.

The trail follows Pretty Creek downstream through a patch of burn. The transition from aspen to majestic towering ponderosa pines happens quickly as the trail weaves along the little stream. When the canyon grows even narrower, the path goes southward, above the stream, into a rolling ponderosa pine parkland. After crossing the grassy park, descend along a small Sids Prong tributary flowing south. At the mouth of this tributary, the trail stays high on the northwest bank of the main prong before finally dropping to streamside.

The wide valley of the prong features grassy benches framed by old-growth pine and fir. These meadows are nearly continuous for the next 3 miles up the prong, rising like stairsteps along the stream. These lush grasslands are home to thousands of busy rodents whose earthen runs are most noticeable in early spring after the melting of the snow. The presence of this subterranean population brings various predators to the valley: red-tailed hawks, bears, and coyotes. The lumpy earth resulting from all this activity makes

Backpacking down Pretty Creek to the junction of Trails 812 and 121.

it difficult to find a suitable tent site, although small campsites are dotted along the lower stream edge.

The trail rises gradually but steadily up the valley. The meadows continue, growing slightly narrower with increasing elevation. There's an old corral about midway up the valley. The stream grows smaller, but the steeper gradient makes lovely little falls between the pools in the upper valley.

At 5.0 miles from the junction on Pretty Creek, the swampy head of the prong marks the end of the string of meadows. Extensive blowdown clutters the upper valley as you approach the Black Range divide. The trail is clear, however, as it climbs to the saddle through the chaos of the wind-punished aspen forest. There's an old stock fence at the saddle, probably of the same vintage as the corral you passed midway up the prong.

In the saddle, turn right onto Trail 79, the Black Range Crest Trail. Very shortly, after some up-and-down hiking, you pass the Quaking Aspen junction. The Black Range Crest Trail is an old jeep road, built in the 1930s as a fire road, which is good news and bad news. The good news is that the signed mileages are accurate because they were based on odometer readings, but the bad news is that it was not engineered with hikers in mind. There are few switchbacks to soften the elevation changes, and the hauls upward or downward are often quite long, 0.5 mile or more. But there are frequent saddles where it is generally open and inviting to pause and enjoy the scenery. There are also rock outcroppings from which to savor the views of western New Mexico. The wind in the big old trees hums or roars, depending on its velocity, so there is soothing background music for your hike.

After seesawing along the crest, you come to the East Canyon Trail in another 0.8 mile. It is in a saddle and signed, although it obviously doesn't get much traffic. The virtue of a crest trail, of course, is that you remain on the crest, so making decisions at junctions is simplified. Between this junction and the trailhead, the Crest Trail ironically avoids the crest itself, and sidehills along the east side or the west side of the Black Range summit mounds, providing good views in both directions. You might encounter some blowdown on the trail, particularly in the early spring, but generally the Crest Trail is open and clear. There is a long uphill section on the west side of the divide, followed by a shady saddle for recovery. As you draw closer to the trailhead, you enter an aspen forest where the trail is relatively flat and wide. At 9.3 miles, you emerge at the trailhead on McKnight Road, ending your canyons and crest exploration.

If you left your vehicle at Pretty Canyon, turn right and hike the final 2.5 miles on the road. This, unfortunately, is not a glamorous finale to a wonderful wilderness outing.

McKnight Trailhead

"Our remnants of wilderness will yield bigger values
to the nation's character and health than they will
to its pocketbook, and to destroy them will be
to admit that the latter are the only values that interest us."

—Aldo Leopold, *Outdoor Life,* 1925

---

24 Flower and Water Canyons

Highlights: Spectacular views of wild, deep canyons, colorful rock formations, and pleasant streams with deep pools and cascades

Type of hike: Loop day hike or two- to three-day backpack

Total distance: 12.6 miles

Difficulty: Strenuous

Best months: May to early October

Maps: Forest Service Aldo Leopold Wilderness Map; Victoria Park USGS quad

Special considerations: In the early spring, check with the Forest Service in Mimbres for road conditions. Snowbanks may linger on FR 152 into May, making the road impassable. The rarely maintained trail into Flower Canyon is extremely rough, steep, and brushy. It is recommended only for experienced hikers as a downhill leg in a longer loop.

Finding the trailhead: On New Mexico 35, 1.5 miles north of the Forest Service Ranger Station in Mimbres, turn right (east) on McKnight Road (signed), also Forest Road 152. The road is maintained gravel for 8 miles, to the junction of FR 537; thereafter it becomes steep and rocky, with hairpin turns. A four-wheel-drive high-clearance vehicle is required. Drive 7 miles beyond the junction, a total of 15 miles, to a large grassy knoll on the right. This is the trailhead for the Black Range Crest Trail, where you will end your loop trip. Your hike begins by walking back on FR 152 about 0.5 mile to the Pretty Canyon trailhead. Because there isn't adequate parking at Pretty Canyon trailhead, we don't suggest leaving your vehicle there.

Parking and trailhead facilities: The signed trailhead has a large unpaved parking area and campsites, but no water. At McKnight Cabin, 0.3 mile farther north on McKnight Road, a spring's flow is trapped in an open cistern, hosting a good crop of algae. The water should be boiled or filtered.

Flower and Water Canyons

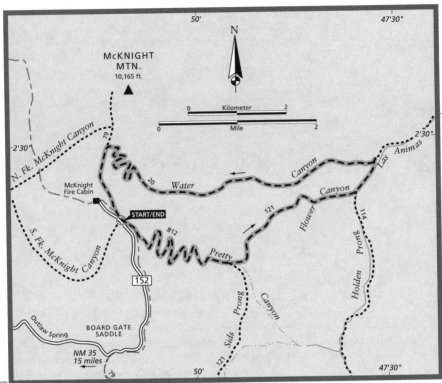

Key points:

0.0	Black Range Crest Trail 79 trailhead at end of McKnight Road.
0.5	Signed trailhead for Pretty Canyon Trail on McKnight Road.
2.9	Trail junction, Sids Prong Trail sign; stay left.
4.7	Dividing ridge between Water and Flower Canyons.
5.7	Signed junction with Holden Prong Trail 114; turn left.
6.2	Mouth of Water Canyon, junction with Water Canyon Trail 20; turn left.
6.9	Lower forks of Water Canyon.
8.4	Upper forks of Water Canyon.
11.4	Signed junction with Black Range Crest Trail 79; turn left (south).
12.2	Trail to McKnight Fire Cabin.
12.6	Black Range Crest Trail 79 trailhead at end of McKnight Road.

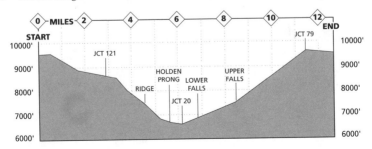

The hike: Walk back along the road 0.5 mile to the Pretty Canyon trailhead on the left (west). After rising over the hummock adjacent to the roadway, Pretty Canyon Trail 812 is all downhill for 2.9 miles to the intersection with the Sids Prong Trail. See Hike 23 for more details on this segment of the hike.

The trail to Flower Canyon (Trail 121) is distinct but unnamed at the junction. It is actually a continuation of the Sids Prong Trail and is identified at the junction only by the inscription JUNCTION TRAIL NO. 114 2.5 and a directional arrow to the left.

This essentially unmaintained route down to Holden Prong is for the well-conditioned adventurer. In places the trail is so steep, rough, and brushy that you'll wonder if you've lost it. These disadvantages are offset to some extent by the spellbinding beauty and solitude of surrounding canyons and formations, and by the opportunities for excellent loop hikes that this trail provides. Because the trail is hard to find in spots, don't forget to bring, and use, the Victoria Park quad map.

From the sign in Pretty Canyon, continue east on the left-hand trail. At first the trail climbs along a grassy hillside and enters a pine forest, reaching the ridge directly above the scenic head of Flower Canyon at 3.3 miles. The ridge top is well marked with rock cairns. For the next 0.5 mile, the brushy trail (white oak and locust) is hard to find as it plunges down a rocky, sandy ridgeline gully to 3.8 miles. The brush makes this a tricky section of trail, but if you angle left (north) to the ridge between Water and Flower Canyons, you'll soon pick up a much more distinct trail.

The trail sidehills up and then around the north slope of hill 8123. Varying between pure route finding and following the occasional rock cairn, the trail offers astounding views of raw, exposed rock formations—great twisted slabs and monumental pillars. The narrow trail widens, with a few blazed trees, but drops steeply on a loose gravelly surface along the left side of the ridge, crossing a saddle into Flower Canyon at mile 4.7.

From the dividing ridge, the trail follows the steep left side of a gully, reaching the bottom of Flower Canyon at 5.2 miles. Appropriately, Flower Canyon treated us to a lovely display of lupine and yellow aster during our early spring hike. Cross the tiny stream and descend gently along the right side before climbing 50 feet above canyon walls. Red rock forms the streambed, with high red rock rims beyond and above Holden Prong. At mile 5.5 the trail climbs high on the left side above a chasm with waterfalls when the stream is running.

This is a confusing spot. Contour straight to a rock cairn and you'll quickly find the trail as it drops to the stream bottom. After crossing to the right, the trail climbs and contours above the narrow drainage down to its junction with the Holden Prong Trail in a ponderosa pine flat at 5.7 miles. You'll appreciate this lovely park next to the delightful pools and rushing water of Holden Prong after your rugged descent from Pretty Canyon. An old wooden sign resting against a blazed tree points downstream toward the Murphy Place (1 mile). Turn left (downstream) toward Water Canyon.

Good campsites abound along this pleasant stretch of Holden Prong. The rocky streambed has little stairstep cascades between deep spellbinding pools. The prong valley is broader here than in its rocky ravine upstream. Stream crossings are frequent; some may be to midcalf in the early spring, so be prepared with appropriate footwear. At the Water Canyon junction (mile 6.2), the Prong Trail bends east as the stream becomes Animas Creek and the valley continues to widen. Your route goes left, up Water Canyon.

When climbing to the crest of the Black Range from lower Holden Prong or Las Animas Creek, Water Canyon is the preferred route. This scenic trail is steep, but the 3,000-foot vertical gain is spread over 5 miles. Unlike Flower Canyon, the Water Canyon Trail is well maintained. Even so, Water Canyon receives light to moderate use, even during busy summer weekends, because of the elevation gain. Water Canyon Trail 20 is shown on the Forest Service wilderness map, but not on the 1963 USGS quad.

A trail junction sign is located just below the mouth of Water Canyon. After crossing the stream, the trail climbs gently along a pine park bench on the right side, crosses Water Canyon, and then climbs through an increasingly diverse forest of oak, box elder, pine, and Douglas fir in a narrowing rocky valley. At mile 6.9 the trail contours around the left side of the left fork of Water Canyon and again crosses the boulder-strewn stream at 7.2 miles. The north side is bound by massive high cliffs. Be alert for poison ivy along this stretch of the creek.

By mile 7.7 the neck-craning canyon closes in, with rock columns and buttresses rising hundreds of feet on both sides. The small stream cascades over shelf rock into deep pools. This deep, secluded canyon is surely one of the most spellbinding in the Black Range.

A photo note is in order here. This narrow, deep, densely vegetated canyon doesn't lend itself to well-exposed canyon shots. The cliff walls are shaded throughout most of the day. It's less frustrating to keep your camera in your pack until you climb high enough for all-encompassing landscape photography.

The good trail weaves back and forth across the creek in dense forest, with small waterfalls and old tree blazes along the way. After 8.4 miles the trail continues up the deep, narrow canyon of the left fork of a second major split in the stream. Climb westerly up the main branch of Water Canyon for another 0.5 mile to a small spring on the left. Just as the canyon becomes more subdued, an amazing array of giant rock fins and balancing rocks appears at 9.0 miles. A small flat used for camping is just to the left as the trail begins climbing more steeply above the stream. After angling steadily up and around a ridge on the right side, you'll once again parallel the cascading stream, crossing again at 9.8 miles.

A small, grassy, early-season spring in an aspen-fir grove is reached after another 0.5 mile of steady climbing, then the trail makes a series of long, well-graded switchbacks up through an aspen forest mixed with conifers on the north side of upper Water Canyon. A small sign for the Water Canyon Trail marks the narrow ridge top of the Black Range Crest and the junction with Crest Trail 79 at 11.4 miles; turn left (south).

The Kelso Place on Las Animas Creek with Massacre Canyon in the background. This is the burial site of fifteen soldiers and scouts killed by Victorio and his Warm Springs Apache band in 1879.

The Crest Trail negotiates the rocky ridge, and then descends via switchbacks to an unmarked junction at 12.2 miles. The trail on the right drops 0.2 mile through the aspen directly to McKnight Fire Cabin. The Crest Trail continues straight along the divide for another 0.4 mile to the trailhead at the end of FR 152, thereby completing this vigorous canyon loop.

Options: If time and energy permit, hike from the mouth of Water Canyon down Las Animas Creek to the Murphy Place or beyond. If camping along Las Animas for a night or two, visit the graves at the Kelso Place below Massacre Canyon (see page 55). The valley widens as the stream enlarges, and frequent grassy flats are ideal for relaxing in this pleasant riparian setting. An additional side hike toward Victoria Park and Canyon from the Murphy Place is possible, although these old trails are no longer maintained and portions are difficult to find.

Note: For information on McKnight Fire Cabin, see Hike 25's Option.

25 McKnight Mountain

Highlights:	Sweeping vistas from the highest peak in the Aldo
Type of hike:	Out-and-back day hike
Total distance:	5.0 miles round-trip
Difficulty:	Moderate
Best months:	May to October
Maps:	Forest Service Aldo Leopold Wilderness Map; Victoria Park USGS quad
Special considerations:	In the early spring, check with the Forest Service in Mimbres for road conditions; snowbanks may linger on FR 152 into May, making the road impassable.

Finding the trailhead: On New Mexico 35, 1.5 miles north of the Forest Service Ranger Station in Mimbres, turn right (east) on McKnight Road (signed), also Forest Road 152. The road is maintained gravel for 8 miles, to the junction of FR 537; thereafter it becomes steep and rocky, with hairpin turns. A four-wheel-drive high-clearance vehicle is required. Drive 7 miles beyond the junction, a total of 15 miles, to a large grassy knoll on the right and the trailhead for the Black Range Crest Trail north to McKnight Mountain.

Parking and trailhead facilities: The signed trailhead has a large unpaved parking area and campsites, but no water. At McKnight Cabin, 0.3 mile farther north on McKnight Road, a spring's flow is trapped in an open cistern, hosting a good crop of algae. The water is potable if boiled or filtered.

Key points:
  0.0   Trailhead on McKnight Road.
  0.4   Path to McKnight Cabin.
  1.2   Junction with Water Canyon Trail 20.
  2.4   McKnight Summit Trail; turn right.
  2.5   McKnight Summit.

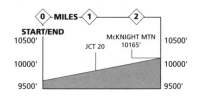

The hike: The day hike to McKnight Summit travels along Black Range Crest Trail 79, weaving on one side of the divide and then the other, so you enjoy the view even before you arrive at the mountaintop. The first part of the hike is on the broad, open trail that is typical of the crest. Much of the rest of the route, however, is on a narrow, rocky path, where it negotiates the rocky crest.

From the trailhead, go straight north on the wide divide through the aspen. At 0.4 mile from the trailhead, an unmarked trail goes left (west) and heads downhill to the McKnight Fire Cabin (see Option). Continuing north, you'll begin an unrelenting climb, via switchbacks, to the rocky crest ridge. The trail drops into a minor saddle at 1.2 miles, where a sign indicates the Water Canyon Trail diving off the ridge to the east. One advantage of a crest hike is that you don't have to worry about what to do at junctions: Stay on the crest. One disadvantage is the undulating nature of the route. You have to gain and regain the same elevation repeatedly. Dropping into a saddle may

McKnight Mountain

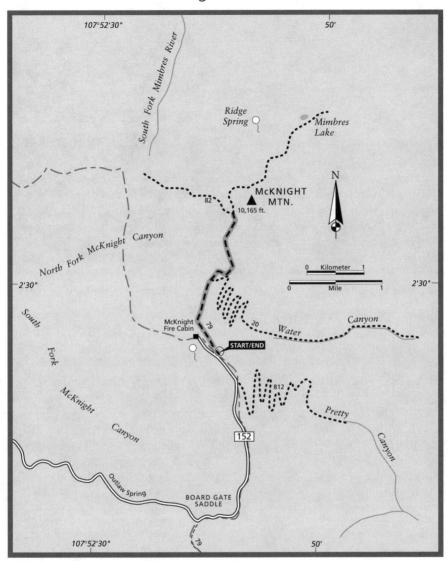

be a temporary relief from the climb, but there is a sinking feeling as well because you'll have to climb again!

So it's up out of the saddle, weaving along the rocky ridge on a narrow rocky trail segment. At 2.4 miles, in a dense aspen grove, is a McKnight Summit sign and a short trail leading right (east) up to the open knoll. The grassy mountaintop is equipped with rocks perfectly contoured for sitting so you can enjoy the view in comfort. At 10,165 feet, McKnight Mountain is the highest point in the Aldo. After you have enjoyed the 360-degree view, return to the trailhead by the same route.

Animas Creek and Hillsboro Peak as seen from McKnight Mountain—the highest point in the Aldo.

Option: On your return trip, you might take a side trip to McKnight Fire Cabin. The facilities at the cabin are very rustic. The cabin, its various outbuildings, and corral are dilapidated, with sagging walls and leaky roofs. The seepy spring is piped to a concrete cistern—actually a watering trough—that catches the spring's flow before it leaks into the swampy meadow. Algae growing in the trough doesn't affect the water's taste, but it should be boiled or filtered. The cabin is unlocked and very untidy. Unlike other Forest Service cabins in the Aldo, which are immaculate and reflect a considerate clientele, this one is a hovel. The area around the cabin is a sloping grassy clearing surrounded by an aspen forest. There is one level campsite at the southern edge of the aspen, near the road. Return to the trailhead by walking 0.3 mile up the road.

26 Mimbres Lake

Highlights:	Views from the Aldo's highest peak, and a remote mountain pond on the Black Range crest
Type of hike:	Out-and-back day hike or overnight backpack
Total distance:	8.8 miles round-trip
Difficulty:	Moderate
Best months:	May to early October
Maps:	Forest Service Aldo Leopold Wilderness Map; Victoria Park USGS quad
Special considerations:	In the early spring, check with the Forest Service in Mimbres for road conditions; snowbanks may linger on FR 152 into May, making the road impassable.

Finding the trailhead: On New Mexico 35, 1.5 miles north of the Forest Service Ranger Station in Mimbres, turn right (east) on McKnight Road (signed), also Forest Road 152. The road is maintained gravel for 8 miles, to the junction of FR 537; thereafter it becomes steep and rocky, with hairpin turns. A four-wheel-drive high-clearance vehicle is required. Drive 7 miles beyond the junction, a total of 15 miles, to a large grassy knoll on the right and the trailhead for the Black Range Crest Trail north to McKnight Mountain.

Parking and trailhead facilities: The signed trailhead has a large unpaved parking area and campsites, but no water. At McKnight Cabin, 0.3 mile farther north on McKnight Road, a spring's flow is trapped in an open cistern, hosting a good crop of algae. The water is potable if boiled or filtered.

Key points:

0.0   Trailhead on McKnight Road.
0.4   Path to McKnight Cabin.
1.2   Junction with Water Canyon Trail 20.
2.4   McKnight Summit Trail.
2.5   Junction with Powderhorn Ridge Trail 82.
2.7   View from overlook.
3.4   Trail to Ridge Spring.
4.4   Mimbres Lake, junction with Lake Trail 110.

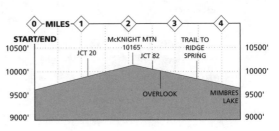

The hike: The hike to Mimbres Lake travels along Black Range Crest Trail 79, weaving on one side of the divide and then the other, so you enjoy the view to both east and west. The first part of the hike is on the broad, open trail that is typical of the crest. Much of the rest of the route, however, is on a narrow, rocky path, where it negotiates the rocky crest. After passing McKnight Mountain, the trail widens again and the route becomes more heavily forested.

Mimbres Lake

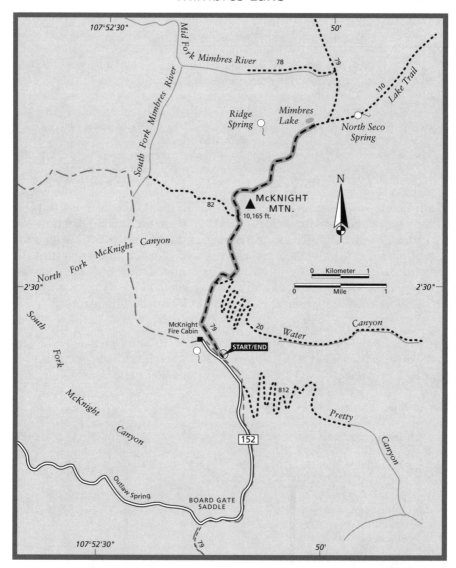

From the trailhead, go straight north on the wide divide through the aspen. At 0.4 mile from the trailhead, an unmarked trail goes left (west) and heads downhill to the McKnight Fire Cabin (see Option). Continuing north, you'll begin an unrelenting climb, via switchbacks, to the rocky crest ridge. The trail drops into a minor saddle at 1.2 miles, where a sign indicates the Water Canyon Trail diving off the ridge to the east. One advantage of a crest hike is that you don't have to worry about what to do at junctions: Stay on the crest. One disadvantage is the undulating nature of the route. You have to gain and regain the same elevation repeatedly. Dropping into a saddle may be a temporary relief from the climb, but there is a sinking feeling as well because you'll have to climb again!

So it's up out of the saddle, weaving along the rocky ridge on a narrow rocky trail segment. At 2.4 miles, in the dense aspen, is a McKnight Summit sign and a short trail leading right (east) up to the open knoll. It is worth a side trip to visit the top, less than 0.1 mile away. The grassy mountaintop is equipped with rocks perfectly contoured for sitting, so you can enjoy the view in comfort. At 10,165 feet, McKnight Mountain is the highest point in the Aldo. After you have enjoyed the 360-degree view, return to the trail and continue north.

Very quickly you will encounter the junction with Powderhorn Ridge Trail 82. Continue to the right on Trail 79. The forest thickens as you go north, but timely openings do exist, enabling you to enjoy the view. One such spot is high on the east side of McKnight Mountain where the trail switchbacks down. There is a stark rocky outcropping adjacent to the trail; it's a lovely place to pause. From this intermission, the steep trail switchbacks down to a saddle, where a side trail leads downhill on the west to Ridge Spring. The spring is 400 feet below the trail, about 0.5 mile away. Continue along the ridge trail to Mimbres Lake. There is a signed junction for the Lake Trail just east of the lake.

Mimbres Lake is a swampy stock pond bounded on three sides by a forest of aspen. It looks lovely from the trail, reflecting the sky and the forest, glistening in the sun. A disintegrating fence surrounds the pond, but no longer creates much of a barrier. The stagnant waters are enjoyed now by wildlife. Look for a variety of tracks in the soft earth near the pond. In the spring, there is lots of bird activity around the pond.

Mimbres Lake on the crest of the Black Range.

Mimbres Lake is a scenic spot for camping, but getting water, which requires treatment, is challenging. Wading in to the proper depth inevitably stirs up silt from the bottom.

Return to the trailhead by the same route.

Option: Take that side trail, 0.4 mile from the trailhead, to drop down to McKnight Fire Cabin. For information on McKnight Fire Cabin, see Hike 25's Option.

27 McKnight–Mimbres

Highlights:	A mostly downhill shuttle backpack from the Black Range crest down the Mimbres River to the CDT trailhead, with majestic views, rugged canyons, and a large perennial stream
Type of hike:	Two- to four-day backpack, shuttle
Total distance:	16.5 miles
Difficulty:	Strenuous
Best months:	May through October
Maps:	Forest Service Aldo Leopold Wilderness Map; Victoria Park and Hay Mesa USGS quads
Special considerations:	In the early spring, check with the Forest Service in Mimbres for road conditions; snowbanks may linger on FR 152 into May, making the road to the beginning trailhead impassable. The road is not plowed or maintained in the winter. You can expect wet foot crossings on the Mimbres River, and brush and downfall in the burned areas of the Middle and South Forks of the Mimbres.

Finding the trailheads: *Beginning trailhead:* On New Mexico 35, 1.5 miles north of the Forest Service Ranger Station in Mimbres, turn right (east) on McKnight Road (signed), also Forest Road 152. The road is maintained gravel for 8 miles, to the junction of FR 537; thereafter it becomes steep and rocky, with hairpin turns. A four-wheel-drive high-clearance vehicle is required. Drive 7 miles beyond the junction, a total of 15 miles, to a large grassy knoll on the right and the trailhead for the Black Range Crest Trail north to McKnight Mountain.

Ending trailhead: From NM 35, 3.0 miles north of the McKnight Road junction, right after milepost 15, turn right on FR 150, also called North Star Mesa Road and NM 61. Cautionary signs at the junction on NM 35 warn of difficult terrain and lack of food, lodging, and gas for 120 miles. Actually the road is graded annually and gets rough only when it dives into or climbs out of canyons via tortuous switchbacks. A high-center two-wheel-drive vehicle can safely negotiate this road. With any vehicle, 10 mph is the average speed. Drive north on the improved gravel road 8 miles to the sign for Mimbres Trail 77 and Continental Divide Trail 74. Turn right and drive on the

McKnight–Mimbres

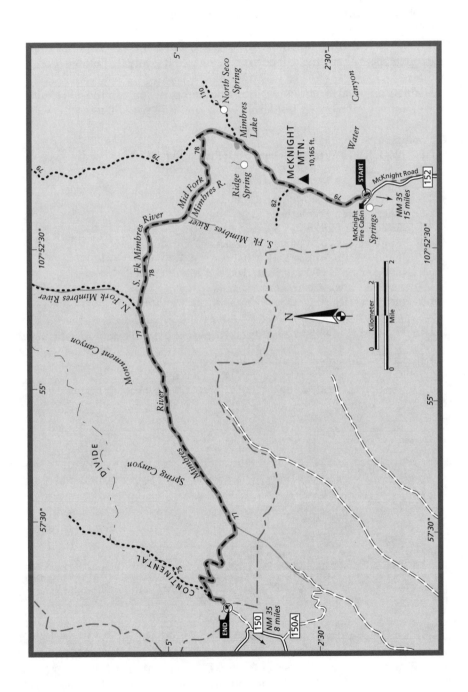

deeply rutted road for 0.75 mile to the corral and primitive campsites on the flat pinyon-juniper mesa at the signed trailhead.

The driving distance between trailheads is 35 miles, of which 3 are paved.

Parking and trailhead facilities: *Beginning trailhead:* The signed trailhead has a large unpaved parking area and campsites, but no water. At McKnight Cabin, 0.3 mile farther north on McKnight Road, a spring's flow is trapped in an open cistern, hosting a good crop of algae. The water is potable if boiled or filtered.

Ending trailhead: Spacious parking and campsites are found here, along with an information board, wilderness sign, and trail signs. There is no water.

Key points:
0.0	Black Range Crest trailhead on McKnight Road.
0.4	Side trail to McKnight Cabin.
1.2	Junction with Water Canyon Trail 20.
2.4	Trail to summit of McKnight Mountain.
2.5	Junction with Powderhorn Ridge Trail 82.
3.4	Unsigned trail to Ridge Spring.
4.4	Mimbres Lake and junction with Lake Trail 110.
5.0	Junction with Middle Fork Mimbres Trail 78; turn left (west).
6.9	Junction of Middle and South Forks of Mimbres Trails; continue downstream.
9.5	Junction of North and South Forks of the Mimbres; continue downstream.
11.8	Mouth of Monument Canyon.
12.6	Corral.
14.1	Last wet foot crossing on Mimbres River.
14.3	New trail up Corral Canyon to CDT trailhead.
16.1	Junction of Mimbres River Trail 77 and CDT 74; turn left to trailhead.
16.5	CDT trailhead.

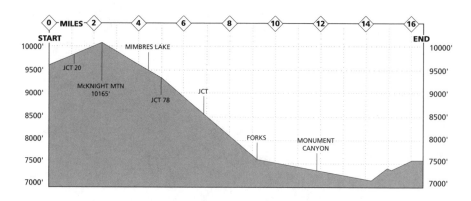

The hike: By starting at the McKnight Road trailhead on the Black Range crest, you enjoy the splendors of the mountain ridge and then travel mostly downhill along the Mimbres River to the CDT trailhead near North Star Mesa Road. From the trailhead, follow the wide trail north through the aspen thicket. At the end of this level section of the ridge, you will pass an unmarked side trail down to McKnight Cabin; continue to the right along the ridge. The trail to McKnight Mountain has rocky sections as it climbs and skirts around the rocky spine of the mountain range, losing its jeep-road quality.

At a minor saddle, the trail into Water Canyon goes off to the right; carry on along the divide. At 2.4 miles from the trailhead, in an aspen grove, is the signed trail to McKnight summit. The grassy mountaintop is equipped with perfectly contoured rocks so you can enjoy the view in comfort. At 10,165 feet McKnight Mountain is the highest point in the Aldo. Drop your pack and take the short stroll up to the summit before continuing to Mimbres Lake.

Just beyond the McKnight summit is a left-hand trail to Powderhorn Ridge. Resist the temptation to take a "shortcut" via Powderhorn and South Fork Mimbres Trails. South Fork Trail 80 is severely fire damaged, with brush and heavy downfall rendering it impassable.

In early spring you can expect scattered snowbanks on the northwest slopes along the Crest Trail. You also will encounter a bit of winter downfall if you are here ahead of the trail crew. The undulating trail is usually clear, however, as it enjoys regularly scheduled visits by the trail crews. Openings in the forest provide exhilarating views, such as when the trail switchbacks down the east side of McKnight Mountain. Excellent seating is available on a rock outcropping right next to the trail, with views to the east.

There are a couple of springs indicated on the quad map between the peak and Mimbres Lake. Ridge Spring has an unsigned trail to it, on the left. You can spot it by watching for log cuts and an opening in the old stock fence. The spring is 0.5 mile downhill from the trail. The second spring trail, closer to Mimbres Lake, is on the right and has been erased by the encroaching forest.

Mimbres Lake is a swampy stock pond bounded on three sides by a forest of aspen. It looks lovely from the trail, reflecting the sky and the forest, glistening in the sun. A disintegrating fence surrounds the pond, but no longer creates much of a barrier. The stagnant waters are enjoyed now by wildlife. Look for a variety of tracks in the soft earth near the pond. Mimbres Lake is a scenic spot for camping, but getting water, which requires treatment, is challenging. Wading in to the proper depth inevitably stirs up silt from the bottom. At the trail junction at the lake, continue north on the ridge trail another 0.6 mile to the next signed junction.

The wide Crest Trail, a former jeep road, is clear. The dense forest of Douglas fir, aspen, spruce, and subalpine fir brackets the trail on either side. You may easily feel dwarfed by the gigantic specimens. The towering giants, soaring to the sky, create the feeling of being in a Gothic cathedral. A deep old-growth forest almost engulfs the Black Range Crest Trail at the head of the Middle Fork of the Mimbres River. Turn left (west) at the signed junction, 0.6 mile north of Mimbres Lake.

The sign on the crest for the Middle Fork Trail accurately indicates 4.5 miles to the Mimbres River, which is the confluence of the North and South Forks. The hike is varied and scenic, but also steep and rough. You'll be glad that you're going down rather than up the Mid and South Forks. At first the trail drops steeply through a diverse forest of mature aspen, spruce, pine, and huge old Douglas fir trees up to 5 feet in diameter, then the descent moderates along the narrow, forested drainage to a dramatic rocky chasm with cascading waterfalls 0.8 mile below the crest. The trail plummets alongside the chasm to a primeval forest on the right side of the narrow streambed. Expect lots of downed trees across this stretch of the leaf-cushioned trail. You'll also encounter high rock cliffs, moss-covered boulders, and a dense forest of pine, Douglas fir, and aspen on down to the confluence of the Mid and South Forks at 6.9 miles. There are streamside campsites here.

Continuing to the right, down the South Fork, the wide trail is passable but slow. Downfall, mountain locust, and other brush combine to make this a very rugged stretch. After 0.4 mile a spring enters from the left. After that, there's more slow going in a recent burn as the trail drops steeply through a maze of blowdown. Don't be in a hurry. It may take close to an hour to get through this 0.7-mile-long obstacle course. One good result of the fire is the ability to actually see the exposed surface geology. Rocky canyons and rock formations stairstepping up the steep slopes are gloriously visible.

After 2.8 miles from the crest, the South Fork Mimbres River and trail make a sharp turn to the left (west) where a major east tributary joins the South Fork (8,120 feet). Continue downstream on the main trail, which winds pleasantly through a parklike forest of stately conifers, with intermittent views to the top of the right canyon rim. Tree blazes and rock cairns appear more often as the trail becomes brushier with some downfall. At 8.5 miles an aspen-lined spring enters from the left, followed by more stream crossings and rock formations high on the right side. The lower 0.3 mile of the South Fork Canyon is especially rugged and ragged, with impressive columns, spires, and shallow caves on the right. Just before reaching the junction at 9.5 miles (7,675 feet), densely forested rock spires dramatically define the dividing ridge between the two forks. At the forks, pass the junction with the North Fork Trail, continuing downstream.

Downstream of the confluence, wet foot crossings will be deeper, but the canyon of the main Mimbres is broader, providing excellent campsites in the grassy meadows. Ponderosa pine parks and gnarly old cottonwoods adorn the valley, with rugged rock formations rising on the canyon walls. Monument Canyon enters from the left 2.3 miles below the forks, and within the next mile you will pass an old corral next to the trail. The valley becomes more open and the stream slows and widens as you progress along the Mimbres. The final crossing of the river is apt to be knee-deep during high water. With a soft silt bottom, it's actually the most challenging of the crossings.

The trail follows the right side of the river through a wide grassy bench dotted with huge ponderosa pines, reaching a trail junction on the western side of the valley. Here you will head uphill, leaving the river for good, on the new trail segment up Corral Canyon to the CDT junction and the trailhead. This new cutover trail is clear and well maintained, but it does feature some steep sections. It is also dry and lacks the pleasant shade you enjoyed in the river valley.

In 2 miles the junction with the CDT is reached; turn left (south) and hike 0.4 mile to the trailhead to complete your trip.

Option: For information on McKnight Fire Cabin, see Hike 25's Option.

28 McKnight–Mimbres Forks

Highlights:	Grand vistas of the Crest Trail, the highest Aldo peaks, and the Forks of the Mimbres with rugged canyons and perennial streams
Type of hike:	Three- to four-day backpack loop
Total distance:	24.7 miles, plus a 2-mile side trip to Reeds Peak
Difficulty:	Strenuous
Best months:	May to early October
Maps:	Forest Service Aldo Leopold Wilderness Map; Hay Mesa, Reeds Peak, and Victoria Park USGS quads
Special considerations:	In the early spring, check with the Forest Service in Mimbres for road conditions; snowbanks may linger on FR 152 into May, making the road impassable. Wet foot crossings are possible along the forks of the Mimbres. Expect brush and blowdown from fires in Forks trails.

Finding the trailhead: On New Mexico 35, 1.5 miles north of the Forest Service Ranger Station in Mimbres, turn right (east) on McKnight Road (signed), also Forest Road 152. The road is maintained gravel for 8 miles, to the junction of FR 537; thereafter it becomes steep and rocky, with hairpin turns. A four-wheel-drive high-clearance vehicle is required. Drive 7 miles beyond the junction, a total of 15 miles, to a large grassy knoll on the right and the trailhead for the Black Range Crest Trail north to McKnight Mountain.

Parking and trailhead facilities: The signed trailhead has a large unpaved parking area and campsites, but no water. At McKnight Cabin, 0.3 mile farther north on McKnight Road, a spring's flow is trapped in an open cistern, hosting a good crop of algae. The water is potable if boiled or filtered.

Key points:

0.0	Black Range Crest trailhead on McKnight Road.
0.4	Side trail to McKnight Cabin.
1.2	Junction with Water Canyon Trail 20.
2.4	Trail to summit of McKnight Mountain.
2.5	Junction with Powderhorn Ridge Trail 82.
3.4	Trail to Ridge Spring.
4.4	Mimbres Lake and junction with Lake Trail 110.
5.0	Junction with Middle Fork Mimbres Trail 78.
8.9	Willow Spring.
9.8	Junction with Spud Patch Trail 111.
10.0	Newman Spring.
10.7	Junction with North Fork Mimbres Trail; turn left, after optional 2-mile side trip to Reeds Peak.
15.2	Forks of the Mimbres River, junction with Trail 78; turn left.
16.9	South Fork bends south, unofficial trail wanders off to the east.
17.8	Junction of Middle and South Forks.
19.7	Black Range crest, junction with Trail 79; turn right.

McKnight–Mimbres Forks

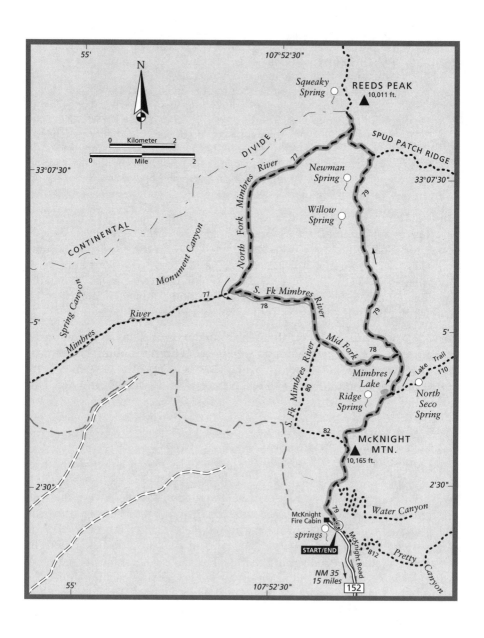

20.3   Mimbres Lake.
22.3   Trail to summit of McKnight Mountain.
24.7   Black Range Crest trailhead on McKnight Road.

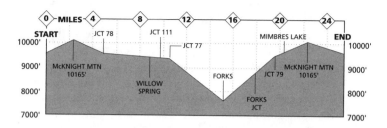

The hike: This backpack takes you along the Black Range crest, with opportunities to visit the two highest peaks on short, packless side hikes. The return route of the loop portion of the trip drops down the North Fork of the Mimbres, then returns to the crest via the South and Middle Forks.

From the trailhead, follow the wide trail north through the aspen thicket. At the end of this level section of the ridge, you will pass an unmarked side trail down to McKnight Cabin; continue along the ridge. The trail to McKnight Mountain has rocky sections as it climbs and skirts around the rocky spine of the mountain range, losing its jeep-road quality.

At a minor saddle, the trail into Water Canyon goes off to the right; carry on along the divide. At 2.4 miles from the trailhead, in an aspen grove, is the signed trail to McKnight Summit. The grassy mountaintop is equipped with perfectly contoured rocks so you can enjoy the view in comfort. At 10,165 feet, McKnight Mountain is the highest point in the Aldo, so it deserves a visit. Drop your pack and take the short stroll up to the summit before continuing to Mimbres Lake.

Just beyond the McKnight summit is the trail to Powderhorn Ridge. Disregard this lightly used trail, and stay to the right on the broad crest route. In early spring you can expect scattered snowbanks on the northwest slopes of the Crest Trail. You also will encounter a bit of winter downfall if you are here ahead of the trail crew, although the undulating trail is usually clear. Openings in the forest provide exhilarating views, such as when the trail switchbacks down the east side of McKnight Mountain. Excellent seating is available on a rock outcropping right next to the trail, with views to the east.

There are a couple of springs indicated on the quad map between the peak and Mimbres Lake. Ridge Spring has an unsigned trail to it on the left; you can spot it by watching for log cuts and an opening in the old stock fence. The spring is 0.5 mile downhill from the trail. The second spring, closer to Mimbres Lake, is on the right and has been erased by the encroaching forest.

Mimbres Lake is a swampy stock pond bounded on three sides by a forest of aspen. It looks lovely from the trail, reflecting the sky and the forest, glistening in the sun. A disintegrating fence surrounds the pond, but no longer creates much of a barrier. The stagnant waters are enjoyed now by wildlife. Look for a variety of tracks in the soft earth near the pond. Camping is possible at Mimbres Lake, with sites along the edge of the woods. Getting water, which requires treatment, is challenging because wading in to the proper depth inevitably stirs up silt from the bottom. There's a trail junction at the lake; continue north on the ridge trail.

The wide Crest Trail, now resembling its original life as a jeep road, is clear because it is usually maintained every other year. The dense forest of Douglas fir, aspen, spruce, and subalpine fir brackets the trail on either side. You may easily feel dwarfed by the gigantic specimens, which make it seem as if you're in a Gothic cathedral. A deep old-growth forest almost engulfs the Black Range Crest Trail at the head of the Middle Fork of the Mimbres River. Continue along the undulating crest northward to Reeds Peak, passing the trail junction that is your return route at the end of the loop.

The trail maintains an overall moderate grade for the next 5 miles, with only a few short steep ups and downs. Dropping into saddles and contouring around steep side slopes keeps the trail between 9,400 and 9,700 feet for most of the distance.

Along the way you'll find some sporadic fire damage, blowdown, and mountain locust, but for the most part the well-defined trail remains in good condition. Most of the high Crest Trail is closed in with old growth, a "hall of trees" with towering monarchs lining the trail. But every so often the forest opens to clear views in both directions that show the amazing contrast between rugged canyons and rock formations to the east and the softer wooded slopes on the west side. When you come across one of these "windows," whether due to a rock outcrop or lightning-caused fire, drop your pack and soak up the scenery. Or pause in the deep woods and sit a while. Only the singing wind, the rustle of squirrels, and the calls of the birds break the stillness.

Willow Spring, 4.5 miles north of Mimbres Lake, is an unreliable source of water. Newman Spring, just north of the Spud Patch Trail junction, is located in a sloping meadow with an expansive view westward. The spring may be little more than a wet meadow seep, but it is usually a reliable water source, except later in the summer during a particularly dry year. Because of a recent fire, expect some blowdown of large blackened Douglas fir trees across the trail as you near the North Fork junction at 10.7 miles.

From the junction, your backpack route goes left down the North Fork on Trail 77. But first, drop your pack and hike a mile up the trail to Reeds Peak (10,011 feet), the highest point on the Continental Divide in the Aldo. The open, rocky apex is surrounded by locust, aspen, and Douglas fir, preventing a complete 360-degree view from the ground. For a commanding view of the entire Aldo Leopold Wilderness and far beyond, climb a few levels of the unmanned lookout tower. The platform just below the lookout cabin has been removed, but if you're looking for a grand view there is certainly no need to climb the very top of the lookout.

You might consider taking your backpack to the peak and camping there. Water is available at Squeaky Spring 0.6 mile away (see Hike 41 for details), and there's a metal cabin next to the lookout. The roomy cabin, complete with table, chairs, bunks, and a wood stove, is open to the public. It is in first-class condition thanks to responsible visitors who clean up after themselves and replenish the wood box. While relaxing in the cabin, out of the wind, take time to read the Reeds Peak cabin log. More than one grateful person thanked Aldo Leopold for his vision, and for his enduring gift of wilderness.

After your visit to the peak, resume your backpack by heading down the North Fork Mimbres. A recent fire at the top of the North Fork valley has left charred Douglas fir snags. The valley is narrow and the trail grade is very steep in several places as it drops to the spring indicated on the map. This spring may be little more than a seep, and you have to descend farther to get to water. About 3 miles from the Black Range crest, you drop to a grassy meadow with a spring adjacent to the small stream. The valley widens a bit, with a mixed conifer forest of spruce, fir, and pine, along with aspen. The valley then becomes a deep, rugged chasm as you drop toward the forks.

If your plans call for camping near the forks, follow the trail downstream on the north side of the Mimbres for about 0.4 mile to a large meadow and a pleasant campsite. Otherwise, take a sharp left at the forks and head upstream on the South Fork (labeled incorrectly as the Mid Fork on the wilderness map). This route to the divide is rougher than the North Fork descent. The stream crossings are more numerous and considerably wetter, and you will be traveling through almost a mile of burned forest, making passage challenging. The burn is one reason for the greater volume of water in this tributary because the naked hillsides allow increased runoff.

From the forks, the trail leads upstream through a canyon with impressive rugged columns, spires, and shallow caves. Densely forested rock spires dramatically define the dividing ridge between the two forks. You will encounter some brush and downfall on this less traveled trail, but cairns and blazes, as well as a noticeable tread, will keep you on track. Within a mile the trail winds pleasantly through a parklike forest of stately conifers with intermittent views to the top of the right canyon rim. After many stream crossings, you arrive at a confluence of two streams, where a large burned area opens to the right (south). Disregard the unofficial trails, left by hunters and firefighters, that spray off to your left. Follow the Forest Service trail across the creek, heading south through the burn.

The trail is passable for the hardy hiker, but slow. Downfall, mountain locust, and other brush combine to make this a very rugged stretch. It is slow going as the trail climbs through a maze of blowdown. You can't do this section in a hurry; it may take close to an hour to get through this 0.7-mile-long obstacle course. One good result of the fire is the ability to see the exposed surface geology. Rocky canyons and rock formations stairstepping up the steep slopes are gloriously visible. Near the end of the burn area, a spring enters from the right, pouring its cool water right out of the hillside. Even beyond the burn, you have to contend with jackstrawed tree trunks because the opening in the forest has permitted the wind to do its work.

Finally, 2.6 miles from the forks, you arrive at the Middle–South Fork trail junction and the confluence of the two streams. If you're thinking about traveling up the South Fork to the divide, reconsider. This patch of burn you just got through is nothing compared to the devastation you can expect on the South Fork Trail. The Forest Service lacks the manpower and the funds to cut out that trail, so it's reverting to wilderness. There are a couple of small

Downfall from a recent fire creates an obstacle course along the Lower South Fork Mimbres River.

campsites near the trail junction along the banks of the creek; these are the best opportunities for camping until you reach Mimbres Lake, 2.5 miles and 1,000 feet in elevation away.

After the junction, the Middle Fork Trail climbs into a dense forest of pine, Douglas fir, and aspen, with high rock cliffs towering above. Expect lots of downfallen trees across this stretch of the leaf-cushioned trail. You rise along the narrow forested drainage through a rocky chasm with waterfalls. The trail departs abruptly from the stream and climbs steeply for 0.3 mile, almost straight up in places, finally reaching the Crest Trail. The sight of blue sky through the forest canopy works like a magnet to draw you upward to the crest.

When you reach the Crest Trail, it's a 5-mile hike back to the trailhead. Although your pack will be lighter due to the food you've consumed, you will find the ups and downs of the crest-line route to be as arduous as they were on the first leg of the journey. Even so, take time to visit McKnight summit again to view the rugged east-side canyons, then continue south to the trailhead.

Note: For more information on McKnight Fire Cabin, see Hike 25's Option.

29 McKnight–North Seco

Highlights:	Panoramas from the crest and the highest point on the Black Range, down North Seco Canyon's Box to the rolling mesas on the east side of the Aldo
Type of hike:	Three-day backpack shuttle
Total distance:	15.3 miles
Difficulty:	Strenuous
Best months:	May to early October
Maps:	Forest Service Aldo Leopold Wilderness map; Victoria Park and Apache Peak USGS quads
Special considerations:	In the early spring, check with the Forest Service in Mimbres for road conditions; snowbanks may linger on FR 152 into May, making the road to the beginning trailhead impassable. There is a possibility of wet foot crossings, depending on water levels. North Seco is a lightly used trail; it is difficult to find in places due to downfall, brush, and rocks. North Seco Spring may not be reliable later in the season. The upper 2 miles of the trail will probably be dry, and the box on North Seco just below Long Canyon must be waded during periods of high water.

Finding the trailheads: *Beginning trailhead:* On New Mexico 35, 1.5 miles north of the Forest Service Ranger Station in Mimbres, turn right (east) on McKnight Road (signed), also Forest Road 152. The road is maintained gravel for 8 miles, to the junction of FR 537; thereafter it becomes steep and rocky, with hairpin turns. A four-wheel-drive high-clearance vehicle is required. Drive 7 miles beyond the junction, a total of 15 miles, to a large grassy knoll on the right and the trailhead for the Black Range Crest Trail north to McKnight Mountain.

Ending trailhead: From Interstate 25, 5 miles north of Truth or Consequences, take NM 52 west 31 miles to Winston. Turn left (south) at Winston through the tiny town toward Chloride. A half mile beyond Winston, turn left (south) on the signed graded gravel road to the St. Cloud Mine, Forest Road 157. Continue southwest for 5 miles. Here the wide, graded county-maintained road continues west to the St. Cloud Mine, and a narrow rough road on the left (south) is signed FR 157. Turn left (south) on FR 157.

Following the contour of the land FR 157, is rough when it follows a canyon or drainage; when on the mesas its quality improves. Travel on FR 157 is slow, averaging about 10 miles an hour. Drive south on FR 157 for 17 more miles. In the middle of a broad valley, some remnant buildings of the defunct town of Hermosa stand on the hillside in front of you. A sign stating PRIVATE PROPERTY. PLEASE STAY ON ROADWAY also indicates this is a private inholding, further reinforced with a steel cable and I-beam post barricade marking the boundary.

Located obscurely about 50 yards east of FR 157 is a tiny sign for FR 732. Continue south on the main road, FR 157, through the former Hermosa. This

McKnight–North Seco

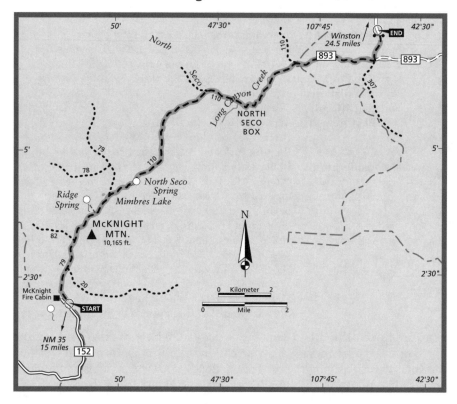

unmaintained stretch of road ends 2.5 miles south of the townsite at a locked gate. This is a rough, four-wheel-drive, high-center road, with steep pitches and deep ruts. Flag Spring has eroded the road severely 1.2 miles south of Hermosa. A small parking slot permits one vehicle to pull off there; parking here will extend the hike 1.3 miles. Otherwise, continue driving on the tortuous road south 1.3 miles to the locked gate atop the mesa north of North Seco Creek, where there is room to turn around and park.

The driving distance between trailheads is about 150 miles, 40 of which are unpaved.

Parking and trailhead facilities: *Beginning trailhead:* The signed trailhead has a large unpaved parking area and campsites, but no water. At McKnight Cabin, 0.3 mile farther north on McKnight Road, a spring's flow is trapped in an open cistern, hosting a good crop of algae. The water is potable, if boiled or filtered.

Ending trailhead: There is a large, flat, unpaved parking area with no protection from sun or wind. The Morgan Creek trailhead, 0.5 mile west of Hermosa on FR 732, is better for camping. There is no water at the trailhead.

Key points:

- 0.0   Black Range Crest trailhead on McKnight Road.
- 0.4   Side trail to McKnight Fire Cabin.
- 1.2   Junction with Water Canyon Trail 20.
- 2.4   Trail to summit of McKnight Mountain.
- 2.5   Junction with Powderhorn Ridge Trail 82.
- 3.4   Trail to Ridge Spring.
- 4.4   Mimbres Lake and junction with Lake Trail 110; turn right (east).
- 4.9   North Seco Spring.
- 9.6   Junction with cutover Trail 87.
- 9.8   North Seco Canyon box.
- 11.9   Wilderness boundary, windmill, junction with Lake Trail 110 and old Forest Road 893.
- 12.0   Springs along trail; valley narrows.
- 12.4   Trail on old roadbed.
- 14.2   Windmill; turn left, cross stream, and follow road uphill.
- 15.3   Locked gate at trailhead.

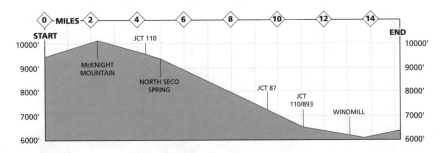

The hike: This outing includes the highest peak in the Aldo and one of the lowest elevation streams on the east side of the divide. After the sweeping views from the crest and McKnight Mountain, you descend into North Seco Canyon. Emerging into the broad valley of the east side, you are in a totally different ecosystem.

From the trailhead, follow the wide trail north through the aspen thicket. At the end of this level section of the ridge, you will pass an unmarked side trail down to McKnight Cabin; continue along the ridge. The trail to McKnight Mountain has rocky sections as it climbs and skirts around the rocky spine of the mountain range, losing its jeep-road quality.

At a minor saddle, the trail into Water Canyon goes off to the right; carry on along the divide. At 2.4 miles from the trailhead, in an aspen grove, is the signed trail to McKnight Summit. The grassy mountaintop is equipped with perfectly contoured rocks so you can enjoy the view in comfort. At 10,165 feet, McKnight Mountain is the highest point in the Aldo, so it deserves a visit. Drop your pack and take the short stroll up to the summit before continuing to Mimbres Lake.

Just beyond the McKnight summit is the trail to Powderhorn Ridge. Disregard this lightly used trail, and stay to the right on the broad crest route.

In early spring you can expect scattered snowbanks on the northwest slopes of the Crest Trail. You also will encounter a bit of winter downfall if you are here ahead of the trail crew. Otherwise, the undulating trail is usually clear. Openings in the forest provide exhilarating views, such as when the trail switchbacks down the east side of McKnight Mountain. Excellent seating is available on a rock outcropping right next to the trail, with views to the east.

There are a couple of springs indicated on the quad map between the peak and Mimbres Lake. Ridge Spring has an unsigned trail to it on the left; you can spot it by watching for log cuts and an opening in the old stock fence. The spring is 0.5 mile downhill from the trail. The second spring, closer to Mimbres Lake, is on the right and has been erased by the encroaching forest.

Mimbres Lake is a swampy stock pond bounded on three sides by a forest of aspen. It looks lovely from the trail, reflecting the sky and the forest, glistening in the sun. A disintegrating fence surrounds the pond, but no longer creates much of a barrier. The stagnant waters are enjoyed now by wildlife. Look for a variety of tracks in the soft earth near the pond. Camping is possible at Mimbres Lake, with sites along the edge of the woods. But getting water, which requires treatment, is challenging because wading in to the proper depth inevitably stirs up silt from the bottom.

The lake is also the location of the signed junction with the Lake Trail, where you turn right (east) and head downhill. It's a little more than 5 miles from here to North Seco Creek, despite what the sign indicates. The trail descends gently through a stately stand of old-growth aspen, spruce, and gigantic Douglas fir more than 4 feet in diameter. A steep drop brings you to the shallow seep of North Seco Spring. The spring is on the north slope of a steep gully that drains to a tiny pool, next to an old broken-down fence shaded by a dark spruce-fir forest. Past the spring, the trail continues its downward gradient. This trail is lightly used, primitive, and obstructed by brush, downfall, and rocks in many places, thereby providing its own brand of isolation and wilderness adventure. The valley widens below the juncture of the North and South Forks of Seco Creek. After passing the remains of an old corral, Long Canyon enters from the south, carrying water in a good snow year.

In the tight gorge below Long Canyon, the stream and the trail are one. In times of high water you will have to get wet. There are no bypass routes to avoid the box. This is a dramatic stretch of North Seco and an appropriate place to linger and appreciate the wonders of the wilderness. The box brings to mind two key characteristics needed in this incredibly rough wildland: respect and humility. The 0.5 mile below the box is particularly rugged, brushy, and hard to find, with constant stream crossings; your reverie will end quickly when you get back to the business of hiking through this country.

Continuing down the valley, you will encounter remnants of the ranchers who tried to make a living here, as well as artifacts of the miners who have also departed. Above it all, ragged cliffs tower in a striking archway formation. The land has outlasted both these efforts to tame it. The trail is at times rugged and brushy, sidehilling and frequently crossing the stream.

North Seco Spring is born in a dense spruce-fir forest.

Entering a wide mountain valley, you may hear an incongruous clanking noise that sounds quite loud after the cloak of silence in the wilderness. Adjacent to a welded 4-foot-tall water storage tank, an energetic eternal windmill continues to pump merrily even though no cows are coming to drink.

The Lake Trail turns north at the windmill, but your route lies down North Seco Creek on former Forest Road 893, which has become a hiking trail. Head east along the stream through an area made soggy by springs alongside the trail. The wide valley changes very quickly. For the next 1.5 miles, the narrow canyon forces the stream into a rocky channel, resulting in noisy stairstep falls and deep pools, especially in early spring runoff. The rustic forest trail stays along the stream.

The valley widens when you get east of the flank of Lake Mountain on the north. The broad, grassy stream valley, bracketed with gently sloping hillsides, makes for easy walking. The earthen trail winds along with the pines and the cottonwoods. Several old campsites exist along the way, usually near stream crossings. Since the former private inholding along North Seco Creek was acquired by the Forest Service, and cattle grazing was terminated, the riparian zone has been nursed back to health. Now the footprints are those of elk, deer, turkey, bear, coyote, and cat. The Forest Service is justifiably proud of this demonstration recovery area.

The trail looks more and more like an old jeep track as you wind your way down the lush valley. A little more than a mile from the first windmill, you will come upon another, also still pumping merrily, keeping a muddy stock pond full. Here there is also an old roadbed running north-south. Turn left (north), cross the creek, and hike uphill another 1.1 mile to the locked gate. This final leg of the outing will be dry, and the sparse vegetation provides no shade. Your hike may have to continue another 1.3 miles beyond the locked gate if your vehicle was unable to negotiate the ruts on the road past Flag Spring. Be sure you have plenty of water with you before departing from North Seco Creek.

Option: An alternative exit would be to hike the 4.4 miles north to Morgan Creek from the first windmill on North Seco Creek (see Hike 4). This alternative requires parking at the Morgan Creek trailhead, which shortens the shuttle distance by 2 miles.

Note: For information on McKnight Fire Cabin, see Hike 25's Option.

Powderhorn Canyon Trailhead

*"I am glad that I shall never be young
without wild country to be young in.
Of what avail are forty freedoms
without a blank spot on the map?"*

—Aldo Leopold, *A Sand County Almanac*, 1949

30 South Fork Powderhorn Canyon

Highlights: Wide diversity, ranging from scenic vistas of the Black Range crest to a pleasant little stream winding through a grassy open forest
Type of hike: Loop day hike
Total distance: 3 miles
Difficulty: Moderate
Best months: April through October
Maps: Forest Service Aldo Leopold Wilderness Map; Hay Mesa USGS quad
Special considerations: The first half of the hike is dry and exposed to wind and sun on a ridge top.

Finding the trailhead: On New Mexico 35, 1.5 miles north of the Forest Service Ranger Station in Mimbres, turn right (east) on McKnight Road (signed). Cross the Mimbres River at the ford. Immediately a sign for Forest Road 151 directs you to turn left; go back across the river and then cross it a third time and head uphill to the northeast on FR 151, atop Kelly Mesa. Pass through a small residential area, reaching the forest boundary at 0.8 mile. At 7 miles, disregard the FOREST TRAIL sign on the right. The road becomes rough as it climbs, requiring a high-clearance four-wheel drive. After another 3 miles the road ends at a wire gate. A sign to the right of the fence indicates the start of the trail.

Parking and trailhead facilities: There is an unpaved parking area, limited camping, and no water.

Key points:
0.0 Trailhead/parking area.
1.5 Trail sign for Powderhorn Ridge Trail 82.
2.7 Stock pond.
3.0 Trailhead/parking area.

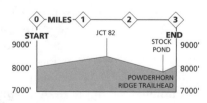

The hike: Although just outside the wilderness boundary, this short loop takes place in a roadless buffer to the Aldo along

South Fork Powderhorn Canyon

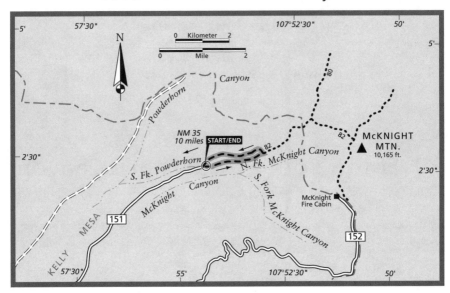

the southwest boundary, and will seem as primitive as many of the trails within the actual wilderness. From a high windy crest to a meandering wooded stream, this hike offers lots of variety within a relatively short distance.

The trail is identified only with a small FOREST TRAIL sign at the road end on a pinyon-juniper ridge between rugged McKnight Canyon and the South Fork Powderhorn Canyon. This good trail starts out in an east to northeast direction along the right (south) side of the ridge. The trail weaves back and forth between the top of the ridge and its right side. Mature stands of ponderosa pine open to grand vistas into McKnight Canyon and on to the crest of the Black Range, which is dominated in this stretch by extensive brushfields from the huge 1951 McKnight Fire. At 1 mile, the trail crests a hilltop overlook, follows the ridgeline, and then sidehills on the right side to a narrow notch at mile 1.5. An old sign on the ground identifies the trail as Powderhorn Ridge Trail 82, pointing beyond to McKnight Mountain.

To continue the loop, turn left and drop into the South Fork of Powderhorn Canyon by following an old blazed trail a short distance down to a grassy stream bottom. The forest is an open mix of pine, oak, and cottonwood interspersed with grassy benches. The tiny stream usually carries water until late spring. This delightful trail follows the stream down to a large stock pond at 2.7 miles. Along the way the trail becomes faint in places, but it is easily regained by simply looking ahead. This shady wooded glen is truly a different world from the exposed, windblown ridge top that you hiked out on. Upon reaching the pond, the trail stays to the right, crosses a fence, and joins a primitive road uphill to the trailhead.

148

The view southeast into McKnight Canyon from the Powderhorn Ridge Trail 82.

31 Powderhorn–McKnight Mountain

Highlights:	A lightly used route to the highest peak in the Aldo Leopold Wilderness with wide vistas of the entire south end of the wilderness, including the Black Range crest and rugged canyons on both sides
Type of hike:	Out-and-back day hike
Total distance:	9.6 miles round-trip
Difficulty:	Strenuous
Best months:	May to early October
Maps:	Forest Service Aldo Leopold Wilderness Map; Hay Mesa and Victoria Park USGS quads
Special considerations:	The entire route is steep, rugged, and dry. The trail follows ridges that are far from any springs or streams. Carry a lot more water than you think you'll need.

Finding the trailhead: On New Mexico 35, 1.5 miles north of the Forest Service Ranger Station in Mimbres, turn right (east) on McKnight Road (signed). Cross the Mimbres River at the ford. Immediately a sign for Forest Road 151 directs you to turn left; go back across the river and then cross it a third time and head uphill to the northeast on FR 151, atop Kelly Mesa. Pass through a small residential area, reaching the forest boundary at 0.8 mile. At 7 miles, disregard the FOREST TRAIL sign on the right. The road becomes rough as it climbs, requiring a high-clearance four-wheel drive. After another 3 miles the road ends at a wire gate. A trail sign to the right of the fence indicates the start of the trail.

Powderhorn–McKnight Mountain

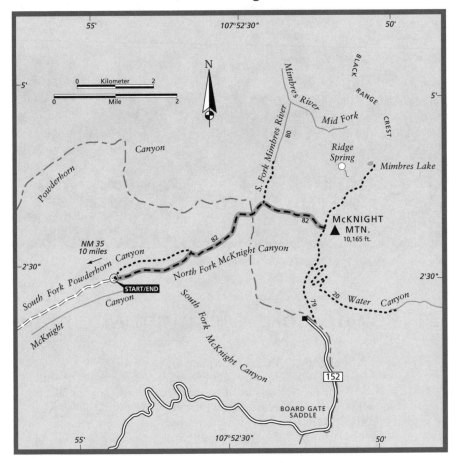

Parking and trailhead facilities: There is an unpaved parking area, limited camping, and no water.

Key points:

0.0	Trailhead/parking area.
1.5	Trail sign for Powderhorn Ridge Trail 82.
3.3	Signed junction of Powderhorn Ridge Trail and South Fork Mimbres Trail 80.
4.7	Signed junction of Powderhorn Ridge Trail and Black Range Crest Trail 79.
4.8	McKnight Mountain (10,165 feet).

The hike: This strenuous route to McKnight Mountain, the "crown" of the Aldo, certainly isn't the easiest way to reach the summit. It's a whole lot longer, drier, and steeper with much more elevation gain than if you were to leave from the McKnight trailhead (see Hike 25). But if you're out for wilderness adventure and lots of healthy exercise, then this hike won't disappoint you.

The trail is identified only with a small FOREST TRAIL sign at the road end on a pinyon-juniper ridge between rugged McKnight Canyon and the South Fork Powderhorn Canyon. This good trail starts out in an east to northeast

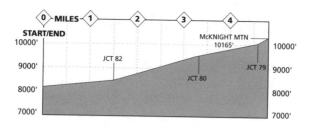

direction along the right (south) side of the ridge. The trail weaves back and forth between the top of the ridge and its right side. Mature stands of ponderosa pine open to grand vistas into McKnight Canyon and on to the crest of the Black Range, which is dominated in this stretch by extensive brushfields from the huge 1951 McKnight Fire. At 1 mile, the trail crests a hilltop overlook, follows the ridgeline, and then sidehills on the right side to a narrow notch at mile 1.5. An old sign on the ground identifies the trail as Powderhorn Ridge Trail 82, pointing beyond to McKnight Mountain.

The left-hand trail drops into the South Fork of Powderhorn Canyon (see Hike 30). Trail 82 continues climbing around the right side of the ridge. It soon joins the main ridge that separates McKnight and Powerhorn Canyons, climbing steeply at times toward the crest of the Black Range. The trail has a well-defined tread, but becomes brushier as elevation is gained. At about 3 miles, the trail sidehills around the north-south ridge that divides Powderhorn Canyon from the Mimbres River. At 3.3 miles, a signed junction is reached with South Fork Mimbres Trail 80 in a grassy saddle ringed by huge Douglas fir with a view southward into McKnight Canyon. The South Fork Mimbres Trail is blocked by heavy brush and downfall, has not been maintained since recent fires, and is not recommended.

From the saddle, take Trail 82 uphill to the right. At first it climbs steeply in a series of short switchbacks through a mixed aspen-conifer forest. The trail gradient moderates a bit as it passes by several grassy openings along the right side. Much of the trail tread is soft dirt, but pesky mountain locust diminishes what would otherwise be pleasurable hiking. After a short downhill stretch and an old fence, the crest of the Black Range is reached at 4.7 miles. A sign proclaims the junction with Black Range Crest Trail 79.

Turn right (south) on the Crest Trail and hike about 0.1 mile to a tiny McKnight Summit sign in an aspen thicket. A short trail leads uphill to the left (east) about 75 yards to the open knoll of the peak. The grassy mountaintop is equipped with perfectly contoured rocks so you can enjoy the magnificent panorama of the whole south end of the Aldo in comfort. At 10,165 feet, McKnight Mountain is the highest point for miles around, so your view is wide open. After you've rested, rehydrated, and enjoyed the 360-degree vista, return to the trailhead by the same route, which is almost all downhill.

Option: If you arrange for someone to meet you at the McKnight trailhead, the final leg of your hike can be a relatively easy 2.5 miles instead of a steep descent of nearly 5 miles. Of course, if you've gone to the trouble of arranging a car shuttle, you might want to start at McKnight and end up at Powderhorn, a mostly downhill hike of about 7.4 miles.

CDT–Mimbres Trailhead

"The elemental simplicities of wilderness travel were thrills . . .
because they represented complete freedom to make mistakes.
The wilderness gave . . . those rewards and penalties for wise
and foolish acts . . . against which civilization
has built a thousand buffers."

—Aldo Leopold, quoted in *Wilderness & Primitive*
Areas in Southwestern National Forests, USFS

---

32 Signboard Saddle

Highlights: Rugged rock formations above the first trail junction, wide views of the Black Range, and pleasant pine parks

Type of hike: Out-and-back day hike

Total distance: 6.6 miles round-trip

Difficulty: Moderate

Best months: April, May, September, and October

Maps: Forest Service Aldo Leopold Wilderness Map; Hay Mesa USGS quad

Special considerations: The entire route is dry, with a long, steep rocky section of trail. Check with the Mimbres Ranger District regarding road conditions on FR 152 in early spring. The road is not plowed or maintained in the winter.

Finding the trailhead: From New Mexico 35, 4.5 miles north of the Forest Service Ranger Station in Mimbres, right after milepost 15, turn right on Forest Road 150, also called North Star Mesa Road and NM 61. Cautionary signs at the junction on NM 35 warn of difficult terrain and lack of food, lodging, and gas for 120 miles. Actually the road is graded annually (whether it needs it or not) and gets rough only when it dives into or climbs out of canyons via tortuous switchbacks. A high-center two-wheel-drive vehicle can safely negotiate this road. With any vehicle, 10 mph is the average speed. Drive north on the improved gravel road 8 miles to the sign for Mimbres Trail 77 and Continental Divide Trail 74. Turn right and drive on the deeply rutted road for 0.75 mile to the corral and primitive campsites on the flat pinyon-juniper mesa at the signed trailhead.

Parking and trailhead facilities: Spacious parking and campsites are found here, along with an information board, wilderness sign, and trail signs. There is no water.

Signboard Saddle

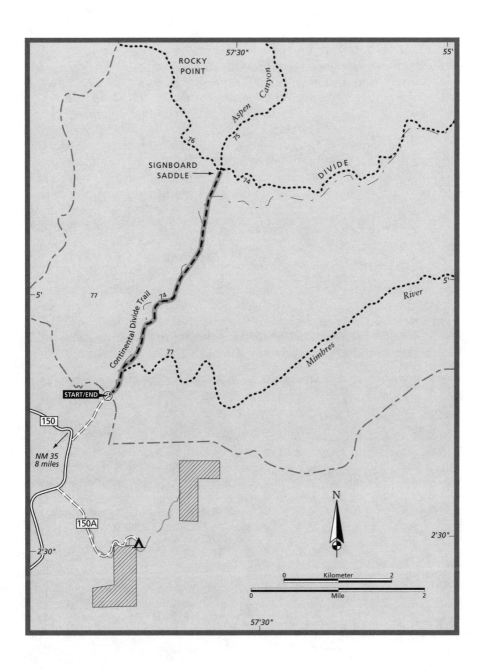

Key points:

0.0	CDT 74 trailhead.
0.4	Signed junction of CDT 74 and Mimbres River Trail 77.
3.3	Signboard Saddle, signed four-way trail junction.

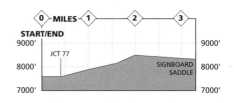

The hike: The CDT/Mimbres River trailhead is also the signed wilderness boundary. The wide, clear trail starts out in open pinyon-juniper and climbs gently up the divide before sidehilling to the signed junction with Mimbres River Trail 77 next to a stock fence. This southern end of the Aldo CDT is more difficult than it appears on the map, with steep exposed pitches and rough rocky sections. Still, because it is part of the popular CDT, it's in good condition, well maintained, and certainly offers some superb views along the divide.

From the signed CDT/Mimbres River trail junction, the wide, rock-strewn trail continues steadily along the Continental Divide in a pinyon-juniper woodland. It veers to the right at 1.0 mile for open vistas of the Black Range crest. After swinging left back to the divide, the good but rocky trail narrows, reaching an open rocky slope at 1.6 miles with grand views back to the south. The CDT steepens in a series of switchbacks to the top of a hill in a mix of pine and oak at 2.0 miles.

For the next mile, the trail parallels an old stock fence as it weaves pleasantly atop and along both sides of the divide. It then drops gently through a grassy ponderosa pine park and passes a stock gate in Signboard Saddle at 3.3 miles. If you don't hear or see wild turkeys or elk in the park, you'll most certainly find telltale tracks and scat here. The actual saddle is a signed

Signboard Saddle on the CDT.

154

four-way trail junction between the Rocky Point Trail to the left, the continuation of CDT 74 to the right, and Aspen Canyon Trail 75 straight ahead to the north.

After enjoying this pleasant pine-studded park, retrace your route back to the CDT/Mimbres River trailhead for a very different perspective of rock spires and columns as you return southward.

Note: A glance at the wilderness map might tempt you to try a CDT–Rocky Point shuttle hike or vice versa. Because the Rocky Point Trail is burned out and very rough in its midsection, we do not recommend this as an option. See Hike 38 for details.

33 Lower Mimbres River

Highlights:	Scenic multicolored rim rock formations, broad vistas of the Black Range and Mimbres River drainage, large stream and riparian community in a wide valley
Type of hike:	Out-and-back day hike or overnighter
Total distance:	7.4 miles round-trip
Difficulty:	Moderate
Best months:	April through October
Maps:	Forest Service Aldo Leopold Wilderness Map; Hay Mesa USGS quad
Special considerations:	Check with the Mimbres Ranger District regarding road conditions on FR 150 in early spring. The road is not plowed or maintained in the winter. There are several short steep pitches on the new cutover portion of Mimbres River Trail 77. Numerous stream crossings are required; wading shoes are recommended.

Finding the trailhead: From New Mexico 35, 4.5 miles north of the Forest Service Ranger Station in Mimbres, right after milepost 15, turn right on Forest Road 150, also called North Star Mesa Road and NM 61. Cautionary signs at the junction on NM 35 warn of difficult terrain and lack of food, lodging, and gas for 120 miles. Actually the road is graded annually and gets rough only when it dives into or climbs out of canyons via tortuous switchbacks. A high-center two-wheel-drive vehicle can safely negotiate this road. With any vehicle, 10 mph is the average speed. Drive north on the improved gravel road 8 miles to the sign for Mimbres Trail 77 and Continental Divide Trail 74. Turn right and drive on the deeply rutted road for 0.75 mile to the corral and primitive campsites on the flat pinyon-juniper mesa at the signed trailhead.

Parking and trailhead facilities: Spacious parking and campsites are found here, along with an information board, wilderness sign, and trail signs. There is no water.

Lower Mimbres River

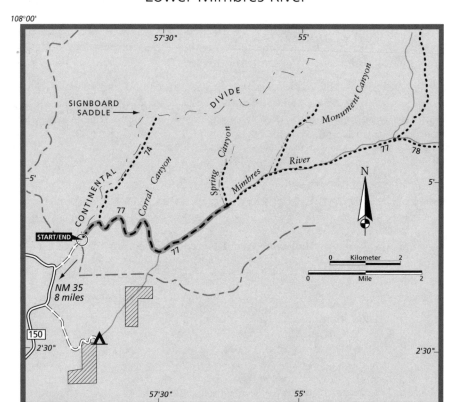

Key points:

- 0.0   CDT 74 trailhead.
- 0.4   Signed junction of CDT 74 and Mimbres River Trail 77; turn right.
- 1.3   Divide between Cooney and Corral Canyons.
- 2.2   New trail section joins the Mimbres River Trail with a sign for Trail 77; bear left.
- 2.4   Trail meets the Mimbres River.
- 3.7   Mouth of Spring Canyon.

The hike: Although steep in a few places, these good trails provide access to varied topography and a lovely river valley, starting from the south end of the CDT within the Aldo. The trailhead is also the signed wilderness boundary. The wide, clear trail starts out in open pinyon-juniper and climbs gently up the divide before sidehilling to the signed junction with Mimbres River Trail 77 next to a stock fence at 0.4 mile.

The first section of Mimbres River Trail 77 is a new cutover trail built recently by the Forest Service to provide public access to the Mimbres River above locked gates on private land. The trail is well maintained and in good condition. From the junction with the CDT, turn right (east) for a steep descent through pine-oak woodland, reaching Cooney Canyon at 0.8 mile. The trail then climbs along the small rocky streambed of Cooney Canyon, crossing the creek at 1.0 mile as majestic cliff rims and spires tower overhead.

The dividing ridge between Cooney and Corral Canyons is reached at 1.3 miles, providing good views toward the river and nearby rock formations. The trail then drops steeply down the wooded gully of Corral Canyon to a sign for the Mimbres River Trail near the river at 2.2 miles. Continue left as the trail follows the left side of the river through a wide grassy bench dotted with huge ponderosa pines.

The first of many wet foot crossings of the Mimbres River, at mile 2.4, is apt to be knee deep with a soft silt bottom during periods of high water. After this relatively deep wade through the river, the trail continues back and forth across the river frequently, climbs high to the left side a couple of times, and then swings wide around a large grassy flat on the left (west) side of the river. The forested canyon is somewhat subdued at first, but occasional glimpses of white tuff and buff-colored mounds foretell of steeper canyon walls ahead. The mouth of aptly named Spring Canyon appears at mile 3.7. The canyon is suggested as a turnaround destination for the hike, but the main idea is to amble anywhere along the lower Mimbres River for an enjoyable out-and-back day trip. If you are backpacking, this stretch of the river has ample grassy flats ideal for camping.

Options: A faint use trail heads up Spring Canyon, which can be explored for a short distance.

Backpacking up from Cooney Canyon on the new section of Mimbres River Trail 77.

34 Mimbres River Forks

Highlights:	A large trout stream and riparian community in a wide valley with ponderosa pine parks, multicolored canyon rim formations, and scenic vistas of the Black Range and Mimbres River drainage
Type of hike:	Out-and-back day hike or overnighter
Total distance:	14.0 miles round-trip
Difficulty:	Strenuous
Best months:	April through October
Maps:	Forest Service Aldo Leopold Wilderness Map; Hay Mesa USGS quad
Special considerations:	Check with the Mimbres Ranger District regarding road conditions on FR 150 in early spring. The road is not plowed or maintained in the winter. There are several short steep pitches on the new cutover portion of Mimbres River Trail 77. Numerous stream crossings are required; wading shoes are recommended.

Finding the trailhead: From New Mexico 35, 4.5 miles north of the Forest Service Ranger Station in Mimbres, right after milepost 15, turn right on Forest Road 150, also called North Star Mesa Road and NM 61. Cautionary signs at the junction on NM 35 warn of difficult terrain and lack of food, lodging, and gas for 120 miles. Actually the road is graded annually and gets rough only when it dives into or climbs out of canyons via tortuous switchbacks. A high-center two-wheel-drive vehicle can safely negotiate this road. With any vehicle, 10 mph is the average speed. Drive north on the improved gravel road 8 miles to the sign for Mimbres Trail 77 and Continental Divide Trail 74. Turn right and drive on the deeply rutted road for 0.75 mile to the corral and primitive campsites on the flat pinyon-juniper mesa at the signed trailhead.

Parking and trailhead facilities: Spacious parking and campsites are found here, along with an information board, wilderness sign, and trail signs. There is no water.

Key points:
- 0.0   CDT 74 trailhead.
- 0.4   Signed junction of CDT 74 and Mimbres River Trail 77; turn right.
- 2.2   New trail section joins the Mimbres River Trail with a sign for Trail 77.
- 3.7   Mouth of Spring Canyon.
- 3.9   Corral No. 9 adjacent to trail.
- 4.7   Mouth of Monument Canyon.
- 7.0   Forks of the Mimbres River, signed trail junction.

The hike: A variety of birds and wildlife rely on the lush habitat of the Mimbres River, which tumbles through a rugged forested valley in a series of deep pools, cascades, and riffles. If time allows, spend a few days base

Mimbres River Forks

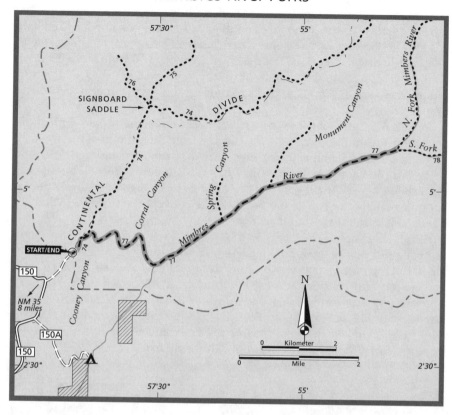

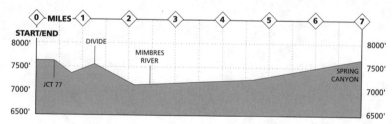

camping about 0.5 mile below the forks to explore side canyons and to relax along the pleasant stream.

The hike begins on the south end of the Aldo portion of the CDT. The trailhead is also the signed wilderness boundary. The wide, clear trail climbs gently up the divide in open pinyon-juniper before sidehilling to the signed junction with the Mimbres River Trail 77 next to a stock fence at 0.4 mile.

Take Trail 77 to the right. You'll climb two dry ridges and drop into two small rocky canyons before finally reaching the green, shady Mimbres valley at 2.2 miles. Here the trail curves on upstream and the stream crossings begin. They become more numerous further along the river. See Hike 35 for details on this section of the hike. Grassy ponderosa pine parks and gnarly old cottonwoods adorn the valley, which becomes more canyonlike with rugged rock formations, especially on the west side.

Monument Canyon enters from the left after 4.7 miles. Once again, the canyon narrows as the trail makes another crossing. Rock hoodoos and goblins appear on the open left slope, where Spanish bayonet cacti contrast with moisture-loving horsetails along the river. Crossings become more frequent in the narrow cottonwood bottom, along with wider views of the surrounding slopes. Deep, dark pools harbor rainbow, cutthroat hybrids, and brown trout.

At mile 6.5, the trail passes by a magnificent large grassy park with abundant campsites adjacent to the river. Judging from the amount of turkey, bear, elk, and mountain lion sign we saw, humans aren't the only critters who enjoy this pleasant spot. For the next 0.5 mile the forest becomes denser as the valley once again closes in. The trail reaches a signed trail junction at 7.0 miles where the North and South Forks converge to form the Mimbres River. This is the turnaround spot for the day hike.

Although camping places are ideal 0.5 mile downstream, there is a small campsite just below the forks, beneath a 70-foot rock bluff. An easy scramble to the top of this outcropping provides excellent views of the surrounding canyon and hillsides. From this junction at the confluence, Trail 77 continues up the North Fork of the Mimbres River to the Black Range crest just south of Reeds Peak. South Fork Trail 78 (shown incorrectly as the Mid Fork on the wilderness map) crosses the river and heads upstream to the right, reaching the crest just north of Mimbres Lake.

Corral No. 9 along Mimbres River Trail 77.

Options: A faint use trail heads up Spring Canyon, which can be explored for a short distance.

A longer side hike is available in Monument Canyon (mile 4.7). A scenic 3-mile round-trip excursion will get you to and from the forks of Monument Canyon. This unofficial use trail (no signs or tree blazes) is faint at first, but quickly becomes well defined as it heads up the left side of the small streambed along a pine-studded bench. Lacking construction, the trail bobs up and down the narrow canyon, mostly on the right side, with monumental rock cliffs and formations rising to the west. The intermittent rocky stream hosts some deep pools in the lower reaches during times of high water. The first major fork in the canyon is reached after 1.5 miles where the trail continues a short distance up the left branch. As with any Aldo hike, you'll make your own discoveries in this remote side tributary to the Mimbres River. During our exploration of the canyon, we surprised an eagle perched on a nearby rock, and later came across the heavy, antlered remains of a bull elk that perhaps died during the winter.

An even more adventurous 5-mile side hike can be made by following the left (west) branch of the canyon, mostly off-trail, another mile north to the Continental Divide.

35 Mimbres–Black Range Crest

Highlights:	Large trout stream and riparian community in a wide river valley with ponderosa pine parks, deep rugged canyons with multicolored formations, scenic vistas of and from the Black Range and Mimbres River drainage, a variety of birds and wildlife
Type of hike:	Four- to five-day backpack loop
Total distance:	29.2 miles
Difficulty:	Strenuous
Best months:	April through October
Maps:	Forest Service Aldo Leopold Wilderness Map; Hay Mesa, Bonner Canyon, Reeds Peak, and Victoria Park USGS quads
Special considerations:	Check with the Mimbres Ranger District regarding road conditions on FR 150 in early spring. The road is not plowed or maintained in the winter. Numerous stream crossings are required; wading shoes are recommended. Some portions of South and Mid Fork Mimbres Trails are blocked with brush and downfall. There is a long dry stretch of trail along the crest.

Finding the trailhead: From New Mexico 35, 4.5 miles north of the Forest Service Ranger Station in Mimbres, right after milepost 15, turn right on Forest Road 150, also called North Star Mesa Road and NM 61.

Mimbres–Black Range Crest

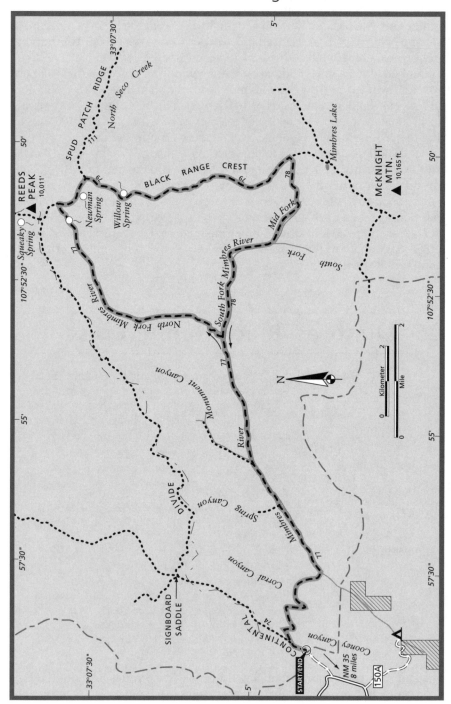

Cautionary signs at the junction on NM 35 warn of difficult terrain and lack of food, lodging, and gas for 120 miles. Actually the road is graded annually and gets rough only when it dives into or climbs out of canyons via tortuous switchbacks. A high-center two-wheel-drive vehicle can safely negotiate this road. With any vehicle, 10 mph is the average speed. Drive north on the improved gravel road 8 miles to the sign for Mimbres Trail 77 and Continental Divide Trail 74. Turn right and drive on the deeply rutted road for 0.75 mile to the corral and primitive campsites on the flat pinyon-juniper mesa at the signed trailhead.

Parking and trailhead facilities: Spacious parking and campsites are at the trailhead, along with an information board, wilderness sign, and trail signs. There is no water.

Key points:
0.0   CDT 74 trailhead.
0.4   Signed junction of CDT 74 and Mimbres River Trail 77; turn right.
2.2   New trail section joins the Mimbres River Trail with a sign for Trail 77.
3.7   Mouth of Spring Canyon.
3.9   Corral No. 9 adjacent to trail.
4.7   Mouth of Monument Canyon.
7.0   Forks of Mimbres River, signed trail junction; bear left up the North Fork.
11.5 Crest of the Black Range, signed junction of trails 77 and 79; turn right.
12.7 Newman Spring and meadow on right (south) side of trail.
12.9 Signed trail junction of Black Range Crest Trail 79 and Spud Patch Trail 111.
13.8 Willow Spring.
17.7 Junction with Mid Fork Mimbres Trail 78; turn right.
19.6 Junction of Mid Fork and South Fork Mimbres Trails; continue downstream.
22.2 Forks of the Mimbres River, junction of North and South Fork Mimbres Trails; continue downstream.
27.0 Trail 77 leaves river valley and joins new cutover trail to CDT.
28.8 Signed junction of Trail 77 and CDT 74; turn left.
29.2 CDT trailhead.

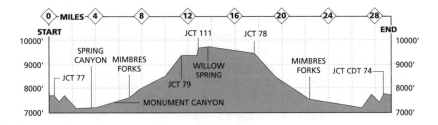

The hike: This hike has it all: the wide valley of the Mimbres River, its rugged forks, and a lofty stretch of the Black Range crest. The CDT trailhead is also the signed wilderness boundary. The wide, clear trail climbs gently up the divide in open pinyon-juniper before sidehilling to the signed junction with Mimbres River Trail 77 at 0.4 mile.

Take Trail 77 to the right. You'll climb two dry ridges and descend into two small rocky canyons before finally reaching the green, shady Mimbres valley at 2.2 miles. Here the trail curves on upstream and the stream crossings begin. The wet foot crossings become more numerous farther up the river. See Hike 33 for details. At 7.0 miles the North and South Forks converge in a steep canyon. The trail junction is marked with a sign. See Hike 34 for details.

Of the three Mimbres Forks trails leading to the crest of the Black Range, North Fork Trail 77 is the most popular. Little wonder: This good trail is well maintained, easy to follow, and is a little less steep due to its longer length. From the junction, hop across the rocks to the other side and follow the trail left up the North Fork. At 7.3 miles the trail passes beneath a sheer 150-foot cliff, marking the start of a narrower rocky canyon densely forested with pine, Douglas fir, and gambel oak. A deep, rugged chasm is quickly reached, followed by a series of moderate pitches and contours along benches above deep pools during high water.

A spring enters from the right (east) at 7.8 miles. The valley soon widens to a pine park with aspen groves, and then climbs steeply to a scenic overlook 100 feet above the right side of a stream chasm at mile 8.2. The trail drops to the stream and soon the valley widens again, with grassy benches and a mixed conifer forest of spruce, fir, pine, and big old Douglas fir along with some aspen. The trail grade is steady but gentle, with only a few crossings. Again the valley narrows as the trail climbs up its right side to a low saddle, across from the rim of the canyon at 9.8 miles.

After losing 100 feet of elevation, the trail comes to a flat grassy meadow with a spring adjacent to the small stream at 10.0 miles. With an open, grassy, pine-studded slope on the left, the trail begins climbing more steeply up the left side of the narrow draw. The spring shown on the map just below the crest is little more than a seep that may dry up before early summer. Before reaching the crest, you'll be able to see the lookout tower on Reeds Peak about 0.5 mile to the north. Mixed with Southwestern white pine, Douglas fir, and aspen, the gully is narrow and the trail grade very steep in several places before it tops out on the Black Range crest at 11.5 miles. Charred Douglas fir snags tell of a recent fire; some blowdown is likely.

The wide trail follows the crest through a thick Douglas fir–aspen forest sprinkled with grand old Southwestern white pine. Along the way, the sloping meadow of Newman Spring opens to an expansive view westward, providing a pleasant break in the otherwise dense forest. The spring might be little more than a wet meadow seep, but it is usually a reliable water source, except later in the summer during a particularly dry year. Just beyond, at mile 12.9, Spud Patch Trail drops steeply to the east. Rocky overlooks at this point provide spectacular views of North Seco and Massacre Canyons, along with Animas Ridge all the way to Hillsboro Peak—the entire southeast quarter of the Aldo! Dense forest continues south from the Spud Patch junction as the crest begins to level off.

Along the way you'll find some sporadic fire damage, blowdown, and mountain locust, but for the most part the well-defined trail remains in good condition. Much of the High Crest Trail is closed in with old growth, a "hall of trees" with towering monarchs lining the trail. But every so often this gothic cathedral of nature opens to clear views in both directions that show the amazing contrast between rugged canyons and rock formations to the east and the softer wooded slopes on the west side. When you come across one of these "windows," whether due to a rock outcrop or lightning-caused fire, drop your pack and soak up the scenery. Or pause in the deep woods and sit a while. Only the singing wind, the rustle of squirrels, and the calls of the birds break the stillness.

The trail maintains an overall moderate grade south of Willow Spring, with only a few short steep ups and downs. Don't expect water at Willow Spring; it has been dry in recent years. Dropping into saddles and contouring around steep side slopes keep the trail between 9,400 and 9,700 feet for most of the distance. At mile 17.7 the trail makes a gradual descent in a mature old-growth forest to the signed junction with Mid Fork Mimbres River Trail 78, where you turn right (west).

The sign on the crest for the Middle Fork Trail accurately indicates 4.5 miles to the Mimbres River, which is the confluence of the North and South Forks. The hike is varied and scenic, but also steep and rough. You'll be glad that you're going down rather than up the Mid and South Forks. At first the trail drops steeply through a diverse forest of mature aspen, spruce, pine, and huge old Douglas fir trees up to 5 feet in diameter, then the descent moderates along the narrow, forested drainage to a dramatic rocky chasm with cascading waterfalls at 18.5 miles. The trail plummets alongside the chasm to a primeval forest on the right side of the narrow streambed. Expect lots of fallen trees across this stretch of the leaf-cushioned trail. You'll also encounter high rock cliffs, moss-covered boulders, and a dense forest of pine, Douglas fir, and aspen until you reach the confluence of the Mid and South Forks at 19.6 miles. Interestingly, both the North and South Forks drain comparably sized watersheds, but the South Fork carries a lot more water. Perhaps this is partly because most of the South Fork has burned during the past fifty years, while the North Fork still contains mostly green forest.

Continuing to the right, down the South Fork, the wide trail is passable but slow. Downfall, mountain locust, and other brush combine to make this a very rugged stretch. After 0.4 mile, a spring enters from the left. Expect more slow going in a recent burn, as the trail drops steeply through a maze of blowdown. Don't be in a hurry. It could take close to an hour to get through this 0.7-mile-long obstacle course. One good result of the fire is the ability to see the exposed surface geology. Rocky canyons and rock formations stairstepping up the steep slopes are gloriously visible.

At 20.5 miles the South Fork Mimbres River and trail make a sharp turn to the left (west) where a major east tributary joins the South Fork. An unsigned, unofficial trail with old log cuts turns right and parallels the left side of this tributary. Continue left on the main trail, which winds pleasantly through a park of stately conifers with intermittent views to the top of the right canyon rim. Tree blazes and rock cairns appear more often as the trail becomes brushier with some downfall. At 21.2 miles an aspen-lined spring enters from the left, followed by more stream crossings and rock formations high on the right side. The South Fork Trail is distinct but far less used than the North Fork. The lower 0.3 mile of the South Fork Canyon is especially rugged and ragged, with impressive columns, spires, and shallow caves on the right. Just before reaching the junction at 22.2 miles, densely forested rock spires dramatically define the dividing ridge between the two forks.

Coming full circle back to the forks completes the loop section of the trip. From the forks, retrace your route down the Mimbres and up to the CDT.

Options: A faint use trail heads up Spring Canyon, which can be explored for a short distance. A longer side hike is possible in Monument Canyon (mile 4.7), where a scenic 3-mile round-trip excursion will get you to and from the forks of the canyon. This unofficial use trail (no signs or tree blazes) is faint at first, but quickly becomes well defined as it heads up the left side of the small streambed along a pine-studded bench. Lacking construction, the trail bobs up and down the narrow canyon, mostly on the right side, with monumental rock cliffs and formations rising to the west. Even so, this horseback-hunter use trail is easier to follow than some of the Forest Service system trails shown on the wilderness maps. The intermittent rocky stream hosts some deep pools in the lower reaches during times of high water. The first major fork in the canyon is reached after 1.5 miles (7,750 feet). The side hike can be made even more adventurous by following the left (west) branch of the canyon, off-trail and all the way north to the Continental Divide. As with any Aldo hike, you'll make your own discoveries in this remote side tributary to the Mimbres River. During our exploration of Monument Canyon, we surprised an eagle perched on a nearby rock, and later came across the heavy, antlered remains of a bull elk that perhaps died during the winter.

From the crest at the head of the North Fork Mimbres River (mile 11.5), Reeds Peak is only 0.5 mile to the north, with a 600-foot climb. This central summit, with its open, well-kept cabin, old lookout, and panoramic views, is well worth the short side trip. Coincidentally, Reeds is exactly the same height as Hillsboro Peak far to the south.

A spring and grassy flat ideal for camping near the North Fork Mimbres River.

36 Mimbres–CDT

Highlights:	A large trout stream and riparian community in a wide river valley with ponderosa pine parks, deep rugged canyons with multicolored formations; scenic vistas of and from the Black Range crest, Continental Divide, and Mimbres River drainage
Type of hike:	Three- to four-day backpack loop
Total distance:	25.8 miles
Difficulty:	Strenuous
Best months:	May through October
Maps:	Forest Service Aldo Leopold Wilderness Map; Hay Mesa, Bonner Canyon, and Reeds Peak USGS quads
Special considerations:	Check with the Mimbres Ranger District regarding road conditions on FR 150 in early spring. The road is not plowed or maintained in the winter. Numerous stream crossings are required; wading shoes are recommended. There is a long dry stretch of trail along the CDT.

Finding the trailhead: From New Mexico 35, 4.5 miles north of the Forest Service Ranger Station in Mimbres, right after milepost 15, turn right on Forest Road 150, also called North Star Mesa Road and NM 61. Cautionary signs at the junction on NM 35 warn of difficult terrain and lack of food, lodging, and gas for 120 miles. Actually the road is graded annually and gets rough only when it dives into or climbs out of canyons via tortuous switchbacks. A high-center two-wheel-drive vehicle can safely negotiate this road. With any vehicle, 10 mph is the average speed. Drive north on the improved gravel road 8 miles to the sign for Mimbres Trail 77 and Continental Divide Trail 74. Turn right and drive on the deeply rutted road for 0.75 mile to the corral and primitive campsites on the flat pinyon-juniper mesa at the signed trailhead.

Parking and trailhead facilities: Spacious parking and campsites are at the trailhead, along with an information board, wilderness sign, and trail signs. There is no water.

Key points:

0.0	CDT 74 trailhead.
0.4	Signed junction of CDT 74 and Mimbres River Trail 77; turn right.
2.2	New trail joins Mimbres River Trail 77.
3.7	Mouth of Spring Canyon.
4.7	Mouth of Monument Canyon.
7.0	Forks of Mimbres River, signed trail junction; bear left up North Fork.
11.5	Crest of Black Range, signed junction of Trails 77 and 79; turn left (north).
12.0	Signed four-way trail junction on west slope of Reeds Peak; turn right.
12.25	Reeds Peak (10,011 feet).

Mimbres–CDT

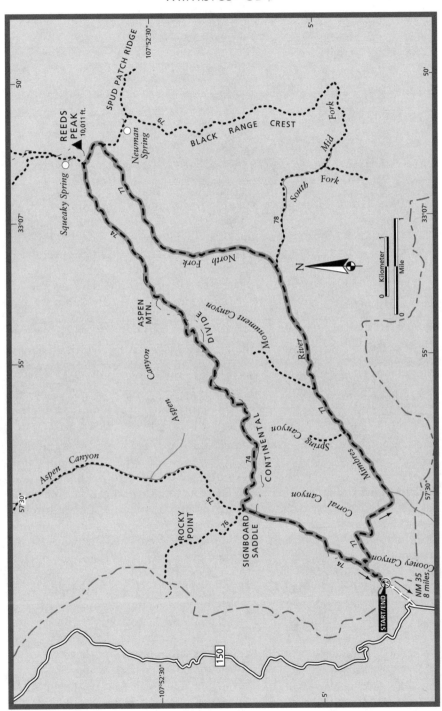

12.5 Signed four-way trail junction on west slope of Reeds Peak; go straight on CDT.
18.0 Aspen Spring site.
22.5 Signboard Saddle.
25.4 Signed junction of CDT 74 and Trail 77.
25.8 CDT 74 trailhead.

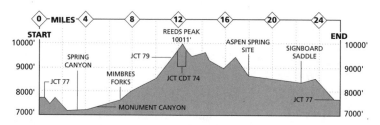

The hike: This long loop traverses the wide valley of the Mimbres River, its rugged north fork, and a long dry stretch of the Continental Divide. The CDT/Mimbres trailhead is also the signed wilderness boundary. The wide, clear trail climbs gently up the divide in open pinyon-juniper before side-hilling to the signed junction with the Mimbres River Trail 77 at 0.4 mile.

Take Trail 77 to the right. You'll climb two dry ridges and descend into two small rocky canyons before finally reaching the green, shady Mimbres valley at 2.2 miles. Here the trail curves on upstream and the stream crossings begin. The wet foot crossings become more numerous farther up the river. See Hike 33 for details on this section of the hike. At 7.0 miles the North and South Forks converge in a steep canyon. The trail junction is marked with a sign. See Hike 34 for more details. Take the North Fork Trail on the left, 4.5 miles to the Black Range crest. See Hike 35 for details on this section of the hike.

Turn left (north) onto the CDT and climb the well-graded trail 0.5 mile to the four-way trail junction on the Continental Divide just west of Reeds Peak. From here a good trail climbs eastward, reaching the summit of Reeds Peak after 0.25 mile. This lofty Continental Divide/Black Range summit rises in the geographical center of the wilderness. Its open, rocky apex is surrounded by locust, aspen, and Douglas fir, preventing a complete 360-degree view from the ground. For a commanding view of the entire Aldo Leopold Wilderness and far beyond, climb a few levels of the unmanned lookout tower. The platform just below the lookout cabin has been removed, but if you're looking for a grand view, there is certainly no need to climb the very top of the lookout.

A metal cabin sits next to the lookout. The roomy cabin, complete with table, chairs, six bunks, and a woodstove, is open to the public. The cabin is in first-class condition, thanks to responsible visitors who clean up after themselves and replenish the wood box. While relaxing in the cabin, out of the wind, take time to read the Reeds Peak cabin log. More than one grateful person thanked Aldo Leopold for his visionary gift of wilderness.

Upon returning to the four-way junction, replenish your water supply by hiking north 0.4 mile to Squeaky Spring. The spring is reliable, even during the dry summer season. Then return to this junction and take the CDT west.

The 10-mile segment of the CDT between the west slope of Reeds Peak and Signboard Saddle is the longest high divide trail in the Aldo without a trail junction and without water. This portion of the CDT is on a biennial maintenance schedule, but the reality of funding and staffing may stretch this out a bit. At least the trail is well marked and well constructed.

The trail quickly passes through an old stock fence and switchbacks down to rejoin the divide at 12.9 miles. The up-and-down nature of high ridges is well represented in this upper segment, where the trail loses and regains elevation before dropping steeply down the open divide to 9,400 feet at 13.5 miles. The up and down continues for another mile, with the elevation back up to 9,600 feet by mile 14.3. After passing through an open pine forest, the trail drops steeply to 9,300 feet at 14.5 miles, followed by a long pleasant section through old-growth Douglas fir. At 15.8 miles the trail cuts right and passes next to large mounds of granite outcrops. After another mile of long steep switchbacks in the Douglas fir forest, the elevation is back up to 9,400 feet on the narrow, open ridge top. Look back for a clear view of the Reeds Peak lookout.

The CDT begins a long descent by sidehilling around the head of Monument Canyon below Aspen Mountain. The woodland of pine and oak is drier, with broad views of the Mimbres River drainage. In places the trail tread is side sloped, but continues to be well marked. Follow a side ridge above the head of Aspen Canyon, then switchback down to a long contour through a picturesque ponderosa pine park to the bottom of a draw at the head of Aspen Canyon. After paralleling the draw, the CDT passes by the Aspen Spring site in an aspen–Douglas fir forest at 18.0 miles. The hard-to-find spring is well concealed in dense brush above the trail and is no longer flowing. The site consists of a concrete cistern sunk deep into the ground with broken pipe next to some old mining debris. It's a disappointment if you're thirsty!

The next 4.5 miles to Signboard Saddle are very pleasant, with only minimal climbing. The trail drops gently through a mixed forest of pine, gambel oak, and Douglas fir, with only the sound of the wind, the chatter of gray squirrels, and the resonating of woodpeckers for company. Every so often the direction of the trail changes abruptly but it's merely following the serpentine path of the Continental Divide. The soft dirt trail is well blazed and easy to follow. After climbing up and down and around a series of grassy pine park draws that feed into Aspen Canyon, the CDT reaches Signboard Saddle at 22.5 miles. True to its name, the saddle is well signed, with the CDT continuing to the left.

The CDT climbs gently through a grassy pine park, weaving pleasantly on both sides of the divide. About 1.3 miles from the saddle, the trail begins a steep switchback descent on a rough, rocky tread for nearly 0.5 mile. Broad vistas open to the crest of the Black Range and to rugged rock formations as the rocky trail drops more gradually in a pinyon-juniper woodland. The signed junction with the new Mimbres River cutover Trail 77 is reached at 25.4 miles. Retracing the final 0.4 mile of CDT completes the return to the trailhead.

A mellow stretch of the Mimbres River just above the mouth of Monument Canyon.

Options: A faint use trail heads up Spring Canyon, which can be explored for a short distance. A longer side hike is possible in Monument Canyon (mile 4.7). A scenic 3-mile round-trip excursion will get you to and from the forks of the canyon. This unofficial use trail (no signs or tree blazes) is faint at first, but quickly becomes well defined as it heads up the left side of the small streambed along a pine-studded bench. Lacking construction, the trail bobs up and down the narrow canyon, mostly on the right side, with monumental rock cliffs and formations rising to the west. Even so, this horseback-hunter use trail is easy to follow. The intermittent rocky stream hosts some deep pools in the lower reaches during times of high water. The first major fork in the canyon is reached after 1.5 miles. The side hike can be made even more adventurous by following the left (west) branch of the canyon, off-trail and all the way north to the Continental Divide.

37 CDT–Black Canyon

Highlights:	A large trout stream and riparian community in a wide river valley with ponderosa pine parks, rugged canyons with multicolored formations, a deep canyon box, and scenic vistas of and from the highest Continental Divide peak in the Aldo
Type of hike:	Three- to five-day backpack loop
Total distance:	32.5 miles
Difficulty:	Strenuous
Best months:	May through October
Maps:	Forest Service Aldo Leopold Wilderness Map; Hay Mesa, Bonner Canyon, and Reeds Peak USGS quads
Special considerations:	Check with the Mimbres Ranger District regarding road conditions on FR 150 in early spring. The road is not plowed or maintained in the winter. The entire CDT within this loop is high and dry. Carry adequate water.

Finding the trailhead: From New Mexico 35, 4.5 miles north of the Forest Service Ranger Station in Mimbres, right after milepost 15, turn right on Forest Road 150, also called North Star Mesa Road and NM 61. Cautionary signs at the junction on NM 35 warn of difficult terrain and lack of food, lodging, and gas for 120 miles. Actually the road is graded annually (whether it needs it or not) and gets rough only when it dives into or climbs out of canyons via tortuous switchbacks. A high-center two-wheel-drive vehicle can safely negotiate this road. With any vehicle 10 mph is the average speed. Drive north on the improved gravel road 8 miles to the sign for Mimbres Trail 77 and Continental Divide Trail 74. Turn right and drive on the deeply rutted road for 0.75 mile to the corral and primitive campsites on the flat pinyon-juniper mesa at the signed trailhead.

CDT–Black Canyon

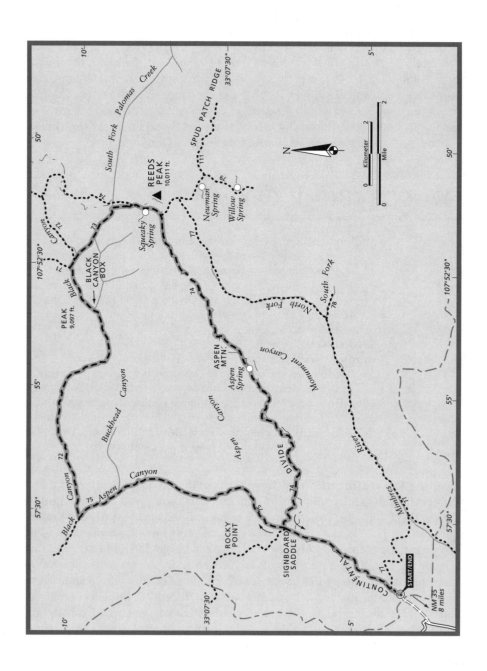

Parking and trailhead facilities: Spacious parking and campsites are at the trailhead, along with an information board, wilderness sign, and trail signs. There is no water.

Key points:
0.0   CDT 74 trailhead.
0.4   Junction of CDT Trail 74 and Mimbres River Trail 77.
3.3   Signboard Saddle; continue straight.
7.2   Buckhead Canyon.
8.6   Junction of Aspen Canyon Trail 75 and Black Canyon Trail 72; turn right.
14.0 Saddle above Black Canyon Box.
15.2 Junction of Black Canyon Trail 72 and Sheep Creek Trail 71.
15.5 Junction of Black Canyon Trail 72 and Falls Canyon Trail 73; bear right.
18.0 Junction of Falls Canyon Trail 73 and CDT 74; turn right.
18.1 Unsigned trail to Squeaky Spring.
18.3 Squeaky Spring.
18.7 Four-way trail junction on west ridge of Reeds Peak; turn left.
19.0 Reeds Peak (10,011 feet).
19.2 Four-way trail junction on west ridge of Reeds Peak; go straight (west) on CDT.
24.7 Aspen Spring site.
29.2 Signboard Saddle; turn left.
32.1 Signed junction of CDT 74 and Mimbres River Trail 77.
32.5 CDT 74 trailhead.

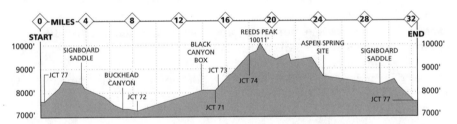

The hike: This extended clockwise lollipop loop dramatizes the contrast between one of the most scenic large stream canyons in the Aldo and the serpentine crest of the Continental Divide. The wide, clear CDT trail starts from the wilderness boundary in open pinyon-juniper. After climbing gently up the divide, it sidehills to the signed junction with Mimbres River Trail 77 next to a stock fence at mile 0.4. This southern end of the Aldo CDT is more difficult than it appears on the map, with steep exposed pitches and rough, rocky sections. Still, because it is part of the popular CDT, it's well maintained, and certainly offers superb views along the divide.

From the junction, the wide, rock-strewn trail continues steadily along the Continental Divide in a pinyon-juniper woodland. After 2.0 miles the CDT climbs a series of steep switchbacks to the top of a hill in a mix of pine and oak. For the next mile the trail parallels an old stock fence as it weaves pleasantly atop and along both sides of the divide. The trail then drops gently through a grassy ponderosa pine park and passes by a stock gate in Signboard Saddle at 3.3 miles. The actual saddle is a signed four-way trail junction between the Rocky Point Trail to the left, the continuation of CDT 74 to the right, and Aspen Canyon Trail 75 straight ahead to the north, which you will take.

The Aspen Canyon Trail is mostly in good condition, providing a pleasant route to Black Canyon. The well-defined trail descends a narrow gully northward in a mixed forest of Douglas fir, Southwestern white pine, and gambel oak. Early in a good water year, the intermittent stream begins flowing after about 0.5 mile. As the trail continues down, notice the contrast between open, scattered forest on the left and the Douglas fir thicket on the right.

The easy-to-follow trail continues to weave in and out of the drainage, where it is washed out or choked with flood-level debris in a few spots. The rocky canyon narrows and then widens, passing along grassy benches with large pine and Douglas fir at mile 5.5. The Bonner Canyon quad shows the Aspen Corral to be somewhere along this flat, but we couldn't find it. In places the trail is faint on the benches, but it is easy to follow with the aid of tree blazes and log cuts. The benches end at mile 5.9 as the canyon tightens up again. Frequent crossings alternate with narrow rocky stretches. By mile 6.4 the lightly used trail becomes more primitive for a short distance.

A small tributary enters from the right at 6.6 miles in a stand of open-grown ponderosa pine. The grassy park continues down to the mouth of Buckhead Canyon at mile 7.2, which can usually be counted on to carry water. Once again the canyon narrows, as the trail avoids rock walls by climbing around to the left side at mile 7.6. The serpentine canyon ends at 8.1 miles, and is followed by a picturesque pine park that extends down to Black Canyon at mile 8.4. The trail crosses a ravine and then Black Canyon, reaching a spacious open meadow dotted with pine and cottonwood as forested slopes rise moderately on both sides. The flat contains a signed junction with the Black Canyon Trail at mile 8.6.

Heading to the right up Black Canyon, the trail climbs over low benches, crosses the gully frequently, and at 9.9 miles reaches a pine bench overseen by towering rock spires on the left (north) side. Musky elk scent hangs heavy in the air, and the sound of gobbling turkeys resonates from nearby hillsides. The trail follows long grassy benches on the left side for nearly a mile, with rugged cliff faces and narrow cave openings on the right side of the stream. Grassy benches suitable for camping continue with pine, Douglas fir, and oak to mile 11.3, where cliffs, spires, and hoodoos dot the steep north slope.

At 11.7 miles a prominent stream enters from the left (north) as the canyon narrows and bends to the right (south). The dense pine-fir forest in the bottom grades rapidly to pinyon-juniper and oak on the adjacent hillsides. Upstream, the tight canyon deepens dramatically, with the stream cutting below rock walls. The trail passes through a recent burn where some blowdown can be expected. Back into green forest, the trail suddenly reaches an open grassy meadow in the otherwise narrow canyon at 12.9 miles. Striking white volcanic tuff is exposed on the left side of the canyon. Grassy flat benches that could be used for small campsites, along with frequent stream

A surprisingly deep pool on a tiny upper tributary to Aspen Canyon.

crossings, continue for another 0.5 mile to a long, dark alcove formed where the stream flows beneath overhanging rock.

At 13.8 miles, pass through an old burn and then climb high above the canyon bottom opposite the mouth of Falls Canyon, which enters from the right (east). The trail steepens as it climbs up the left (west) side of the valley to a low saddle at 14.0 miles. The saddle is bound by a wonderland of massive granite formations to the immediate right of the trail directly above Black Canyon Box. These intricate formations will enchant you. High above, the north rim is defined by a long series of jagged spires and towers just below peak 9097 as shown on the Bonner Canyon quadrangle. The box is one of the deepest and most scenic chasms in the Black Range. Find a rocky perch and enjoy the splendor of unusual rock formations on all sides. The bottom of the box lies partially hidden 200 feet below. A maze of pathways weaves between balancing boulders, mushroom-shaped rocks, and great fin-shaped mounds.

From the saddle above the box, the trail drops through open pine forest to a grassy bottom near the stream. It then climbs gently along grassy pine benches, becoming obscure in a burn, before reaching the signed junction with Sheep Creek Trail 71 at 15.2 miles. The sign indicates a distance of 2.5 miles to the Continental Divide up Sheep Creek, but this would be a long 2.5 miles because the trail is choked with downfall and is rarely maintained. This lower end of the Sheep Creek Trail is completely buried under downfall and, for all practical purposes, has been erased by nature. Instead, continue right (east) on the main Black Canyon Trail toward Reeds Meadow. Even this stretch of the trail could be obstructed with downfall where it passes through a burn. The next trail junction is reached at mile 15.5 in an aspen–Douglas fir forest. The trail sign sits to the right and is easy to miss if you're hiking down the Falls Canyon Trail to this junction.

When traveling between Black Canyon and Reeds Peak, by far the best of three possible routes is Falls Canyon Trail 73, which is direct, scenic, and well maintained. It is steep and rocky, but passes mostly through green forest, thereby minimizing the amount of blowdown.

Trail 73 climbs through a mosaic of green and burned pine-fir forest in a series of short, steep switchbacks, reaching the dividing ridge between Black and Falls Canyons at 16.2 miles. Striking gray rock formations rise above Black Canyon to the north. At mile 16.3 the trail contours to an overlook of the falls on the north branch of Falls Canyon. Its 200-foot drop, off cliffs and down steep rock chutes, amplifies the sound of the small stream plummeting over the falls. A rocky perch just below the trail offers a great photo op.

The trail wraps around the canyon and climbs to a narrow notch above the falls at 16.5 miles. Open rocky ledges below the trail provide spectacular views of the falls and the mostly burnt slopes of Falls Canyon. The trail then climbs steadily up the left side of the stream, and in the stream at times, crossing to the right side as it enters a mature aspen–Douglas fir forest. At 17.3 miles you'll come to a bowl-shaped meadow ringed with aspen, pine, and fir. When you reach this lovely interlude in the forest, you'll see why Whitmore, an early pioneer, built his cabin here so long ago. Part of the original stone foundation of the cabin sits on the north side of the meadow

The trail is faint at the upper end of the meadow. A more distinct but unofficial trail heads up to the left, providing an easy shortcut to the CDT if you're going north. Otherwise, keep to the right and look for old blazes and log cuts. Poke around the northeast end of the meadow and you'll soon find a distinct trail going south up the left side of a draw. The trail quickly reenters the burn with a short but rough section. Fortunately, the upper end of the trail is pleasant, surrounded by a live spruce-fir forest.

At 18.0 miles the Falls Canyon Trail joins the CDT. Signs point north to Diamond Peak (8.5 miles) and south to Reeds Peak (0.75 mile). This CDT junction is adjacent to an old stock fence in a forest of spruce, fir, and aspen. If the trail hasn't been cut out above the meadow, expect about 0.5 mile of slow going almost up to the divide. Continue right (south) on the CDT to a broad, grassy park draping the divide after 0.1 mile. From here there are two ways to reach the summit of Reeds Peak. The first is to take the main left-hand trail straight up the divide and into the burn where it's marked with rock cairns. The better choice is to go first to Squeaky Spring for water and then contour south to the Continental Divide just west of the peak. For lack of a better name, we'll call this the Reeds Peak Bypass Trail.

The bypass to the spring is worth taking, but it's hard to find because it is unsigned and indistinct. The best way to find it is to head southwest across the meadow. The trail becomes obvious toward the edge of the meadow near an aspen thicket suitable for camping. An old corral encircles the head of Squeaky Spring just below the aspen, where you'll find a small cement-lined cistern filled with water. And sure enough, a broken squeaky pipe faucet sits nearby. This is an essential side trip to fetch water; don't forget to re-place the heavy cement lid on the cistern.

From the spring at mile 18.3, an old trail climbs uphill about 50 yards and intersects the "bypass" trail. This trail is well constructed, but expect some downfall where it passes through the burn. It climbs gradually, reach-ing the Continental Divide at 18.7 miles. This is also the west ridge of Reeds Peak and a signed four-way trail junction. Significantly, the junction marks the intersection between the two main "high-line" trails of the Aldo: the CDT and the Black Range Crest Trail. From here the Continental Divide turns sharply west, as does the CDT. This point is also the northern terminus of the Black Range Crest Trail. Of course, the actual topographic turning point between the Continental Divide and the crest of the Black Range is Reeds Peak—230 feet and 0.25 mile to the immediate east.

The peak's open, rocky apex is surrounded by locust, aspen, and Dou-glas fir, preventing a complete 360-degree view from the ground. For a com-manding view of the entire Aldo Leopold Wilderness and far beyond, climb a few levels of the unmanned lookout tower. The platform just below the lookout cabin has been removed, but if you're looking for a grand view, there is certainly no need to climb the very top of the lookout.

A metal cabin sits next to the lookout. The roomy cabin, complete with table, chairs, six bunks, and a woodstove, is open to the public. The cabin is in first-class condition thanks to responsible visitors who clean up after themselves and replenish the wood box. While relaxing in the cabin, out of the wind, take time to read the Reeds Peak cabin log. More than one grate-ful person thanked Aldo Leopold for his visionary gift of wilderness.

From the signed junction, continue west on the CDT. The 10-mile seg-ment of the CDT between the west slope of Reeds Peak and Signboard Sad-dle is the longest high divide trail in the Aldo without a trail junction and without water. This portion of the CDT is on a biennial maintenance sched-ule, but the reality of funding and staffing may stretch this out a bit. At least the trail is well marked and well constructed.

The trail quickly passes through an old stock fence and switchbacks down to rejoin the divide at 19.6 miles. The up-and-down nature of high ridges is well represented in this upper segment, where the trail loses and regains elevation before dropping steeply down the open divide to 9,400 feet at 20.2 miles. After another mile, the elevation is back up to 9,600 feet. The trail passes through an open-grown pine forest, then drops steeply to 9,300 feet at 21.2 miles. This is followed by a long pleasant section through old-growth Douglas fir. At 22.5 miles the trail cuts right and passes next to large mounds of granite outcrops. After another mile of long steep switchbacks in the Dou-glas fir forest, the elevation is back up to 9,400 feet on the narrow, open ridge top. Look back for a clear view of the Reeds Peak lookout.

The CDT begins a long descent by sidehilling around the head of Monu-ment Canyon below Aspen Mountain. The woodland of pine and oak is drier, with broad views of the Mimbres River drainage. In places the trail tread is side sloped, but continues to be well marked. Follow a side ridge above the head of Aspen Canyon, then switchback down to a long contour through a picturesque ponderosa pine park to the bottom of a draw at the head of the canyon. After paralleling the draw, the CDT passes by the Aspen Spring site in an aspen–Douglas fir forest at 24.7 miles. The hard-to-find spring is well concealed in dense brush above the trail and is no longer flowing. The site consists of a concrete cistern sunk deep into the ground with broken pipe—and no water—next to some old mining debris.

The next 4.5 miles to Signboard Saddle are very pleasant, with only minimal climbing. The trail drops gently through a mixed forest of pine, gambel oak, and Douglas fir, with only the sound of the wind, the chatter of gray squirrels, and the resonating of woodpeckers for company. Every so often the direction of the trail changes abruptly, but it's merely following the serpentine path of the Continental Divide. The soft dirt trail is well blazed and easy to follow. After climbing up and down and around a series of grassy pine park draws that feed into Aspen Canyon, the CDT reaches Signboard Saddle at 29.2 miles. True to its name, the saddle is well signed, with the CDT continuing to the left.

The CDT climbs gently through a grassy pine park, weaving pleasantly on both sides of the divide. About 1.3 miles from the saddle, the trail begins a steep switchback descent on a rough, rocky tread for nearly 0.5 mile. Broad vistas open to the crest of the Black Range and to rugged rock formations as the rocky trail drops more gradually in a pinyon-juniper woodland. The signed junction with the new section of Mimbres River Trail 77 is reached at 32.1 miles. Retracing the final 0.4 mile of the CDT completes the return to the trailhead.

Option: For an alternate route to the CDT that adds 1.7 miles, stay on the Black Canyon Trail another 1.4 miles, climbing 400 feet to Reeds Meadow. This large sloping meadow usually has water in its lower end. Turn right (south) onto the CDT and continue another 2.8 miles, with a gain of 1,060 feet, to the Falls Canyon Trail junction. Much of the CDT south of Reeds Meadow passes through burns with heavy brush and blowdown.

Rocky Point Trailhead

*"Wilderness is the raw material out of which man
has hammered the artifact called civilization."*

—Aldo Leopold, *A Sand County Almanac*, 1949

38 Rocky Point

Highlights: A challenging route to the CDT at Signboard Saddle
Type of hike: Out-and-back day hike
Total distance: 9 miles round-trip
Difficulty: Strenuous
Best months: April to October
Maps: Forest Service Aldo Leopold Wilderness Map; North Star Mesa and Hay Mesa USGS quads
Special considerations: In the early spring, check with the Mimbres Ranger District regarding road conditions on FR 150, which is not plowed or maintained in the winter, and about the conditions on Trail 76. The parking area across the road from the trailhead is soft sand. Don't get stuck! Sections of the trail were under construction in 2001. The trail goes through several burn areas; you can expect downfall on the trail. There is no water on this trail.

Finding the trailhead: From New Mexico 35, 4.5 miles north of the Forest Service Ranger Station in Mimbres, right after milepost 15, turn right on Forest Road 150, also called North Star Mesa Road and NM 61. Cautionary signs at the junction on NM 35 warn of difficult terrain and lack of food, lodging, and gas for 120 miles. Actually the road is graded annually, getting rough only when it dives into or climbs out of canyons via tortuous switchbacks. A high-center two-wheel-drive vehicle can safely negotiate this road. With any vehicle, 10 mph is the average speed. Drive north on the improved gravel road 13 miles to the faded FOREST TRAIL 76 sign on the right, 2 miles north of Rocky Canyon Forest Camp.

Parking and trailhead facilities: There is limited parking at the trailhead. The nearest campsites are at Rocky Canyon, 2 miles south. There is no water at the trailhead.

Key points:
0.0   Trailhead on FR 150.
0.4   New trail ends.
0.8   Blue flagged route joins original Trail 76.
1.0   Ridge top.

Rocky Point

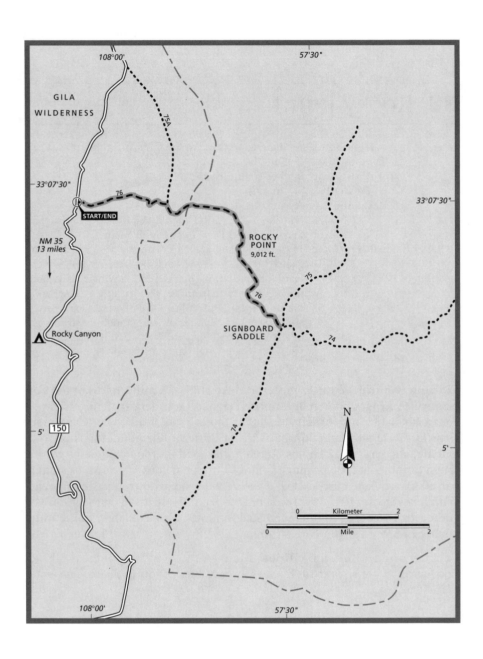

1.2	Start of a 0.2-mile burned area.
1.8	Junction with Trail 754.
1.9	Start of a 2-mile burned area.
2.1	Wilderness boundary.
3.0	Trail sidehills below Rocky Point.
3.2	Burned area.
4.5	Signboard Saddle; junction with Aspen Canyon Trail 75 and CDT Trail 74.

The hike: The Forest Service has plans for the Rocky Point Trail to become part of the CDT, as a link to a new Rocky Canyon segment west of FR 150 in the Gila Wilderness. When finally established, these trails will allow through hikers to avoid long stretches of road hiking. Although there is a CDT sticker on the hiker sign at the side of the road, and the Rocky Canyon section is under construction, there is no other indication that Trail 76 deserves the honor of being part of the CDT. The trail has experienced numerous fires and has had very little rehabilitation. The route goes straight up steep ridges and sidehills around the tops of steep valleys on narrow tracks that threaten to collapse and send you into the ravine below. These obstacles are combined 3 miles from the trailhead. The steep west-facing sidehill section just east of Rocky Point is blocked by fallen burned trees. Adding to the challenge, this is a hot, dry trail with very little shade.

The first 0.4 mile of the Rocky Point Trail has been reconstructed in broad switchbacks up the slope at the trailhead. The second 0.4 mile might not yet exist on the ground; the route is marked with blue flags as it wraps around to the north side of the hill and joins the original trail. On your return to the trailhead after the day hike, you might take the old trail for a shortcut to the road. One could easily wonder why new trails are created when the old trail seems fine, at least in this stretch.

The old trail slopes upward through ponderosa pine and gambel oak, topping out at 1.0 mile on a ridge with a view of the rolling Continental Divide to the east. Here an old signpost carries the distinctive signature of a bear: The sign and post are chewed and clawed to pieces. Continue along the ridge into a burned area. Blazes are less visible on the burned and downed trunks, and the trail tread is faint on the broiled ground. The trail stays on the crest of the ridge, heading northeast. By 1.4 mile you get beyond the fire, curling around the south slope to reach a cairn atop another ridge at 1.6 miles. The trail contours around the head of a valley, maintaining its elevation before dropping to a faint junction with Trail 754 at 1.8 miles. A sign in the saddle assures you that Signboard Saddle is 3 miles away.

The trail continues up the ridge, gaining 400 feet in 0.3 mile. In addition to the elevation gain, this stretch has also been burned; it requires some

The Continental Divide forms the horizon two miles east as seen from Rocky Point Trail 76.

detective work to spot cairns and blazes on blackened trunks. At the ridge top (8,650 feet) you cross the invisible wilderness boundary. A burned ponderosa pine trunk carries a barely legible, blackened metal PREVENT FOREST FIRES—IT PAYS sign. What irony.

The trail goes east. After losing 150 hard-earned feet of elevation, you climb back to 8,600 feet at the next saddle. From here the trail leads south, barely clinging to the same contour while you skirt along the steep western side of Rocky Point (9,012 feet). For an out-and-back day hike of 6 miles, Rocky Point would be a scenic spot to explore, then return to the trailhead from here. Beyond Rocky Point, where there is no room to maneuver, a blockade of burnt, bristling downfall blocks the hillside. If you get beyond that obstacle, a 140-foot climb to the saddle south of Rocky Point puts you in a position for the downhill roll on the final mile through ponderosa pine to Signboard Saddle.

This is a tough day hike with a light pack. As the first leg of a backpack, it would be brutal with a heavy load. On the final leg of a long excursion, it would also be challenging because it's a long way to water. Because of this we recommend starting from the CDT/Mimbres River trailhead for longer backpack trips that include accessing the Continental Divide and points beyond.

Black Canyon Trailhead

"Wilderness areas are first of all a series of sanctuaries
for the primitive arts of wilderness travel,
especially canoeing and packing."

—Aldo Leopold, *A Sand County Almanac*, 1949

39 Black Canyon

Highlights: A gentle stream in a broad valley
Type of hike: Out-and-back day hike
Total distance: 8 miles round-trip
Difficulty: Moderate
Best months: April to October
Maps: Forest Service Aldo Leopold Wilderness Map; Middle Mesa and Bonner Canyon USGS quads
Special considerations: Check with the Mimbres Ranger District regarding road conditions on FR 150 in early spring. The road is not plowed or maintained in the winter. Expect stream crossings on the hike.

Finding the trailhead: From New Mexico 35, 4.5 miles north of the Forest Service Ranger Station in Mimbres, right after milepost 15, turn right on Forest Road 150, also called North Star Mesa Road and NM 61. Cautionary signs at the junction on NM 35 warn of difficult terrain and lack of food, lodging, and gas for 120 miles. Actually the road is graded annually and gets rough only when it dives into or climbs out of canyons via tortuous switchbacks. A high-center two-wheel-drive vehicle can safely negotiate this road. With any vehicle, 10 mph is the average speed. Drive north on the improved gravel road 20 miles. On the left is Black Canyon Primitive Campground. A silty pond is adjacent to the road on the west next to the campground. Continue across the Black Canyon Creek bridge to the Forest Trail sign 0.2 mile north at the second gated road on the right. You can either park along the road 0.1 mile south of this gate, or turn down the road, closing the light metal hinged gate after you pass through, and drive 0.2 mile to the rough, unpaved sloping parking area just south of a shallow creek crossing. A Forest Trail sign at the eastern edge of the parking area to the right of the barbed wire fence marks the trail.

Parking and trailhead facilities: There is limited parking at the trailhead, and no campsites. Use the Black Canyon Campground across the road. Water can be obtained in Black Canyon Creek; treat before using.

Black Canyon

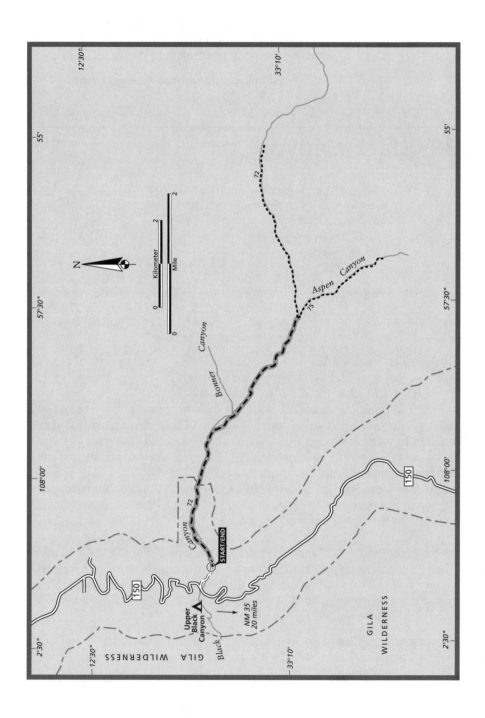

Key points:

0.0　Head east on old two-track at Forest Trail sign.
0.2　Trail sign for Aspen Canyon.
1.0　Stream crossings begin.
1.8　Mouth of Bonner Canyon.
4.0　Aspen Canyon; junction with Trail 75.

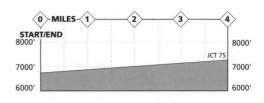

The hike: The 4-mile stretch of Black Canyon is a delightful, gentle valley with a wide wandering stream. The meadows are ringed with ponderosa pines, and strips of cottonwoods line the stream banks. From the parking area at the trailhead, the Forest Trail sign beckons you east. A long-deserted two-track hugs the south canyon wall, skirting what used to be a large private inholding, the Diamond Bar Ranch. Now the only land that remains in private hands is the modest ranch house, which you can see across the pasture about 0.5 mile from the trailhead. The trail stays to the right (south) of the ranch fence for the first mile, skirting the posted private land. Where the fenceline ends, cross the unsigned wilderness boundary and begin crossing the shallow stream. This isn't a rocky stream, so it lacks handy stepping-stones. Although it isn't deep at the crossings, you can count on getting your feet wet.

Black Canyon Creek is one of several streams where Gila trout have been reestablished by the New Mexico Department of Game and Fish. In spring 2001, another chapter in the Gila trout saga was written. A joint Forest Service and Game and Fish team planted hundreds of willow slips along 2 miles of lower Black Creek. It is hoped that they will eventually provide shady

Black Canyon looking southeast about 2.8 miles above the trailhead.

187

pools for the new trout. All the years of cattle grazing stripped the stream of the native willows; this project is part of the effort to return the valley to its original condition.

It is easy to see why early ranchers, especially those here at the Diamond Bar, thought this was such great country for cattle. The broad valley floor is lush with grass. It's hard to believe that you're in the arid southwest. In the spring, the happy songs of birds fill the air; they can't believe it either!

The earthen path takes a very direct route up the valley. The crossings are not terribly numerous, but are about right if it's a warm day. The soft trail, the shade of the pines and cottonwoods, the ready access to a gentle stream—this is a wonderful outing for dogs, one of the few in the Aldo.

At 1.8 miles, the mouth of Bonner Canyon is on your left. From here to the Aspen Trail junction, the valley grows a little narrower, and dramatic rock outcroppings jut from the walls as the gentle gradient continues. Suddenly you'll encounter a trail sign in a ponderosa flat, and you've arrived at the Aspen Canyon junction. The confluence of the streams is to your right, around the base of a 40-foot ridge that protrudes across the valley floor here. A faint trail leads around the ridge and up the edge of Aspen Canyon Creek. Where the two streams meet, you might notice a rusty folded bedspring. Before returning to the trailhead downstream, enjoy the quiet mountain valley. With such grand surroundings, one could even envy the person who used that uncomfortable bed!

Option: Either before or after taking a hike up Black Canyon Creek, stop at the upper Black Canyon Campground on the west side of FR 150, immediately south of the bridge over the creek. There might not be a sign, but you'll notice a silted pond next to the driveway. There are two campsites next to the stream, and a pit toilet. The picnic tables feature unique designs using native stone. In the stream below them, evidence of nature's engineer, the beaver, is displayed in a string of dams, also using native materials. These rodents, who have apparently moved on, decimated the cottonwoods while creating a stairstep of pools that even ducks enjoy.

Just upstream from the beaver dams, human engineers have built a gabion dam that limits the flow of Black Canyon Creek. An informative board by the road provides an explanation for this unnatural barricade that appears so incongruous in this setting: Ash resulting from the Black Range fires of 1995 and 1996 wiped out the fish in the upper Black Canyon drainage. This provided New Mexico Game and Fish an opportunity to reestablish native Gila trout, a state and federally protected species. The gabion dam was built by a variety of agencies and volunteers who support fishing to prevent more aggressive nonnative trout downstream from intruding in the Gila habitat above the dam.

40 Black Canyon Box

Highlights: From gentle valley to majestic rock formations, along a perennial stream with a deep canyon box
Type of hike: Two- to three-day out-and-back backpack
Total distance: 18.8 miles round-trip
Difficulty: Moderate
Best months: April through October
Maps: Forest Service Aldo Leopold Wilderness Map; Middle Mesa and Bonner Canyon USGS quads
Special considerations: Check with the Mimbres Ranger District regarding road conditions on FR 150 in early spring. The road is not plowed or maintained in the winter. Expect numerous stream crossings.

Finding the trailhead: From New Mexico 35, 4.5 miles north of the Forest Service Ranger Station in Mimbres, right after milepost 15, turn right on Forest Road 150, also called North Star Mesa Road and NM 61. Cautionary signs at the junction on NM 35 warn of difficult terrain and lack of food, lodging, and gas for 120 miles. Actually the road is graded annually and gets rough only when it dives into or climbs out of canyons via tortuous switchbacks. A high-center two-wheel-drive vehicle can safely negotiate this road. With any vehicle, 10 mph is the average speed. Drive north on the improved gravel road 20 miles. On the left is Black Canyon Primitive Campground. A silty pond is adjacent to the road on the west next to the campground. Continue across the Black Canyon Creek bridge to the Forest Trail sign 0.2 mile north at the second gated road on the right. You can either park along the road 0.1 mile south of this gate, or turn down the road, closing the light metal hinged gate after you pass through, and drive 0.2 mile to the rough, unpaved sloping parking area just south of the creek. A Forest Trail sign at the eastern edge of the parking area to the right of the barbed wire fence marks the trail.

Parking and trailhead facilities: There is parking for a half dozen vehicles. No campsites are at the trailhead; use the Black Canyon Campground across the road. Water can be obtained in Black Canyon Creek; treat before using.

Key points:
0.0 Head east on old two-track at Forest Trail sign.
0.2 Trail sign for Aspen Canyon.
1.0 Stream crossings begin.
1.8 Mouth of Bonner Canyon.
4.0 Aspen Canyon; junction with Trail 75.
9.4 Saddle above Black Canyon Box.

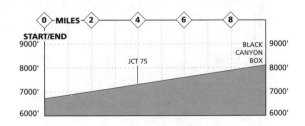

Black Canyon Box

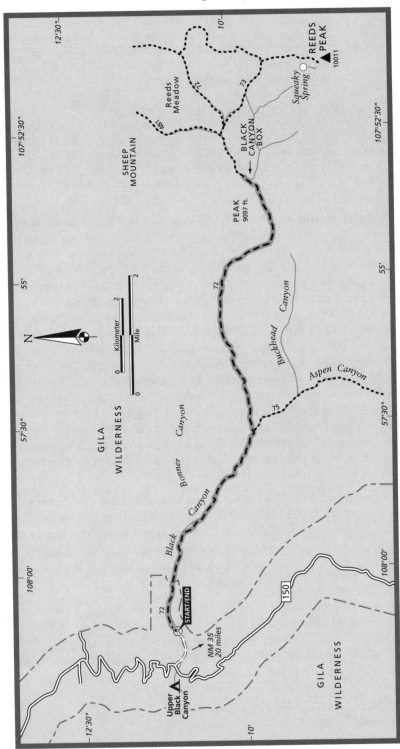

The hike: The lower 4 miles of the Black Canyon Trail, up to Aspen Creek, wind along the babbling brook through a broad grassy valley. Stream crossings begin at mile 1 and continue all the way to Aspen Creek. Be prepared for shallow but wet foot crossings. See Hike 39 for details on this section of the hike. At the trail junction, marked with a sign in the middle of a large ponderosa pine park, remain on the trail going east up Black Canyon.

The trail climbs over low benches, crosses the stream frequently, and at 5.3 miles reaches a pine bench overseen by towering rock spires on the left (north) side. Musky elk scent hangs heavy in the air, and the sound of gobbling turkeys resonates from nearby hillsides. The trail follows long grassy benches on the left side for nearly a mile, with rugged cliff faces and narrow cave openings on the right side of the stream. Grassy benches suitable for camping continue with pine, Douglas fir, and oak to mile 6.7, where cliffs, spires, and hoodoos dot the steep north slope.

At 7.1 miles a prominent tributary enters from the left (north) as the canyon narrows and bends to the right (south). The dense pine-fir forest in the bottom grades rapidly to pinyon-juniper and oak on the adjacent hillsides. Upstream, the tight canyon deepens dramatically, with the stream cutting below rock walls. The trail passes through a recent burn where some blowdown can be expected. Back into green forest, the trail suddenly reaches an open grassy meadow in the otherwise narrow canyon at 8.3 miles. Striking white volcanic tuff is exposed on the left side of the canyon. Grassy flat benches that could be used for small campsites, along with frequent stream crossings, continue for another 0.5 mile to a long, dark alcove formed where the stream flows beneath overhanging rock.

At 9.2 miles, pass through an old burn and then climb high above the canyon bottom opposite the mouth of Falls Canyon, which enters from the right (east). The trail steepens as it climbs up the left (west) side of the valley to a low saddle at 9.4 miles. The saddle is bound by a wonderland of massive granite formations to the immediate right of the trail directly above Black Canyon Box. These intricate formations will enchant you. High above, the north rim is defined by a long series of jagged spires and towers just below peak 9097 as shown on the Bonner Canyon quadrangle. The box is one of the deepest and most scenic chasms in the Black Range. Find a rocky perch and enjoy the splendor of unusual rock formations on all sides. The bottom of the box lies partially hidden 200 feet below. A maze of pathways weaves between balancing boulders, mushroom-shaped rocks, and great fin-shaped mounds. Across from the box, a large burned area marks the far slope of Falls Canyon.

From the box, return to the trailhead by the same route.

Option: Either before or after taking a hike up Black Canyon Creek, stop at the upper Black Canyon Campground on the west side of FR 150, immediately south of the bridge over the creek. There might not be a sign, but you'll notice a silted pond next to the driveway. There are two campsites next to the stream, and a pit toilet. The picnic tables feature unique designs using native stone. In the stream below them, evidence of nature's engineer, the beaver, is displayed in a string of dams, also using native

The ridge above the Black Canyon Box contains a wonderland of climbing boulders and weaving pathways.

materials. These rodents, who have apparently moved on, decimated the cottonwoods while creating a stairstep of pools that even ducks enjoy.

Just upstream from the beaver dams, human engineers have built a gabion dam that limits the flow of Black Canyon Creek. An informative board by the road provides an explanation for this unnatural barricade that appears so incongruous in this setting: Ash resulting from the Black Range fires of 1995 and 1996 wiped out the fish in the upper Black drainage. This provided New Mexico Game and Fish an opportunity to reestablish native Gila trout, a state and federally protected species. The gabion dam was built by a variety of agencies and volunteers who support fishing to prevent more aggressive nonnative trout downstream from intruding in the Gila habitat above the dam.

41 Black Canyon–CDT

Highlights:	A large trout stream and riparian community in a wide river valley with ponderosa pine parks, rugged canyons with multicolored formations, a deep canyon box, scenic vistas of and from the highest Continental Divide peak in the Aldo, and a variety of birds and wildlife along Black Canyon
Type of hike:	Three- to four-day backpack loop
Total distance:	33.9 miles
Difficulty:	Strenuous
Best months:	May through October
Maps:	Forest Service Aldo Leopold Wilderness Map; Middle Mesa, Bonner Canyon, Reeds Peak, and Hay Mesa USGS quads
Special considerations:	Check with the Mimbres Ranger District regarding road conditions on FR 150 in early spring. The road is not plowed or maintained in the winter. Wading shoes are recommended for frequent stream crossings. The entire CDT portion of the hike is high and dry; fill up at Squeaky Spring.

Finding the trailhead: From New Mexico 35, 4.5 miles north of the Forest Service Ranger Station in Mimbres, right after milepost 15, turn right on Forest Road 150, also called North Star Mesa Road and NM 61. Cautionary signs at the junction on NM 35 warn of difficult terrain and lack of food, lodging, and gas for 120 miles. Actually the road is graded annually and gets rough only when it dives into or climbs out of canyons via tortuous switchbacks. A high-center two-wheel-drive vehicle can safely negotiate this road. With any vehicle, 10 mph is the average speed. Drive north on the improved gravel road 20 miles. On the left is Black Canyon Primitive Campground. A silty pond is adjacent to the road on the west next to the campground. Continue across the Black Canyon Creek bridge to the For-

Black Canyon–CDT

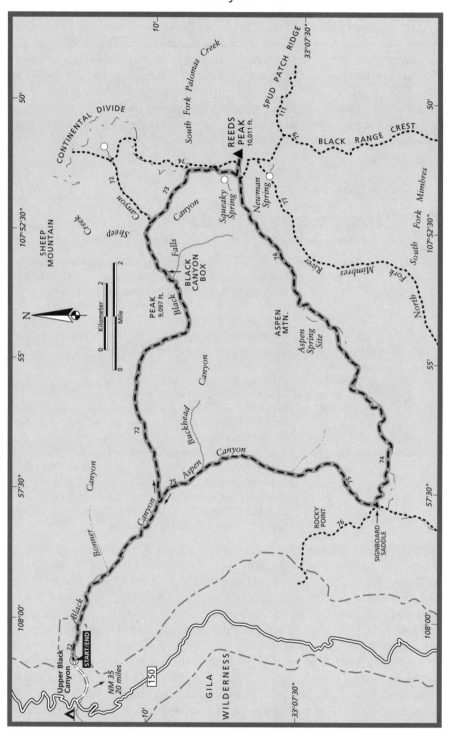

est Trail sign 0.2 mile north at the second gated road on the right. You can either park along the road 0.1 mile south of this gate, or turn down the road, closing the light metal hinged gate after you pass through, and drive 0.2 mile to the rough unpaved sloping parking area just south of the creek. A Forest Trail sign at the eastern edge of the parking area to the right of the barbed wire fence marks the trail.

Parking and trailhead facilities: There is parking for a half dozen vehicles. No campsites are at the trailhead; use the Black Canyon Campground across the road. Water can be obtained in Black Canyon Creek; treat before using.

Key points:
- 0.0   Head east on old two-track at Forest Trail sign.
- 0.2   Trail sign for Aspen Canyon.
- 1.0   Stream crossings begin.
- 4.0   Signed junction of Aspen Canyon Trail 75 and Black Canyon Trail 72; continue left.
- 9.4   Saddle above Black Canyon Box.
- 10.6   Signed junction of Black Canyon Trail 72 and Sheep Creek Trail 71.
- 10.9   Signed junction of Black Canyon Trail 72 and Falls Canyon Trail 73; bear right.
- 12.7   Whitmore cabin site.
- 13.4   Signed junction of Falls Canyon Trail 73 and CDT 74; turn right (south).
- 13.5   Unsigned trail to Squeaky Spring.
- 13.7   Squeaky Spring.
- 14.1   Four-way trail junction on west ridge of Reeds Peak.
- 14.3   Reeds Peak (10,011 feet).
- 14.6   Four-way trail junction on west ridge of Reeds Peak; go straight (west) on the CDT.
- 20.1   Aspen Spring site.
- 24.6   Signboard Saddle; turn right on Aspen Canyon Trail 75.
- 28.5   Mouth of Buckhead Canyon.
- 29.9   Junction of Aspen Canyon and Black Canyon Trails; turn left (west).
- 33.9   Black Canyon trailhead at Forest Trail sign.

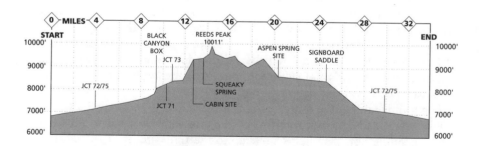

The hike: This extended loop dramatizes the natural diversity between one of the most scenic large stream canyons in the Black Range and the highest Continental Divide summit in the Aldo.

The lower 4 miles of the Black Canyon trail, up to Aspen Creek, wind along the babbling brook through a broad grassy valley. Stream crossings begin at mile 1 and continue all the way to Aspen Creek. Be prepared for shallow but wet foot crossings. See Hike 39 for details on this section of the hike. At the trail junction, marked with a sign in the middle of a large ponderosa pine park, remain on the trail going east up Black Canyon.

The canyon becomes narrower and more dramatic, with spires, cliffs, and fanciful hoodoos adorning its walls. At 9.4 miles you reach a low saddle directly above the Black Canyon Box. See Hike 40 for details on this section of the hike.

From the saddle above the box, the trail drops through open pine forest to a grassy bottom near the stream. It then climbs gently along grassy pine benches, becoming obscure in a burn, before reaching the signed junction with Sheep Creek Trail 71 at 10.6 miles. This lower end of the rarely maintained Sheep Creek Trail is completely buried under downfall and, for all practical purposes, has been erased by nature. Instead, continue right (east) on the main Black Canyon Trail toward Reeds Meadow. Even this stretch of the trail could be obstructed with downfall where it passes through a burn. The next trail junction is reached at mile 10.9 in an aspen–Douglas fir forest. The trail sign sits to the right and is easy to miss if you're hiking down the Falls Canyon Trail to this junction.

When traveling between Black Canyon and Reeds Peak, by far the best of three possible routes is Falls Canyon Trail 73, which is direct, scenic, and well maintained. It is steep and rocky, but passes mostly through green forest, thereby minimizing the amount of blowdown.

Trail 73 climbs steeply through a mosaic of green and burned pine-fir forest, reaching the dividing ridge between Black and Falls Canyons at 11.6 miles. Striking gray rock formations rise above Black Canyon to the north. At mile 11.7 the trail contours to an overlook of the falls on the north branch of Falls Canyon. Its 200-foot drop, off cliffs and down steep rock chutes, amplifies the sound of the small stream plummeting over the falls. A rocky perch just below the trail offers a great photo op.

The trail wraps around the canyon and climbs to a narrow notch above the falls at 11.9 miles. Open rocky ledges below the trail provide spectacular views of the falls and the mostly burnt slopes of Falls Canyon. The trail then climbs steadily up the left side of the stream, and in the stream at times, crossing to the right side as it enters a mature aspen–Douglas fir forest. At 12.7 miles you'll come to a bowl-shaped meadow ringed with aspen, pine, and fir. Part of the original stone foundation of the Whitmore cabin sits on the north side of the meadow.

The trail is faint at the upper end of the meadow. A more distinct but unofficial trail heads up to the left, providing an easy shortcut to the CDT if you're heading north. Otherwise, keep to the right and look for old blazes and log cuts. Poke around the northeast end of the meadow and you'll soon find a distinct trail going south up the left side of a draw. The trail quickly reenters the burn with a short but rough section. Fortunately, the upper end of the trail is pleasant, surrounded by a live spruce-fir forest.

At 13.4 miles the Falls Canyon Trail joins the CDT. Signs point north to Diamond Peak (8.5 miles) and south to Reeds Peak (0.75 mile). This CDT junction is adjacent to an old stock fence in a forest of spruce, fir, and aspen. If the trail hasn't been cut out above the meadow, expect about 0.5 mile of slow going almost up to the divide. Continue right (south) on the CDT to a broad, grassy park draping the divide after 0.1mile. From here there are two ways to reach the summit of Reeds Peak. The first is to take the main left-hand trail straight up the divide and into the burn where it's marked with rock cairns. The better choice is to go first to Squeaky Spring for water and then contour south to the Continental Divide just west of the peak.

This bypass to the spring is worth taking, but it's hard to find. The unsigned trail fades in the meadow. The best way to find it is to head southwest across the meadow. The trail becomes obvious toward the far edge, near an aspen thicket suitable for camping. An old corral encircles the head of Squeaky Spring just below the aspen, where you'll find a small cement-lined cistern filled with water. And sure enough, a broken squeaky pipe faucet sits nearby. This is an essential side trip to fetch water; don't forget to replace the heavy cement lid on the cistern.

From the spring at mile 13.7, an old trail climbs uphill about 50 yards and intersects the bypass trail. This trail is well constructed, but expect some downfall where it passes through the burn. It climbs gradually, reaching the Continental Divide at 14.1 miles. This is also the west ridge of Reeds Peak and a signed four-way trail junction. Significantly, the junction marks the intersection between the two main "high-line" trails of the Aldo: the CDT and the Black Range Crest Trail. From here the Continental Divide turns sharply west, as does the CDT. This point is also the northern terminus of the Black Range Crest Trail. Of course, the actual topographic turning point between the Continental Divide and the crest of the Black Range is Reeds Peak—230 feet higher and 0.25 mile to the immediate east.

The open, rocky apex is surrounded by locust, aspen, and Douglas fir, preventing a complete 360-degree view from the ground. For a commanding view of the entire Aldo Leopold Wilderness and far beyond, climb a few levels of the unmanned lookout tower. The platform just below the lookout cabin has been removed, but if you're looking for a grand view, there is certainly no need to climb the very top of the lookout. A metal cabin sits next to the lookout. The roomy cabin, complete with table, chairs, six bunks, and a wood stove is open to the public. The cabin is in first-class condition thanks to responsible visitors who clean up after themselves and replenish the wood box. While relaxing in the cabin, out of the wind, take time to read the Reeds Peak cabin log. More than one grateful person thanked Aldo Leopold for his visionary gift of wilderness.

From the signed junction, continue west on the CDT. The 10-mile segment of the CDT between the west slope of Reeds Peak and Signboard Saddle is the longest high divide trail in the Aldo without a trail junction and without water. This portion of the CDT is on a biennial maintenance schedule, but the reality of funding and staffing may stretch this out a bit. At least the trail is well marked and well constructed.

Squeaky Spring is a reliable water source, hidden in a grassy glade high above Black Canyon.

The trail quickly passes through an old stock fence and switchbacks down to rejoin the divide. The up-and-down nature of high ridges is well represented in this upper segment, where the trail loses and regains elevation before dropping steeply down the open divide at 15.6 miles. Elevation gain and loss continues for another mile. After passing through an open-grown pine forest, the trail loses 300 feet of elevation in only 0.2 mile, followed by a long pleasant section through old-growth Douglas fir. At 17.9 miles the trail cuts right and passes next to large mounds of granite outcrops. After another mile of long steep switchbacks in the Douglas fir forest, the trail has regained nearly 400 feet of elevation, reaching a narrow, open ridge top. Look back for a clear view of the Reeds Peak lookout.

The CDT begins a long descent by sidehilling around the head of Monument Canyon below Aspen Mountain. The woodland of pine and oak is drier, with broad views of the Mimbres River drainage. In places the trail tread is side sloped, but continues to be well marked. Follow a side ridge above the head of Aspen Canyon, then switchback down to a long contour through a picturesque ponderosa pine park to the bottom of a draw at the head of the canyon. After paralleling the draw, the CDT passes by the Aspen Spring site in an aspen–Douglas fir forest at 20.1 miles. The hard-to-find spring is well concealed in dense brush above the trail and is no longer flowing. The site consists of a concrete cistern sunk deep into the ground with broken pipe, next to some old mining debris. If you're thirsty, you will be disappointed with Aspen Spring.

The next 4.5 miles to Signboard Saddle are very pleasant, with only minimal climbing. The trail drops gently through a mixed forest of pine, gambel oak, and Douglas fir, with only the sound of the wind, the chatter of gray squirrels, and the resonating of woodpeckers for company. Every so often the direction of the soft dirt trail changes abruptly, but it's merely following the serpentine path of the Continental Divide. After climbing up and down and around a series of grassy pine park draws that feed into Aspen Canyon, the CDT reaches Signboard Saddle at 24.6 miles. True to its name, the saddle is well signed, with the trail down Aspen Canyon turning to the right (north).

The Aspen Canyon Trail is mostly in good condition, providing a pleasant route to Black Canyon. The well-defined trail descends a narrow gully northward in a mixed forest of Douglas fir, Southwestern white pine, and gambel oak. Early in a good water year, the intermittent stream begins flowing after about 0.5 mile. As the trail continues down, notice the contrast between open, scattered forest on the left and the Douglas fir thicket on the right.

The easy-to-follow trail continues to weave in and out of the drainage, where it is washed out or choked with flood-level debris in a few spots. The rocky canyon narrows and then widens, passing along grassy benches with large pine and Douglas fir at mile 26.8. The Bonner Canyon quad shows the Aspen Corral to be somewhere along this flat, but we couldn't find it. In places the trail is faint on the benches, but it is easy to follow with the aid of tree blazes and log cuts. The benches end at mile 27.2 as the canyon tightens up again. Frequent crossings alternate with narrow rocky stretches. By mile 27.7 the lightly used trail becomes more primitive for a short distance.

The grassy park continues down to the mouth of Buckhead Canyon at mile 28.5, which can usually be counted on to carry water. Once again the canyon narrows, as the trail avoids rock walls by climbing around to the left side at mile 28.9. The serpentine canyon ends at 29.4 miles, and is followed by a picturesque pine park that extends down to Black Canyon at mile 29.6. The trail crosses a ravine and then Black Canyon, reaching a spacious open meadow dotted with pine and cottonwood as forested slopes rise moderately on both sides. The flat contains a signed junction with the Black Canyon Trail at mile 29.9.

Upon returning to this grassy pine park, you've spanned some 3,000 feet of vertical relief spread across 30 miles of rugged trails. Continuing left down Black Canyon for the remaining 4 miles to the trailhead will seem like a walk in the park.

Option: For an alternate route to the CDT that adds 1.7 miles, stay on the Black Canyon Trail another 1.4 miles, climbing 400 feet to Reeds Meadow. This large sloping meadow usually has water in its lower end. Turn right (south) onto the CDT and continue another 2.8 miles, with a gain of 1,060 feet, to the Falls Canyon Trail junction. Much of the CDT south of Reeds Meadow passes through burns with heavy brush and blowdown. This loop at the head of Black Canyon and along the CDT is best enjoyed as a day hike from a nearby campsite.

Either before or after the long loop, stop at the upper Black Canyon Campground on the west side of FR 150, immediately south of the bridge over Black Canyon Creek. There might not be a sign, but you'll notice a silty pond next to the driveway. There are two campsites next to the stream, and a pit toilet. The picnic tables feature unique designs using native stone. In the stream below them, evidence of nature's engineer, the beaver, is displayed in a string of dams, also using native materials. These rodents, who have apparently moved on, decimated the cottonwoods while creating a stairstep of pools that even ducks enjoy.

Just upstream from the beaver dams, human engineers have built a gabion dam that limits the flow of Black Canyon Creek. An informative board by the road provides an explanation for this unnatural barricade that appears so incongruous in this setting: Ash resulting from the Black Range fires of 1995 and 1996 wiped out the fish in the upper Black drainage. This provided the New Mexico Department of Game and Fish an opportunity to reestablish native Gila trout, a state and federally protected species. The gabion dam was built by a variety of agencies and volunteers who support fishing to prevent more aggressive native trout downstream from intruding in the Gila habitat above the dam.

42 Black Canyon–Mimbres

Highlights: Water and a view: two large perennial streams of the west Aldo with rugged canyons and a box; the highest Continental Divide point in the Aldo, Reeds Peak (10,011 feet)

Type of hike: Three- to four-day shuttle backpack

Total distance: 26.6 miles

Difficulty: Strenuous

Best months: April to early October

Maps: Forest Service Aldo Leopold Wilderness Map; Middle Mesa, Bonner Canyon, Reeds Peak, and Hay Mesa USGS quads

Special considerations: Check with the Mimbres Ranger District regarding road conditions on FR 150 in early spring. The road is not plowed or maintained in the winter. Expect numerous wet foot crossings on the streams.

Finding the trailheads: *Beginning trailhead:* From New Mexico 35, 4.5 miles north of the Forest Service Ranger Station in Mimbres, right after milepost 15, turn right on Forest Road 150, also called North Star Mesa Road and NM 61. Cautionary signs at the junction on NM 35 warn of difficult terrain and lack of food, lodging, and gas for 120 miles. Actually the road is graded annually and gets rough only when it dives into or climbs out of canyons via tortuous switchbacks. A high-center two-wheel-drive vehicle can safely negotiate this road. With any vehicle, 10 mph is the average speed. Drive north on the improved gravel road 20 miles. On the left is Black Canyon Primitive Campground. A silty pond is adjacent to the road on the west next to the campground. Continue across the Black Canyon Creek bridge to the Forest Trail sign 0.2 mile north at the second gated road on the right. You can either park along the road 0.1 mile south of this gate, or turn down the road, closing the light metal hinged gate after you pass through, and drive 0.2 mile to the rough, unpaved sloping parking area just south of the creek. A Forest Trail sign at the eastern edge of the parking area to the right of the barbed wire fence marks the trail.

Ending trailhead: The exit trailhead is 12 miles south of Black Canyon on FR 150. The large trailhead sign and turn are 8 miles from the NM 35–North Star Mesa intersection. At the sign for Mimbres Trail 77 and Continental Divide Trail 74, turn east and drive on the deeply rutted road for 0.75 mile to the end of the road. A corral and primitive campsites are on the flat pinyon-juniper mesa at the signed trailhead.

The driving distance between trailheads is 13 miles, none of which is paved.

Parking and trailhead facilities: *Beginning trailhead:* There is limited parking. No campsites are at the trailhead; use the Black Canyon Campground across the road. Water can be obtained in Black Canyon Creek; treat before using.

Black Canyon–Mimbres

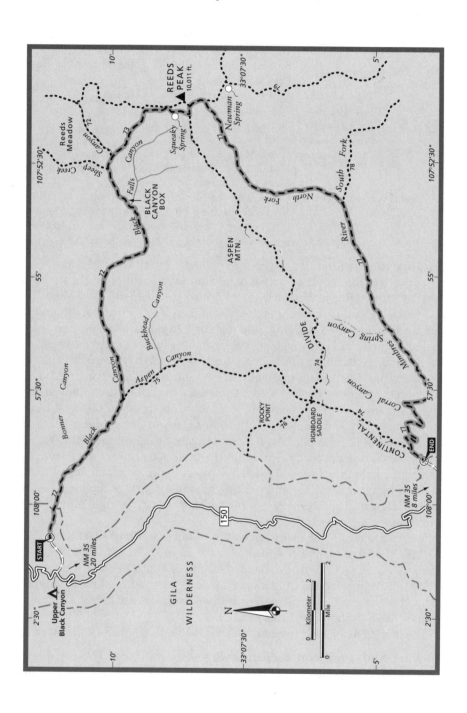

Ending trailhead: The trailhead has spacious parking, campsites, an information board, wilderness sign, and trail signs. There is no water.

Key points:
  0.0   Head east on old two-track at Forest Trail sign.
  0.2   Trail sign for Aspen Canyon.
  1.0   Stream crossings begin.
  1.8   Mouth of Bonner Canyon.
  4.0   Signed junction of Aspen Canyon Trail 75 and Black Canyon Trail 72.
  9.4   Saddle above Black Canyon Box.
  10.6 Signed junction of Black Canyon Trail 72 and Sheep Creek Trail 71.
  10.9 Signed junction of Black Canyon Trail 72 and Falls Canyon Trail 73.
  12.7 Whitmore cabin site.
  13.4 Signed junction of Falls Canyon Trail 73 and CDT 74.
  13.5 Unsigned trail to Squeaky Spring.
  13.7 Squeaky Spring.
  14.1 Four-way trail junction on west ridge of Reeds Peak.
  14.3 Reeds Peak (10,111 feet).
  14.6 Four-way trail junction on west ridge of Reeds Peak.
  15.1 Junction of Black Range Crest Trail 79 and North Fork Mimbres Trail 77; turn right.
  16.6 Flat grassy meadow with spring adjacent to North Fork.
  19.6 Forks of the Mimbres; junction with Middle Fork Trail 78.
  21.9 Mouth of Monument Canyon.
  22.7 Old corral next to the trail.
  24.2 Last crossing of the Mimbres.
  24.4 Join new trail up Corral Canyon to CDT and the trailhead.
  26.2 Junction of Mimbres Trail 77 and CDT; turn left.
  26.6 CDT/Mimbres River trailhead.

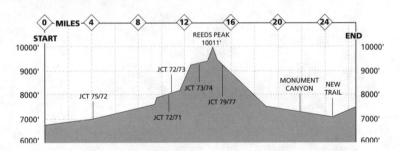

The hike: This shuttle half loop, which travels along the two major permanent streams that drain westward off the divide, is one of the wettest in the Aldo. Only two short segments of the route take you away from water.

The lower 4 miles of the Black Canyon Trail, up to Aspen Creek, wind along the babbling brook through a broad grassy valley. Stream crossings begin at mile 1 and continue all the way to Aspen Creek. Be prepared for shallow but wet foot crossings. See Hike 39 for details on this section of the hike. At the trail junction, marked with a sign in the middle of a large ponderosa pine park, remain on the trail going east up Black Canyon.

An intriguing rock profile towers above upper Black Canyon.

The canyon becomes narrower and more dramatic, with spires, cliffs, and fanciful hoodoos adorning its walls. At 9.4 miles you reach a low saddle directly above the Black Canyon Box. See Hike 40 for details on this section of the hike. Continue on the Black Canyon Trail another 1.5 miles to the junction with Falls Canyon Trail 73. Turn right and climb up to the CDT. Turn right (south) toward Reeds Peak. Just short of the peak, you can decide whether to stop by Squeaky Spring before climbing the peak. Reeds Peak, on the Continental Divide, has a comfortable cabin available for use by backpackers. For details on this segment, the route to the spring, and details about the cabin, see Hike 41.

From the peak, hike south 0.3 mile to the CDT/Black Range Crest Trail junction, and continue south on the Black Range Crest Trail, which angles around the south slope of the peak with vistas to the south. The good trail switchbacks down to the burn at the head of the North Fork Mimbres River and trail junction. Because of a recent fire, you can expect some blowdown of large blackened Douglas fir trees across the trail. Of the three Mimbres Forks trails leading from the crest of the Black Range, North Fork Trail 77 is the most popular. Little wonder, this good trail is well maintained, easy to follow, and is a little less steep due to its longer length.

Turn right onto the North Fork Mimbres Trail, dropping steeply down a narrow gully of aspen and Douglas fir. The spring shown on the map just below the crest is little more than a seep that could dry up by early summer. The trail continues dropping rapidly, reaching a flat grassy meadow with a spring next to a small stream 1.5 miles below the crest. After climbing a low saddle across from the rim of the canyon, the trail descends a narrow valley on a steady but gentle grade, with only a few stream crossings.

As the valley widens, grassy benches and a mixed conifer forest appear. A lovely pine park with aspen groves precedes a scenic overlook 100 feet above the left side of the canyon chasm. A spring enters from the left (east) 3.7 miles below the crest, followed by a series of moderate pitches and contours along benches above deep pools. The chasm becomes deeper and more rugged; its most impressive feature is a sheer 150-foot cliff rising above the dense forest and narrow canyon 0.3 mile above the forks. The forks of the Mimbres are reached at mile 19.6, with a junction sign across the North Fork on the right side.

The main Mimbres River Trail 77 continues downstream on the right. Below the confluence, wet foot crossings will be deeper, but the canyon of the main Mimbres is broader, providing excellent campsites in the grassy meadows. Grassy ponderosa pine parks and gnarly old cottonwoods adorn the valley as rugged rock formations rise on the canyon walls. Monument Canyon enters from the right after 2.3 miles, and within the next mile you will pass an old corral next to the trail. The valley becomes more open and the stream slows and widens as you progress along the Mimbres. The final crossing of the river may be knee deep during times of high water. With its soft silt bottom, it's actually the most challenging of the crossings.

The trail follows the right side of the river through a wide grassy bench dotted with huge ponderosa pines to a trail junction on the western side of the valley. Here you will head uphill, leaving the river for good, on the new trail segment up Corral Canyon to the CDT junction and the trailhead. This new cutover trail is clear and well maintained. It does feature some steep sections, however; it is also dry and lacks the pleasant shade you enjoyed in the river valley.

In 2 miles the junction with the CDT is reached; turn left (south) and hike 0.4 mile to the trailhead to complete your extended backpack.

Option: An interesting side hike is possible in Monument Canyon (mile 21.9). A scenic 3-mile round-trip excursion will get you to and from the forks of the canyon. This unofficial use trail (no signs or tree blazes) is faint at first, but quickly becomes well defined as it heads up the left side of the small streambed along a pine-studded bench. Lacking construction, the trail bobs up and down the narrow canyon, mostly on the right side, with monumental rock cliffs and formations rising to the west. The intermittent rocky stream hosts some deep pools in the lower reaches during times of high water. The first major fork in the canyon is reached after 1.5 miles, where the trail continues up the left branch. As with any Aldo hike, you'll make your own discoveries in this remote side tributary to the Mimbres River.

43 Black and Morgan Canyons

Highlights:	A large trout stream and riparian community in a wide river valley with ponderosa pine parks, rugged canyons with multicolored formations, a deep canyon box, scenic vistas of and from the highest Continental Divide peak in the Aldo, a variety of birds and wildlife along Black Canyon, and spectacular east-side canyon scenery from Spud Patch Ridge
Type of hike:	Three- to four-day backpack shuttle
Total distance:	24 miles
Difficulty:	Strenuous
Best months:	May through October
Maps:	Forest Service Aldo Leopold Wilderness Map; Middle Mesa, Bonner Canyon, Reeds Peak, Victoria Park, and Sugarloaf Peak USGS quads
Special considerations:	Check with the Mimbres Ranger District regarding road conditions on FR 150 in early spring. The road is not plowed or maintained in the winter. Wading shoes are recommended for frequent stream crossings. The Spud Patch Ridge Trail is dry; fill up at Squeaky Spring.

Finding the trailheads: *Beginning trailhead:* From New Mexico 35, 4.5 miles north of the Forest Service Ranger Station in Mimbres, right after milepost 15, turn right on Forest Road 150, also called North Star Mesa Road and

NM 61. Cautionary signs at the junction on NM 35 warn of difficult terrain and lack of food, lodging, and gas for 120 miles. Actually the road is graded annually and gets rough only when it dives into or climbs out of canyons via tortuous switchbacks. A high-center two-wheel-drive vehicle can safely negotiate this road. With any vehicle, 10 mph is the average speed. Drive north on the improved gravel road 20 miles. On the left is Black Canyon Primitive Campground. A silty pond is adjacent to the road on the west next to the campground. Continue across the Black Canyon Creek Bridge to the Forest Trail sign 0.2 mile north at the second gated road on the right. You can either park along the road 0.1 mile south of this gate, or turn down the road, closing the light metal hinged gate after you pass through, and drive 0.2 mile to the rough, unpaved sloping parking area just south of the creek. A Forest Trail sign at the eastern edge of the parking area to the right of the barbed wire fence marks the trail.

Ending trailhead: From Interstate 25, 5 miles north of Truth or Consequences, take NM 52 west 31 miles to Winston. Turn left (south) at Winston through the tiny town toward Chloride. A half mile beyond Winston, turn left (south) on the signed road to the St. Cloud Mine, FR 157. This road is graded gravel. Continue southwest for 5 miles. Here the wide, graded county-maintained road continues west to the St. Cloud Mine, and a narrow rough road on the left (south) is signed FR 157. Turn left (south) on FR 157.

Following the contour of the land, FR 157 is rough when it follows canyons or drainages; when on the mesas its quality improves. Travel on FR 157 is slow, averaging about 10 mph. Drive south on FR 157 for an additional 17 miles. In the middle of a broad valley, some remnant buildings of the defunct town of Hermosa stand on the hillside in front of you. A sign stating PRIVATE PROPERTY. PLEASE STAY ON ROADWAY also indicates this is a private inholding, further reinforced with a steel cable and I-beam post barricade indicating the boundary.

Located obscurely about 50 yards east of FR 157 is a tiny sign for FR 732. The main road, FR 157, continues south through the former Hermosa. Turn right (northeast) on FR 732, following Morgan Creek up the great bowl valley. The newly constructed trailhead is 0.5 mile west of Hermosa in a large flat area beneath towering cottonwoods and ponderosa pines. This short section of road is softer and kinder than FR 157 is. There is one shallow ford across Morgan Creek just before the trailhead, which is on the left, marked with a large kiosk.

The driving distance between the two trailheads, going around the north end via FR 150, NM 59, and NM 52, is 105 miles, 42 of which are paved. The roads are rough, slow, and winding, so allow ample time for the car shuttle.

Parking and trailhead facilities: *Beginning trailhead:* There is parking for a half dozen vehicles, but no campsites at the trailhead. Use the Black Canyon Campground across the road. Water can be obtained from Black Canyon Creek; treat before using.

Ending trailhead: There is a kiosk at the trailhead, along with flat campsites and a spacious parking area. There is water in Morgan Creek; treat before using.

207

Black and Morgan Canyons

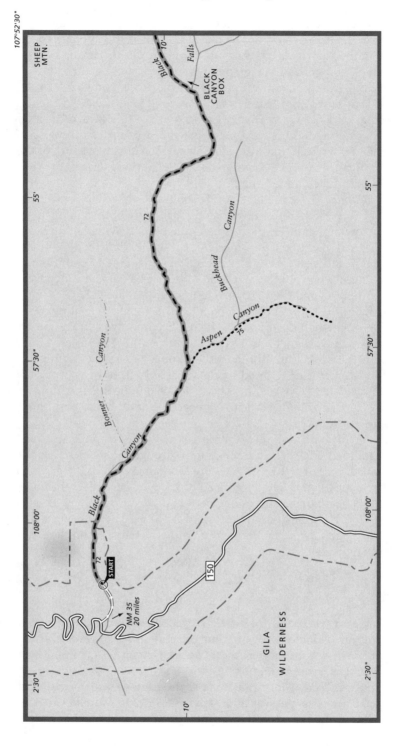

Black and Morgan Canyons

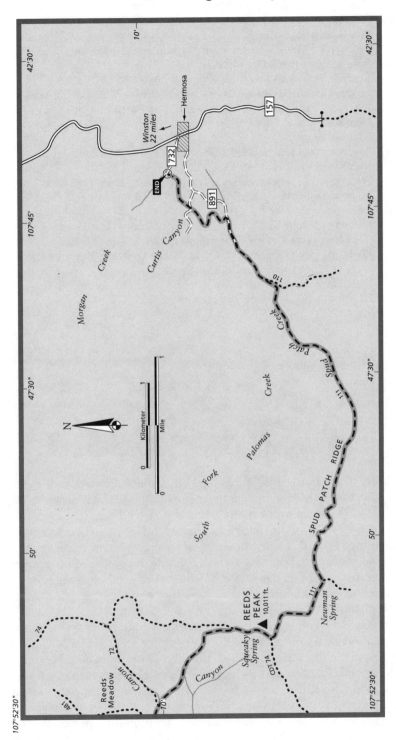

Key points:

- 0.0 Head east on old two-track at Forest Trail sign.
- 0.2 Trail sign for Aspen Canyon.
- 1.0 Stream crossings begin.
- 1.8 Mouth of Bonner Canyon.
- 4.0 Junction of Aspen Canyon Trail 75 and Black Canyon Trail 72.
- 9.4 Saddle above Black Canyon Box .
- 10.6 Junction of Black Canyon Trail 72 and Sheep Creek Trail 71.
- 10.9 Junction of Black Canyon Trail 72 and Falls Canyon Trail 73; bear right.
- 13.4 Junction of Falls Canyon Trail 73 and CDT 74; turn right.
- 13.5 Unsigned trail to Squeaky Spring.
- 13.7 Squeaky Spring.
- 14.1 Four-way trail junction on west ridge of Reeds Peak; turn left.
- 14.3 Reeds Peak (10,011 feet).
- 14.6 Four-way trail junction on west ridge of Reeds Peak; turn left.
- 15.1 Junction of North Fork Mimbres Trail 77 and Black Range Crest Trail 79.
- 15.8 Newman Spring south of trail.
- 16.0 Junction of Crest Trail 79 and Spud Patch Trail 111; turn left.
- 19.0 Hard-to-find trail drops right (south) to North Seco Creek.
- 21.7 Junction of Spud Patch Trail 111 and Lake Trail 110; continue left.
- 22.3 Sign for FR 891 in South Palomas Creek.
- 22.8 Trail leaves stream with hiker sign pointing north to new trail.
- 24.0 New trailhead alongside Morgan Creek.

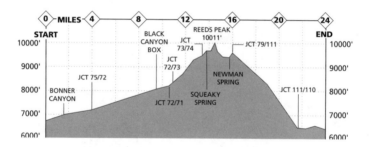

The hike: This shuttle hike across the wilderness dramatizes the contrast among one of the most scenic large streams in the Black Range, the highest Continental Divide summit in the Aldo, and rugged east-side canyons.

The lower 4 miles of the Black Canyon trail, up to Aspen Creek, wind along the babbling brook through a broad grassy valley. Stream crossings begin at mile 1 and continue all the way to Aspen Creek. Be prepared for shallow but wet foot crossings. See Hike 39 for details on this section of the hike. At the trail junction, marked with a sign in the middle of a large ponderosa pine park, remain on the trail going east up Black Canyon.

The canyon becomes narrower and more dramatic, with spires, cliffs, and fanciful hoodoos adorning its walls. At 9.4 miles you reach a low saddle directly above the Black Canyon Box. See Hike 40 for more details on this section of the hike. Continue on the Black Canyon Trail another 1.5 miles to the junction with Falls Canyon Trail 73. Turn right and climb up to the CDT. Turn right (south) toward Reeds Peak. Just short of the peak, you can decide whether to stop by Squeaky Spring before climbing the peak. Reeds Peak, on the Continental Divide, has a comfortable cabin available for use by back-packers. For details on this segment, the route to the spring, and details about the cabin, see Hike 41.

From the peak, hike south to the CDT/Black Range Crest Trail junction, and continue south, staying on the Black Range Crest Trail past the junction with the North Fork Mimbres Trail. The wide trail follows the crest through a thick Douglas fir–aspen forest sprinkled with grand old Southwestern white pine. Along the way, the sloping meadow of Newman Spring opens to an expansive view westward, providing a pleasant break in the otherwise dense forest. The spring might be little more than a wet meadow seep, but is usually a reliable water source, except later in the summer during a par-ticularly dry year.

Just beyond, at mile 16.0, Spud Patch Trail drops steeply to the east. Rocky overlooks at this point provide spectacular views of North Seco and Massacre Canyons, along with Animas Ridge all the way to Hillsboro Peak—the entire southeast quarter of the Aldo! The sign accurately reads 8.5 miles to the Her-mosa townsite by way of Spud Patch Ridge Trail 111 ("the Spud"). From the crest, turn left onto the Spud where it drops through a diverse forest of Dou-glas fir, subalpine fir, ponderosa pine, and lots of thorny mountain locust. For the next 3 miles the trail rapidly loses elevation, with only a couple of mod-est rises, to a saddle where a hard-to-find trail drops south into North Seco Creek. After climbing out of the saddle, the trail wraps around and down into the head of Spud Patch Creek, where the pine-fir forest changes to a dense mantle of pinyon-juniper and mountain mahogany. Monumental rock faces guard side tributaries to the north. After contouring around these gullies, the trail sidehills steadily downhill above and along the creek. Picturesque rock shelves form the lower reaches of the streambed. The rocky drainage narrows down to its confluence with Marshall Creek and the signed junc-tion with Lake Trail 110 at 21.7 miles. You'll be glad you backpacked the steep and rugged Spud downhill.

From the junction, turn left (north) onto the soft needle-cushioned path that drops gently down Marshall Creek. After 0.5 mile the trail exits the wilder-ness and passes by a Lake Trail sign, followed quickly by a sign for Road 891 next to bubbling South Fork Palomas Creek. Here the trail coincides with the old two-track of Road 891 and is well marked with rock cairns at each of the many stream crossings. Canyon walls soar on the south side. At mile 22.8, a tiny hiker sign points left to the section of trail that leads north from South Fork Palomas Creek to Morgan Creek. This is a newly constructed trail that provides public access to and from the wilderness around private land owned by the Ladder Ranch.

At 23.4 miles the soft dirt trail crosses an ungated fence near the rocky head of Curtis Canyon. Soon after leaving the canyon, good views open east-ward to the old townsite of Hermosa. The trail contours around side gullies and across rolling pinyon-juniper foothills that were purchased from the Lad-der Ranch by the Forest Service in 1993. The new trail reaches a ridge and second gated fence, overlooking Morgan Creek Canyon, with a short 100-yard descent to the new trailhead and kiosk on Morgan Creek.

Meown Hill Trailhead

"Mechanized recreation already has seized nine-tenths
of the woods and mountains; a decent respect
for minorities should declare the other tenth to wilderness."

—Aldo Leopold, *A Sand County Almanac,* 1949

44 Meown Hill

> Highlights: Wide, scenic vistas of the crest of the Black Range
> along the Continental Divide; from mesa to South
> Diamond Creek, a diversity of ecosystems
> Type of hike: Out-and-back day hike or overnighter
> Total distance: 8 miles round-trip
> Difficulty: Strenuous
> Best months: April to October
> Maps: Forest Service Aldo Leopold Wilderness Map;
> Middle Mesa and Bonner Canyon USGS quads
> Special considerations: Check with the Mimbres Ranger District regarding
> road conditions on FR 150 in early spring. The road
> is not plowed or maintained in the winter.

Finding the trailhead: From New Mexico 35, 4.5 miles north of the Forest Service Ranger Station in Mimbres, right after milepost 15, turn right on Forest Road 150, also called North Star Mesa Road and NM 61. Cautionary signs at the junction on NM 35 warn of difficult terrain and lack of food, lodging, and gas for 120 miles. Actually the road is graded annually and gets rough only when it dives into or climbs out of canyons via tortuous switchbacks. A high-center two-wheel-drive vehicle can safely negotiate this road. With any vehicle, 10 mph is the average speed. Drive north on the improved gravel road 24 miles to the unsigned Y at the crest of the hill north of Moore Canyon. The traffic to and from the Forest Service facility makes this junction hard to miss; the road to the right appears as dominant as the main route 150, which is on the left. Bear right at the Y and go by the Forest Trail sign next to the cattle guard. Follow the road through the Forest Service facility and out to the mesa to the east. Drive through the open gate and continue 0.4 mile to the Aldo Leopold Wilderness signboard. There is a flat parking area just before the sign.

Parking and trailhead facilities: The trailhead has a large unpaved parking area and space for camping, but no water. There is an Aldo Leopold Wilderness sign, but no trail sign.

Meown Hill

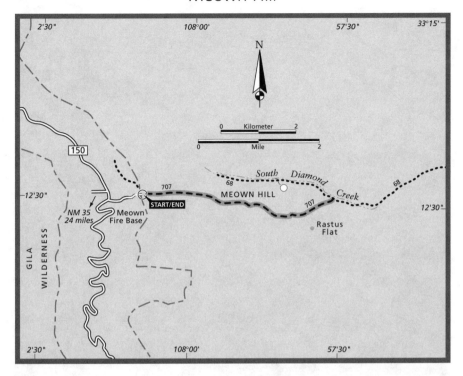

Key points:

0.0	Trailhead east of Meown Fire Base.
0.25	Stock pond north of trail.
1.8	Meown Hill.
2.5	Y junction; go left.
2.75	Y junction; go left.
3.0	Edge of South Diamond Canyon.
4.0	South Diamond Creek; junction with South Diamond Trail 68.

The hike: This hike follows an aged jeep trail along a narrow finger of the pinyon-juniper mesa, rising very gradually for 1.8 miles. A muddy stock pond is on the left a short distance from the trailhead. There is no water on the trail until you get down to South Diamond Creek, which may be dry in its middle stretch. Just beyond the fringe of widely scattered trees, sometimes only yards to the north, is the wide forested chasm cut by South Diamond Creek. The track of Trail 707 is easy to follow, even without blazes in the scattered pinyon-juniper. On your return to the trailhead, however, some of the runoff gullies resemble trails, so watch for footprints on the tread.

The slope of Trail 707 increases as you near Meown Hill, a forested knob on the mesa. Great old gnarly alligator junipers bracket the trail as it curls around the hill's southern flank. A sudden change occurs in the forest just east of the hill. It is a different world of rolling ponderosa pine parkland.

The view up South Diamond Creek from Trail 707 above the trailhead.

This area, identified as Rastus Flat on the maps, is a favorite of elk hunters. Their camps dot the area and their trails might cause confusion. There are, in fact, two Ys in the trail east of Meown Hill. At both Ys, bear to the left to stay on the blazed Forest Service trail. The hunter trails are more heavily used, with a wider track on the ground, but they'll take you south to Meown Tank at the head of Diamond Bar Canyon.

Staying left at each junction brings you to the brink of the South Diamond Creek Canyon. From here it is a long zigzag drop into Diamond Creek, more than 700 feet below. The heavily forested canyon walls are punctuated with stark hoodoos and spires that jut between patches of ponderosa pine on the cooler south slope and the pinyon-juniper on the hotter north slope.

For a day hike, drop to the creek, anticipating the climb back up that same day. A longer outing allows the steep descent to fade a bit in your memory. A camp on South Diamond Creek permits you to explore upstream on Trail 68 before returning to the parking area by the same route.

Option: For an adventurous 10-mile loop trip, turn left at South Diamond Creek and head downstream on Trail 68, which is hard to follow in places. Keep going for about 5 miles to the first prominent side canyon entering from the left (south). Climb off-trail up the canyon bottom or up the ridge on either side to intersect the Meown Trail near the trailhead. You'll definitely need the Middle Mesa USGS quad and map navigation skills to successfully negotiate this off-trail conclusion of the loop.

South Diamond Creek Trailhead

"Wilderness is a resource which can shrink but not grow."

—Aldo Leopold, *A Sand County Almanac*, 1949

45 South Diamond Creek

Highlights: Short evening or morning stroll for wildlife viewing
Type of hike: Out-and-back day hike
Total distance: 2.0 to 4.0 miles round-trip
Difficulty: Easy
Best months: April to October (April and May are usually best for bird-watching)
Maps: Forest Service Aldo Leopold Wilderness Map; Wall Lake USGS quad
Special considerations: Check with the Mimbres Ranger District regarding road conditions on FR 150 in early spring. The road is not plowed or maintained in the winter. Do not count on water in South Diamond Creek.

Finding the trailhead: From New Mexico 35, 4.5 miles north of the Forest Service Ranger Station in Mimbres, right after milepost 15, turn right on Forest Road 150, also called North Star Mesa Road and NM 61. Cautionary signs at the junction on NM 35 warn of difficult terrain and lack of food, lodging, and gas for 120 miles. Actually the road is graded annually and gets rough only when it dives into or climbs out of canyons via tortuous switchbacks. A high-center two-wheel-drive vehicle can safely negotiate this road. With any vehicle, 10 mph is the average speed. Drive north on the improved gravel road 31 miles to the Trail 68 sign. Turn right. Drive about 1.5 miles on the unimproved dirt road to a vehicle barrier at the road end and trailhead where there is a wilderness boundary sign.

Parking and trailhead facilities: The trailhead has a large unpaved parking area and a flat area for camping. There is no water.

Key points:
0.0   Trailhead at end of road.
1.0   Windmill; turnaround spot.

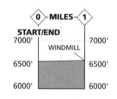

The hike: The broad valley of South Diamond Creek with its scattered ponderosa pine groves is an outstanding place to watch wildlife. It is not a heavily visited area; in fact, the trail is hard to find in some spots. The trail begins as an old two-track road used by ranchers in the past. On this wildlife ramble, of course, it is not necessary to stay on the trail at all.

A quiet outing in the early morning or late in the day toward evening could reward you with sightings of elk, coyotes, or turkeys in the valley. In the early spring, bird-watchers will also enjoy visiting South Diamond.

South Diamond Creek

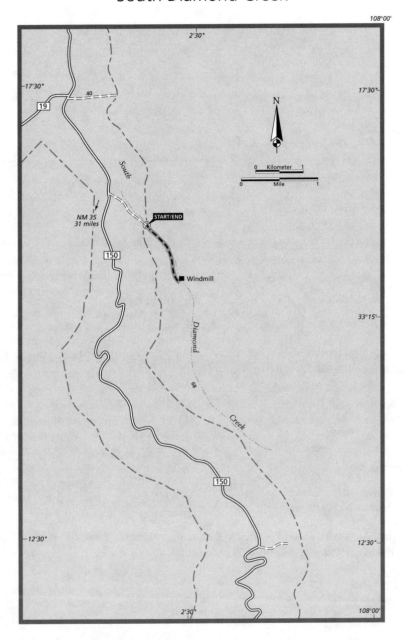

You can mosey up the valley as far as you wish before turning around. At the old windmill, stay on the main South Diamond Creek, bearing right to the south. If you plan to venture farther than 2 miles, you'll need the Middle Mesa quad with you as well. Return to the trailhead by the same route when you have gone far enough.

Diamond Creek Trailhead

". . . the creation of new wilderness in the full sense of the word is impossible."

—Aldo Leopold

46 Diamond Creek

Highlights: Flat open valley, opportunity for wildlife viewing
Type of hike: Out-and-back day hike
Total distance: 3.0 to 5.0 miles round-trip
Difficulty: Easy
Best months: April to October (April and May are usually best for bird-watching)
Maps: Forest Service Aldo Leopold Wilderness Map; Wall Lake USGS quad
Special considerations: Check with the Mimbres Ranger District regarding road conditions on FR 150 in early spring. The road is not plowed or maintained in the winter.

Finding the trailhead: From New Mexico 35, 4.5 miles north of the Forest Service Ranger Station in Mimbres, right after milepost 15, turn right on Forest Road 150, also called North Star Mesa Road and NM 61. Cautionary signs at the junction on NM 35 warn of difficult terrain and lack of food, lodging, and gas for 120 miles. Actually the road is graded annually and gets rough only when it dives into or climbs out of canyons via tortuous switchbacks. A high-center two-wheel-drive vehicle can safely negotiate this road. With any vehicle, 10 mph is the average speed. Drive north on the improved gravel road 32.5 miles and turn right at the faded Forest Trail sign at the intersection with FR 225, which goes west. Drive east about 0.5 mile on the dirt road to the wilderness boundary sign and metal vehicle barrier.

Parking and trailhead facilities: The trailhead has a large flat parking area and space for camping. There is no water.

Key points:

0.0   Trailhead/wilderness boundary at end of road.
0.4   Dry Diamond Creek on the left (north).
1.2   Stock tank.
1.5   Middle Diamond Creek on right (south).

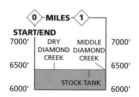

The hike: Like the wildlife stroll along South Diamond, this outing into the main Diamond Creek valley offers an opportunity to spot elk that make this gentle valley their home. Wandering up the wide valley in the early morning or late in the day,

Diamond Creek

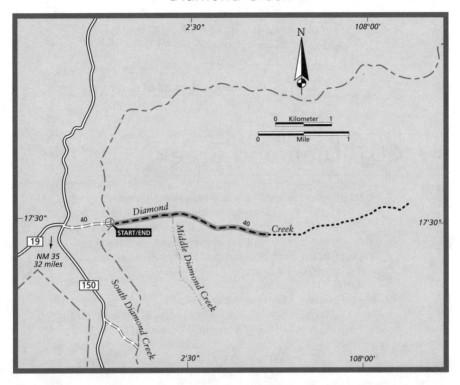

you might come across a herd of these ungulates, especially if you travel silently into the wind. One successful method of spotting these shy critters is to settle yourself in one of the ponderosa pine groves, next to a tree trunk so your silhouette won't be noticeable. Just sit and wait. If your timing is good, you might see elk moving across the valley ahead of you. You could spot other wildlife as well, such as turkeys, coyotes, or bobcats, along with a variety of birds.

Diamond Creek could be flowing early in a good snow year, but the trail does not get near the stream until you're close to the stock tank. Carry water with you.

Hike from the wilderness boundary, marked with a fence, up the valley as far as time and energy permit. When you decide to turn around, retrace your route to the trailhead.

Turkey Run Trailhead

*". . . a militant minority of wilderness-minded
citizens must be on watch throughout the nation
and vigilantly available for action."*

—Aldo Leopold, *A Sand County Almanac,* 1949

47 CDT–Diamond Creek

Highlights: Scenic views of canyons and peaks from the
Continental Divide, a bubbling trout stream with
deep pools, unusual rock formations, and a
waterfall, all accessible on good trails

Type of hike: Day hike or short backpack loop

Total distance: 9.7 miles

Difficulty: Strenuous

Best months: May through October

Maps: Forest Service Aldo Leopold Wilderness Map;
Lookout Mountain USGS quad

Special considerations: The first two-thirds of the hike will be high and dry
until reaching Diamond Creek. There are a few
rough sections of the CDT in burned areas along
the divide.

Finding the trailhead: From paved New Mexico 59, 16 miles east of the
Beaverhead Work Center, or 14.5 miles west of the junction with NM 52,
turn south on signed Forest Road 226, located at Burnt Cabin Flat, which is
also identified with a sign. This turn is between mileposts 14 and 15 on NM
59. Go south on FR 226, an improved gravel two-wheel-drive high-center
road. At 4 miles, 226A intersects on the left. Stay on 226 south. Another 3
miles brings you to a left turn for 226; continue straight on FR 500 for 8.7
miles to the end of the road. At first the low standard road switchbacks down
into Turkey Run and then follows the tiny stream to the unsigned Caledonia Trail trailhead at the end of the road about 16 miles from NM 59. The
Turkey Run Road is not maintained as frequently as other roads; it is vul-
nerable to erosion and washouts, so four-wheel drive is recommended.

Parking and trailhead facilities: There is abundant space for parking and
camping along the tiny stream of Turkey Run just below the end of the road.
Water that must be treated can be obtained from the stream in Turkey Run.

Key points:
0.0   Unsigned Caledonia Trail 42 at end of Turkey Run Road 500.
1.7   Junction of Caledonia Trail and CDT 74; turn right.
3.0   Signed wilderness boundary on CDT.

CDT–Diamond Creek

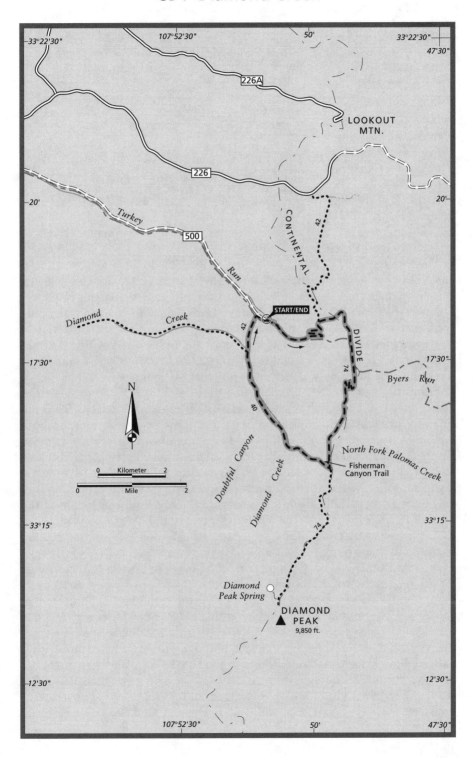

3.5   Unsigned junction with Byers Run Trail.
5.7   Junction with North Fork Palomas Trail and Fisherman Trail; turn right.
6.7   Junction of Fisherman Canyon Trail and Diamond Creek Trail 140; bear right.
7.2   Doubtful Canyon.
8.4   Junction of Diamond Creek Trail and Caledonia Trail 42; bear right.
9.4   Road 500 in Turkey Run.
9.7   End of Road 500.

The hike: Although steep in places, this loop segment in Fisherman Canyon, Diamond Creek, and Caledonia is a joy to hike, with trails in good to excellent condition. Adding

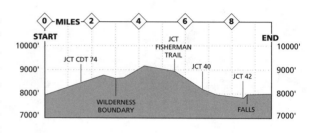

to the enjoyment are the varied landforms, from the Continental Divide to upper Diamond Creek.

The low standard but well-used Turkey Run Road 500 passes by numerous pleasant grassy campsites along the tiny stream near a large vehicle closure sign where the Caledonia Trail intersects the road from Diamond Creek. The two-track road ends after 0.3 mile. The unsigned but good Caledonia Trail gently climbs up the left side of Turkey Run, followed by a series of new switchbacks and intersections with closed off sections of the old trail. It joins the CDT in a narrow saddle at mile 1.7. To reassure you, a small sign just below the junction identifies the trail as Caledonia #42.

From the big CDT 74 sign, continue to the right on the new, clear trail that is easy to follow with the aid of small CDT emblems on trees. The trail sidehills through a pine forest where spot fires have occurred, rejoining both the old trail and the Continental Divide at 2.5 miles. This section of original trail is rough and narrow, with brush and downfall where it sidehills along the east side of the divide. A small metal sign announces the wilderness boundary at 3.0 miles, where the trail passes below a large rock outcrop. The trail improves as it sidehills around the head of Turkey Run to a saddle at the head of Byers Run at 3.5 miles. This upper end of the Byers Run Trail is unsigned, most likely consumed in a recent fire. The faint trail drops steeply from the divide down the right side of Byers Run.

From the saddle, a new CDT section switchbacks to the top and then along the divide, reaching the south ridgeline of Byers Run at 4.4 miles. After passing through part of a burn, the trail drops around the west side of an elevated plateau guarded by sheer 200-foot-high cliffs of reddish gray igneous rock. Spectacular views unfold westward, high above Fisherman Canyon. The trail then descends steeply, levels out along the narrow rock-lined divide, and joins the signed junction with the North Fork Palomas Trail at 5.7 miles. According to the sign, the trail ends 4 miles below and to the left (east) at Road 727. The sign is there, but the trail isn't. Nonuse and the passage of time have erased the upper end of the North Palomas Trail. A few yards ahead,

Looking south from the head of Byers Run to new switchbacks on CDT 74.

a small DIAMOND CREEK 1 MILE sign identifies the Fisherman Canyon Trail. Take this trail as it drops sharply to the right (west).

The good trail is easy to follow, but it is very steep with some loose gravel. It loses more than 600 feet of elevation in 0.6 mile to the narrow stream bottom of Fisherman Canyon, then follows the streambed down. Unusual rock formations appear on the right (north) at 6.4 miles and line the trail down to the canyon mouth. The intricately eroded bedrock is dotted with turrets and pocketed with alcoves. The temptation is to drop the pack and scramble for a while. The trail joins the Diamond Creek Trail at 6.7 miles; a sign points back up to the "Fisherman's Trail." Don't be tempted by the upper Diamond Creek Trail to the left; it isn't regularly maintained and is in pretty rough shape.

From the junction, continue right down the Diamond Creek Trail. The small stream is bound by low-lying forested hills. Winding through pine, fir, and aspen, the trail parallels Diamond Creek. Low rock walls on the right (east) side are riddled with mysterious dark alcoves and slits in the rock. At 7.2 miles Doubtful Canyon enters from the left (south). An old trail up the canyon has been abandoned by the Forest Service and is marked only with a rock cairn. It is still used once in a while by a hunter or livestock permittee on horseback.

All of a sudden, tiny Diamond Creek is flowing higher, with trout water big enough to lure anglers down Fisherman Trail. The trail continues pleasantly along the stream below canyon rims and molded rock mounds. Small cascades tumble over logs into deep rounded pools. If backpacking, there are several open benches that would accommodate small campsites along this stretch of the creek. At mile 8.4 the trail joins with Caledonia Trail 42. Turn right at a small sign pointing right to the Caledonia Trail and Road 500. The Diamond Creek Trail splits left at a 45-degree angle and is easy to miss. It follows the drainage westward for another 15 miles down to North Star Mesa Road 150.

Clearly, the Caledonia Trail to Road 500 receives more use, and this lower end has recently been relocated. The trail climbs gradually uphill to the right, reaching a small water slide, overseen by jagged "shark's teeth" rock formations. At 8.7 miles a thin 50-foot waterfall enters from a side canyon as the trail switchbacks steeply to a grassy ponderosa pine flat. From the lip of the flat, the trail descends gently down a grassy draw dotted with majestic old Douglas fir and ponderosa pine, leaving the wilderness at mile 9.4, marked with a small sign and low-slung cable fence. The trailhead on Road 500 is 50 yards beyond, marked with a vehicle closure sign and hiker symbol. Turn right and hike about 0.3 mile to the end of the road to complete this varied trip in the upper north end of the Aldo.

Options: Explore the old abandoned trail up Doubtful Canyon (mile 7.2) or take a side hike another mile or two down Diamond Creek below the Caledonia Trail junction (mile 8.4). The trail provides pleasant hiking, and the north side of the stream is bound by scenic rock formations.

A short, easy out-and-back hike would be to head south on the Caledonia Trail from Road 500, reaching Diamond Creek after only 1 mile. This is a popular direct route for hiking, camping, and fishing along upper Diamond Creek.

Caledonia Trailhead

". . . raw wilderness gives definition and meaning to the human enterprise."

—Aldo Leopold, *A Sand County Almanac,* 1949

48 Upper Caledonia Trail

Highlights: Vistas of northern Black Range on route to the
Continental Divide
Type of hike: Out-and-back day hike
Total distance: 7.6 miles round trip
Difficulty: Moderate
Best months: April to October
Maps: Forest Service Aldo Leopold Wilderness Map;
Lookout Mountain USGS quad
Special considerations: FR 226 between Monument Park and Chloride is not
recommended for any vehicle.

Finding the trailhead: From paved New Mexico 59, 16 miles east of the
Beaverhead Work Center, or 14.5 miles west of the junction with NM 52,
turn south on signed Forest Road 226, located at Burnt Cabin Flat, which is
also identified with a sign. This turn is between mileposts 14 and 15 on NM
59. Go south on FR 226, an improved gravel two-wheel-drive high-center
road. At 4 miles 226A intersects on the left; stay on 226 south. After another
3 miles, turn left (east) to remain on FR 226. Drive 9 miles to the large Caledonia Trail signboard adjacent to the road on the right (south), right after
you cross the usually dry Chloride Creek.

Parking and trailhead facilities: There is very limited parking at the trailhead. There is room for one vehicle in a flat spot 0.1 mile west of the trail, back
near the creek crossing. Lovely campsites are plentiful in Monument Park, 1.0
mile east of the trailhead. The park also has a pit toilet; the cabin there is closed
to the public. To get water from the cistern, you will need a bucket and a rope.

Key points:
0.0   Caledonia trailhead.
0.3   Climb above
Chloride Creek.
0.8   Join South Fork of
Chloride Creek.
2.0   Stone chimney next
to trail.
2.4   Enter burn area
along stream.
2.6   Sign for NEW TRAIL NO. 42; begin switchbacks.

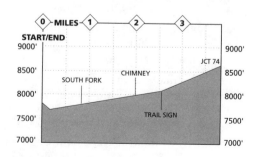

225

Upper Caledonia Trail

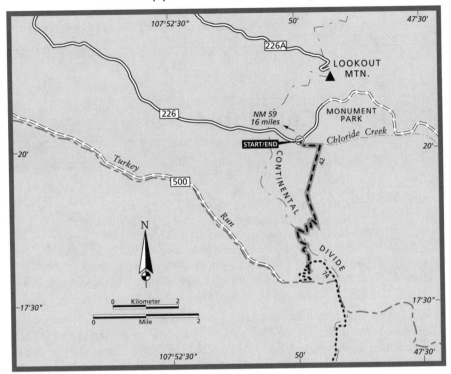

3.0 Ridge top respite; switchbacks continue.
3.8 Junction with CDT Trail 74 in saddle.

The hike: The old trailhead for the CDT at the northern end of the Black Range still exists on the Forest Service wilderness map and on the USGS quad. It has been officially erased on the ground, although the old blazes, the footpath, and the gate through the fence on the Monument Park road are still discernible. The new trailhead, about a mile to the west, is well marked, more convenient, and more pleasant. The new trail segment leads down the shady little valley of Chloride Creek, where you might encounter water, at least in early spring.

Another improvement in this northernmost leg of the CDT is at the upper end, near the junction with Crest Trail 74. About 1.2 miles of new switchbacks have been constructed through a vast burn, softening the 450-foot elevation gain and eliminating junctions with defunct trails.

From the large new CALEDONIA TRAIL #42 sign, pass through the stock gate and follow the trail, dropping 20 feet to Chloride Creek, which it follows east for 0.25 mile through the mixed pine woods. The trail is marked, not with traditional blazes or the old square wooden CDT plaques, but with snappy new blue and white CDT medallions. These clever signs are conspicuous from a distance so you can spot them. They are also informative: The T is an arrow, and a twist of the medallion indicates a turn. They are an excellent innovation in CDT signage.

226

From the creek, the trail climbs gradually along the south slope to meet the original CDT on the point above the forks of Chloride Creek. The old trail turns south through a mix of oak, pine, and juniper on the east-facing slope. The anonymous tributary of Chloride Creek babbles along 50 feet below the trail, creating a shiny ribbon in the V-shaped valley. After maintaining its contour above the stream for 0.4 mile, the trail descends to meet the stream in a grassy forest glade.

For more than a mile, you will enjoy a winding forest path up the open ponderosa pine park along the stream. There are areas where understory fires have swept the slopes above the trail. The ponderosa pine grasslands of the stream bottom continue, with cozy campsites located in stream bends. Some of the adjacent hillside and ravines, now stripped of their cloak of vegetation, reveal intricate rock formations: puffy pastel sandstone castles, pockmarked sandstones, and displays of selective erosion, as if attacked by a huge rock-gouging woodpecker.

The valley gradually narrows as you continue south. At 2.0 miles, a stone chimney stands next to the trail, looking like the world's largest cairn. Because there are no smoke stains, it's probably never been used. This is a thought-provoking artifact. Onward up the creek in the deep old pine-fir forest, the tiny stream may be only a trickle. Skinny-fingered dry tributaries trace down from side gullies of barren rock. Entering a wider section in the upper end of the valley, you'll encounter a burn that has cleared the hillsides west of the creek. Continuing along the creek bottom would be impossible with the fire debris and the brush. Just in time, a NEW TRAIL NO. 42 sign appears and off you go, uphill on switchbacks, climbing the fire-blasted slope.

Volcanic tuff formation above Caledonia Trail 42 2 miles south of the trailhead.

With its forest removed, the hillside trail provides great views of Lookout Mountain to the north. The trail reaches an intermediate ridge at 3.0 miles. A couple of pines that survived the fire offer a shady respite from the climb. CDT medallions direct you to the trail, which continues its zigzag path through the burn, ever upward, eventually reaching the saddle on the divide and the junction with Trail 74.

A couple of signs greet you. The TRAIL 74 sign is new, large, and highly informative, providing mileages to nine trails, peaks, and passes to the south. The Caledonia Trail continues south. Its sign is very courteous: PLEASE USE NEW TRAIL NO. 42. The trail is cut out and clear, so if you're going that way, how could you refuse?

From this saddle it's an easy roll downhill back to the trailhead for a day hike outing.

Option: At the point of land at the confluence of the forks of Chloride Creek, drop down the slope east of the trail to investigate the gorge below. The South Fork has cut its way through the basement metamorphic rock that underlies the Black Range, sculpting sinuous curves with its centuries of seasonal water. You'll discover some of this same rock formation beneath your feet on the trail up Chloride Creek to the trailhead. Even this tiny stream has the power to change the landscape.

49 Diamond Peak

Highlights:	Spectacular vistas of rugged canyon rock formations, the northern Black Range, and the Continental Divide from a prominent wilderness peak
Type of hike:	Two- to three-day backpack, out and back
Total distance:	23.6 miles round-trip
Difficulty:	Strenuous
Best months:	May through October
Maps:	Forest Service Aldo Leopold Wilderness Map; Lookout Mountain and Reeds Peak USGS quads
Special considerations:	Driving the extremely rough FR 226 east of the trailhead, between Monument Park and Chloride, is not recommended by anyone. The entire section of the CDT is dry to Diamond Peak Spring; carry ample water. Some sections of the CDT are steep, brushy, and impacted by fire, particularly in older sections not yet reconstructed.

Finding the trailhead: From paved New Mexico 59, 16 miles east of the Beaverhead Work Center, or 14.5 miles west of the junction with NM 52, turn south on signed FR 226, located at Burnt Cabin Flat, which is also identified with a sign. This turn is between mileposts 14 and 15 on NM 59. Go south on FR 226, an improved gravel two-wheel-drive high-center road. At

Diamond Peak

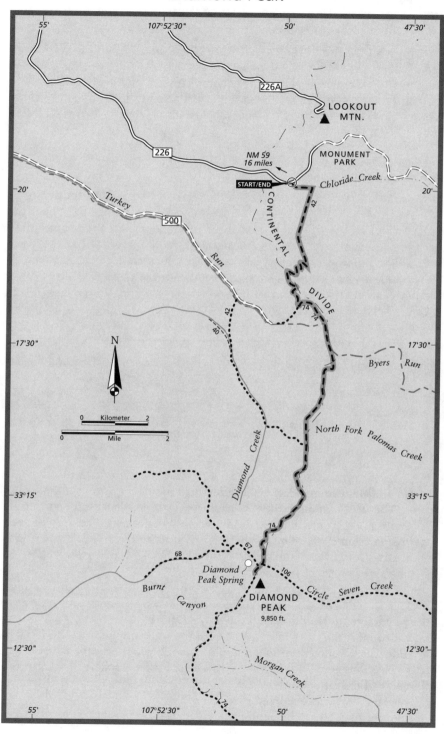

4 miles 226A intersects on the left; stay on 226 south. After another 3 miles, turn left (east) to remain on FR 226. Drive 9 miles to the large Caledonia Trail signboard adjacent to the road on the right (south), right after you cross the usually dry Chloride Creek.

Parking and trailhead facilities: There is very limited parking at the trailhead. There is room for one vehicle in a flat spot 0.1 mile west of the trail, back near the creek crossing. Lovely campsites are plentiful in Monument Park, 1.0 mile east of the trailhead. The park also has a pit toilet; the cabin there is closed to the public. To get water from the cistern, you will need a bucket and a rope.

Key points:
- 0.0   Caledonia trailhead.
- 0.8   Join South Fork of Chloride Creek.
- 2.6   Sign for NEW TRAIL NO. 42; begin switchbacks.
- 3.8   Junction with CDT Trail 74 in saddle; turn left.
- 5.1   Signed wilderness boundary.
- 5.6   Unsigned junction with Byers Run Trail.
- 7.8   Junction with North Fork Palomas Trail and Fisherman Canyon Trail.
- 11.3 Junction of CDT 74 and Circle Seven Creek Trail 106.
- 11.5 Diamond Peak sign, fence, and spring.
- 11.8 Diamond Peak.

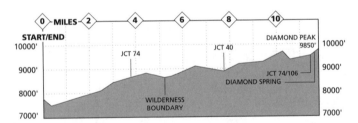

The hike: From the large new CALEDONIA TRAIL #42 sign, pick up the well-marked trail that drops along Chloride Creek before it turns south, within a mile. The well-marked pathway leads you up a gentle streambed to mile 2.6. At this point, you will begin climbing via switchbacks through a burned area, rising from the stream to the high ridge that takes you to the Continental Divide and the intersection with CDT Trail 74. See Hike 48 for details on this segment of the hike.

This northernmost leg of the CDT within the Aldo starts out in a high saddle, marked with an elaborate new sign stating distances to nine successively longer destinations, all the way south to Emory Pass (47.5 miles). The Caledonia CDT to Diamond Peak is the only segment of the CDT in the Aldo that receives annual maintenance. Still, there are some steep brushy sections and inevitable downfall in burns, especially where the original trail hasn't been relocated. The CDT is much improved wherever new construction has occurred.

From the big CDT 74 sign, the new, clear trail is easy to follow with the aid of small CDT emblems on trees. The trail sidehills through a pine forest where spot fires have occurred, rejoining both the old trail and the Continental Divide at 4.6 miles. This section of original trail is rough and narrow, with brush and downfall where it sidehills along the east side of the divide. A small metal sign announces the wilderness boundary at 5.1 miles, where the trail passes below a large rock outcrop. The trail improves as it sidehills around the head of Turkey Run to a saddle at the head of Byers Run at 5.6 miles. This upper end of the Byers Run Trail is unsigned.

From this saddle, a new CDT section switchbacks to the top and then along the divide, reaching the south ridgeline of Byers Run. After passing through part of a burn, the trail drops around the west side of an elevated plateau guarded by sheer 200-foot-high cliffs of reddish gray igneous rock. Spectacular views unfold westward, high above Fisherman Canyon. The trail then descends steeply, levels out along the narrow rock-lined divide, and reaches the signed junction with the North Fork Palomas Trail at 7.8 miles. According to the sign, the trail ends 4 miles below and to the left (east) at Road 727. The sign is there, but the trail isn't. Nonuse and the passage of time have erased the upper end of the North Palomas Trail. A few yards ahead, a small DIAMOND CREEK 1 MILE sign identifies the Fisherman Canyon Trail, which drops sharply to the right (west).

Just beyond the Fisherman Canyon Trail, the CDT passes through a stock gate and starts uphill. This scenic stretch of trail then switchbacks up about 200 feet and wraps around the head of Fisherman Canyon to mile 8.3. More switchbacks up through the burned forest offer sweeping vistas on both sides of the divide. The trail curves around the west side of burned-off peak 9635 at 9.4 miles, passing by white volcanic tuff rock with stunning views of the high cliffs enclosing Deadman Canyon. After dropping steeply to another saddle, climb steadily to the divide, regaining elevation lost within the burn. After briefly leveling off, the trail again plunges to another saddle at mile 10.4, with more views of gigantic multicolored cliffs and formations in Circle Seven Creek to the southeast.

After all this up and down in mostly burned forest, the next mile of the new CDT trail feels like a superhighway! This delightful "contour cruise" continues to the signed junction for the Circle Seven Creek Trail at mile 11.3 in a notch just below Diamond Peak. This stretch is often frequented by elk, bear, and mountain lion, and maybe even a rare wolf. The mournful howl of wolves greeted us as we approached the saddle—or was it the unending wind whistling through hollow burned snags?

Various cattle brands, including the Diamond Bar, are etched into the sign for Diamond Peak. From the opening in the stock fence on the CDT, the Circle Seven Creek Trail falls steeply off the east side. Old fallen trees across the trail are a sure sign of infrequent maintenance. From the divide, continue on the CDT to the right and uphill, where more blowdown from the fire might be encountered. At 11.5 miles (9,640 feet), the trail reaches a fence and a sign for the Diamond Creek Trail to the right. Despite the sign, the upper end of Diamond Creek Trail 40 no longer exists. In fact, due to lack of maintenance, the upper Diamond Creek Trail from the spring down to

An eagle's view all the way down North Fork Palomas Creek from the CDT.

the mouth of Fisherman Canyon is not recommended. Interestingly, Spring Mountain Trail 67 isn't signed, but it's easy to find, taking off to the right (north) just above the fence next to the Diamond Creek Trail sign.

Diamond Peak Spring sits just above the sign to the left of the trail. The spring is a shallow 4-foot-wide pool fed slowly by seepage from above. The tiny spring is a reliable water source early in the season, but would be questionable by early summer. The Forest Service trail crew wisely stockpiles jugs of water along the trail. As the CDT climbs above the spring, it passes along the lower edge of a large grassy alpine meadow. The meadow slopes toward the spring and is ringed by aspen and a mix of both dead and live Douglas fir. Only 0.3 mile northwest of Diamond Peak, this high meadow is campable, especially if the spring is flowing.

The 9,850-foot peak is reached at mile 11.8. Rising high above the surrounding mountains, this northern sentinel of the Aldo presents commanding views in every direction. The narrow ridge-top summit is encircled by locust and a few pine and fir trees, but opens enough for panoramas south to Hillsboro Peak and eastward down Circle Seven Creek. Almost all of the Aldo can be seen from this prominent peak. Especially impressive is the extent of burned forest across a maze of rough-hewn canyons all the way to Hillsboro Peak. The CDT continues just west of the Diamond Peak summit to a CDT trail sign pointing south to Reeds Peak (9 miles).

Your return trip along the high divide will be equally challenging and rewarding, presenting new perspectives on this remote north end of the Aldo.

Options: If you have an extra day at Diamond Peak, consider hiking the 8.6-mile Spring Mountain–Diamond Creek loop (see Hike 51).

For a closer look at the monumental "gates" of Deadman Canyon, drop down the Circle Seven Creek Trail (mile 11.3) about 1.5 miles. This entails a drop of about 2,000 vertical feet, so the word "steep" doesn't quite do it justice.

The return trip to the Caledonia Trailhead can also be varied by dropping down Fisherman Canyon to Diamond Creek and then connecting back up on the Caledonia Trail (see Hike 50).

50 Diamond Peak–Diamond Creek

Highlights: Spectacular vistas of rugged canyon formations, the northern Black Range, and the Continental Divide from a prominent wilderness peak; a pleasant stream in a rocky canyon
Type of hike: Three- to four-day backpack loop
Total distance: 25 miles
Difficulty: Strenuous
Best months: May through October
Maps: Forest Service Aldo Leopold Wilderness Map; Lookout Mountain and Reeds Peak USGS quads
Special considerations: Driving the extremely rough FR 226 between Monument Park and Chloride is not recommended by anyone. This entire section of the CDT is dry to Diamond Peak Spring; carry ample water. Some sections of the CDT are steep, brushy, and impacted by the fire, particularly in older sections not yet reconstructed.

Finding the trailhead: From paved New Mexico 59, 16 miles east of the Beaverhead Work Center, or 14.5 miles west of the junction with NM 52, turn south on signed Forest Road 226, located at Burnt Cabin Flat, which is also identified with a sign. This turn is between mileposts 14 and 15 on NM 59. Go south on FR 226, an improved gravel two-wheel-drive high-center road. At 4 miles, 226A intersects on the left; stay on 226 south. After another 3 miles, turn left (east) to remain on FR 226. Drive 9 miles to the large Caledonia Trail signboard adjacent to the road on the right (south), right after you cross the usually dry Chloride Creek.

Parking and trailhead facilities: There is very limited parking at the trailhead. There is room for one vehicle in a flat spot 0.1 mile west of the trail, back near the creek crossing. Lovely campsites are plentiful in Monument Park, 1.0 mile east of the trailhead. The park also has a pit toilet; the cabin there is closed to the public. To get water from the cistern, you will need a bucket and a rope.

Diamond Peak–Diamond Creek

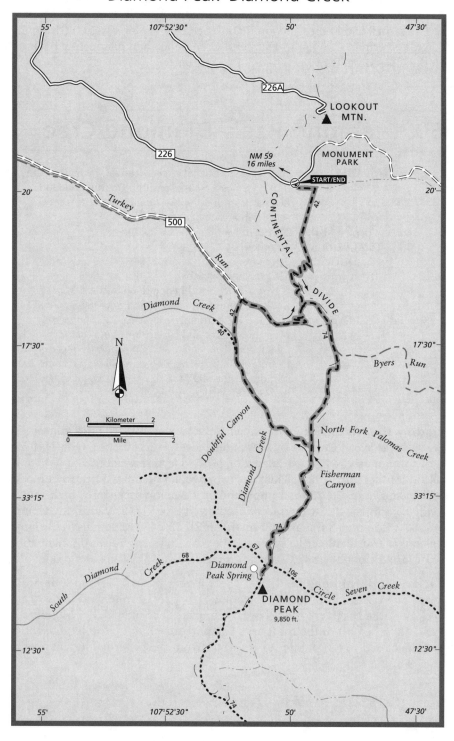

Key points:

0.0   Caledonia trailhead.
0.8   Join South Fork of Chloride Creek.
2.6   Sign for NEW TRAIL NO. 42; begin switchbacks.
3.8   Junction with CDT Trail 74 in saddle; turn left.
5.1   Signed wilderness boundary.
5.6   Unsigned junction with Byers Run Trail.
7.8   Junction with North Fork Palomas Trail and Fisherman Trail.
11.3   Junction of CDT 74 and Circle Seven Creek Trail 106.
11.5   Diamond Peak sign, fence, and spring.
11.8   Diamond Peak.
15.8   Junction with Fisherman Trail; turn left.
16.8   Junction of Fisherman Trail and Diamond Creek Trail; turn right.
18.5   Junction of Diamond Creek Trail and Caledonia Trail 42; bear right.
19.2   Leave wilderness boundary at Road 500 in Turkey Run; turn right.
19.8   End of Road 500, continuation of Caledonia Trail 42.
21.2   Signed junction with CDT 74; continue on Caledonia Trail 42.
25.0   Caledonia trailhead.

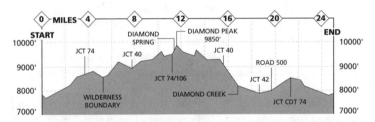

The hike: This double-stem lollipop loop traverses varied terrain, from one of the highest Continental Divide peaks, to rugged canyons, to a delightful stream and a picturesque waterfall. A high camp just below Diamond Peak and a low camp along Diamond Creek, combined with good trails, make this hike especially enjoyable. From the large new CALEDONIA TRAIL #42 sign, pick up the well-marked trail that drops along Chloride Creek before it turns south, within a mile. The well-marked pathway leads you up a gentle streambed to mile 2.6. At this point, you begin climbing via switchbacks through a burned area, rising from the stream to the high ridge that takes you to the Continental Divide and the intersection with CDT Trail 74. See Hike 48 for details on this segment of the hike.

Turn left along the ridge line on the CDT Trail, winding along the wild divide for 8 miles to Diamond Peak. You will pass several trail junctions on the way to the peak. At 4 miles along the divide trail you reach the signed junction of the North Fork Palomas Trail on the left, and the Fisherman Canyon Trail (signed DIAMOND CREEK 1 MILE) on the right. This is the trail you'll be taking on the return leg of the loop from Diamond Peak. Continue south on the CDT for 4 more miles to Diamond Peak. See Hike 49 (page 228) for details on this segment of the hike.

After spending a high country night or two camping near the summit, return to the Fisherman Canyon Trail. Turn left on the steep trail, losing more than 600 feet of elevation in 0.6 mile to the narrow stream bottom of

Fisherman Canyon. Eroded bedrock dotted with turrets and alcoves appears on the right (north) after 0.7 mile and continues down to the canyon mouth. This is a great place to drop the pack and scramble for a while. The trail joins the Diamond Creek Trail 1.0 mile below the divide, with a sign pointing back up to the "Fisherman's Trail." The upper Diamond Creek Trail to the left isn't regularly maintained and is in pretty rough shape.

From the junction, continue to the right down the Diamond Creek Trail. Winding through pine, fir, and aspen, the trail parallels Diamond Creek on its right side. Low rock walls on the right (east) side are riddled with mysterious dark alcoves and slits in the rock. At mile 17.3, Doubtful Canyon enters from the left (south). An old trail up the canyon has been abandoned by the Forest Service and is marked only with a rock cairn.

Suddenly, Diamond Creek is carrying a lot more water, with trout-filled pools big enough to lure anglers down Fisherman Trail. The trail continues pleasantly along the stream, with views of canyon rims and molded rock mounds. At mile 18.5 the trail meets Caledonia Trail 42. Turn right at a small sign pointing right to the Caledonia Trail and Road 500. The Diamond Creek Trail splits left at a 45-degree angle and is easy to miss.

Clearly, the Caledonia Trail to Road 500 receives more use; its lower end has recently been relocated. The trail climbs gradually uphill to the right, passing a small water slide. At 18.8 miles a wispy 50-foot waterfall enters from a side canyon as the trail switchbacks steeply to a grassy ponderosa pine flat. From the lip of the flat, the trail descends gently down a grassy draw. It leaves the wilderness boundary at mile 19.8, marked with a small sign and a low-slung cable fence. The trailhead on Road 500 is 50 yards be-

Perfect campsites abound at the junction of Caledonia Trail 42 and FR 500 on Turkey Run.

yond, marked with a vehicle closure sign. The low standard but popular road winds up Turkey Run, where there are numerous grassy campsites.

Turn right (southeast) on the two-track road and follow it to its end after another 0.3 mile. The unsigned but good Caledonia Trail gently climbs up Turkey Run, followed by a series of new switchbacks and intersections with closed-off sections of the old trail. It joins the CDT in the narrow saddle at mile 21.2, thereby completing the Caledonia CDT–Diamond Creek loop. To reassure you, a small sign just below the junction identifies the trail as Caledonia #42. The final 3.8 miles to the trailhead retrace the northern "stem" of the lollipop.

Options: If you have an extra day at Diamond Peak, consider hiking the 8.6 mile Spring Mountain–Diamond Creek loop, thereby making the overall trip a double lollipop (see Hike 51).

For a closer look at the monumental "gates" of Deadman Canyon, drop down the Circle Seven Creek Trail about 1.5 miles (starting from mile 11.3 or 12.3 in the hike). This entails a drop of about 2,000 vertical feet, so the word "steep" doesn't quite do it justice.

If you plan your hike for some extra time along Diamond Creek, consider a short side stroll below the turnoff for the Caledonia Trail (mile 18.5). The gentle grade of the trail permits enjoyment of the scenic canyon, especially rugged on its north side.

51 Diamond Peak–South Diamond

Highlights:	Spectacular vistas of rugged canyon rock formations, the northern Black Range, and the Continental Divide from a prominent wilderness peak; a tumbling stream in a rocky canyon and high remote mesas
Type of hike:	Three- to five-day backpack loop
Total distance:	32.2 miles
Difficulty:	Strenuous
Best months:	May through October
Maps:	Forest Service Aldo Leopold Wilderness Map; Lookout Mountain and Reeds Peak USGS quads
Special considerations:	Driving the extremely rough FR 226 east of the trailhead, between Monument Park and Chloride, is not recommended by anyone. This entire section of the CDT is dry to Diamond Peak Spring; carry ample water. Some sections of the CDT are steep, brushy, and impacted by the fire, particularly in older sections not yet reconstructed. Some sections of the Spring Mountain and South Diamond Trails are hard to find.

Diamond Peak–South Diamond

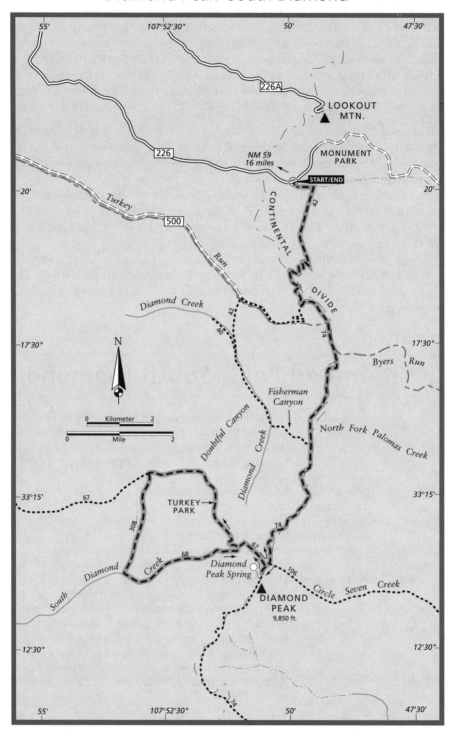

Finding the trailhead: From paved New Mexico 59, 16 miles east of the Beaverhead Work Center, or 14.5 miles west of the junction with NM 52, turn south on signed Forest Road 226, located at Burnt Cabin Flat, which is also identified with a sign. This turn is between mileposts 14 and 15 on NM 59. Go south on FR 226, an improved gravel two-wheel-drive high-center road. At 4 miles 226A intersects on the left; stay on 226 south. After another 3 miles, turn left (east) to remain on FR 226. Drive 9 miles to the large Caledonia Trail signboard adjacent to the road on the right (south), right after you cross the usually dry Chloride Creek.

Parking and trailhead facilities: There is very limited parking at the trailhead. There is room for one vehicle in a flat spot 0.1 mile west of the trail, back near the creek crossing. Lovely campsites are plentiful in Monument Park, 1.0 mile east of the trailhead. The park also has a pit toilet; the cabin there is closed to the public. To get water from the cistern, you will need a bucket and a rope.

Key points:

0.0	Caledonia trailhead.
2.6	Sign for NEW TRAIL NO. 42; begin switchbacks.
3.8	Junction with CDT Trail 74 in saddle; turn left.
5.1	Signed wilderness boundary.
5.6	Unsigned junction with Byers Run Trail.
7.8	Junctions with North Fork Palomas Trail and Fisherman Trail 40.
11.3	Junction of CDT 74 and Circle Seven Creek Trail 106.
11.5	Diamond Peak sign, fence, and spring.
11.8	Diamond Peak.
12.1	Junction of CDT 74 and Spring Mountain Trail 67 near Diamond Peak Spring; turn left.
12.7	Unsigned junction with South Diamond Creek Trail 68.
13.7	Turkey Park.
14.3	Unsigned junction with Doubtful Canyon Trail.
15.5	Junction with Trail 308; turn left.
17.4	Trail 308 reaches South Diamond Creek; bear left.
20.1	Unsigned junction with Spring Mountain Trail 67.
20.7	Return to trail junction next to Diamond Peak Spring.
24.4	Junctions with North Fork Palomas and Fisherman Trails.
28.4	Junction with CDT and Caledonia Trail 42; turn right.
32.2	Caledonia trailhead.

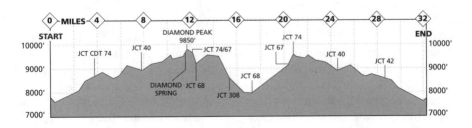

The hike: This lollipop loop into the north-central heart of the Aldo traverses varied terrain, from one of the highest Continental Divide peaks, to rugged canyons, to a rushing stream. Good campsites range from near Diamond Peak Spring to a pine bench along upper South Diamond Creek.

From the large new CALEDONIA TRAIL #42 sign, pick up the well-marked trail that drops along Chloride Creek before it turns south, within a mile. The well-marked pathway leads you up a gentle streambed to mile 2.6. At this point, you begin climbing via switchbacks through a burned area, rising from the stream to the high ridge that takes you to the Continental Divide and the intersection with CDT Trail 74. See Hike 48 for details on this segment of the hike.

Turn left along the ridge line on the CDT Trail, winding along the wild divide for 8 miles to Diamond Peak. You will pass several trail junctions on your way to the peak. At Diamond Peak Spring, take note of Spring Mountain Trail, which is unsigned. It's easy to find, taking off to the right (northward) just above the fence next to the Diamond Creek Trail sign. Continue south on the CDT to Diamond Peak. See Hike 49 for details on this segment of the hike.

The loop of the lollipop begins at the upper end of the Spring Mountain Trail, which is surprisingly good considering that it is completely unsigned in its upper 3.4 miles. It starts from a switchback just below Diamond Peak Spring (hike mile 12.1) and is faint and overgrown at first. The trail quickly becomes evident, with good tread and cut logs as it heads northwest. It drops through a burned forest to a saddle at 12.7 miles. Maintenance is infrequent, so expect a fair amount of downfall. The upper end of the South Diamond Trail meets this saddle, but the sign is missing and the trail easy to miss. The junction is marked only with a rock cairn; if you search carefully, you'll find a few cut logs at the head of the trail.

The Spring Mountain Trail continues up the left side of the dividing ridge between Diamond and South Diamond Creeks and then crosses to the right side of the ridge above Diamond Creek. After sidehilling through the burn, the brushy trail climbs steeply to green forest on top of the ridge, reaching the grassy slope of Turkey Park at 13.7 miles. To locate the faint trail through the park, simply follow the stock fence north for about 0.2 mile to where the trail is again blazed and more evident. The well-defined trail then drops through a burn to the head of Doubtful Canyon at 14.3 miles. The abandoned Doubtful Canyon Trail is distinct and cut out in its upper end. The Spring Mountain Trail continues uphill to the left.

Soon the trail becomes hard to find in places, although it's easier to locate when going downhill. Look ahead for tree blazes and a dirt track. After sidehilling, the trail follows a ridge down to a small clearing surrounded by ponderosa pine. Continue across the grassy flat, look for blazes, and follow the trail as it continues downhill. A junction is soon reached at mile 15.5, where a Spring Mountain Trail sign lies on the ground. The Spring Mountain Trail continues to the right (west); turn left on the distinct but unsigned trail. This is Trail 308, which follows a small stream southward to South Diamond Creek.

Trail 308 is surprisingly good despite a lack of regular maintenance. The canyon soon narrows amid a dense live forest of Douglas fir, Southwestern white pine, and gambel oak. The small stream usually carries early season water in its upper reaches well above the springs shown on the wilderness map. The descent is pleasant, and mostly clear all the way to South Diamond Creek, although it's a bit rougher in the lower end of the twisting, rocky canyon, and requires frequent stream crossings. At 16.8 miles the trail passes by a stock fence that crosses the streambed. Trail 308 meets South Diamond Creek at mile 17.4 in a thick pine-fir-aspen forest.

The well-defined South Diamond Trail continues downstream, but the South Diamond Trail heading upstream is very hard to find at this intersection. As you exit this unnamed north tributary to South Diamond that Trail 308 descends, look for cut logs and a faint trail that wraps around the toe of the ridge to South Diamond Creek. The actual signed junction is another 0.3 mile downstream. If you're hiking up South Diamond to complete the loop, there is no need to hike down to the junction because the trail going back up is buried under brush and downfall through this entire stretch, especially in the burn.

Don't make the mistake of going up nearby Burnt Canyon. The aptly named Burnt Canyon Trail is in equally bad shape. By hiking up South Diamond, you'll find a faint trail that will gradually improve by the time it leaves the burn after about 0.4 mile. A well-defined tread and blazes will reassure you that you're on the right track. The narrow, forested canyon contains deep pools with native Gila cutthroat trout. Look for them darting into the shadows.

Sculpted rock mounds at the head of Deadman Canyon along the CDT.

241

After about 1.5 miles the trail begins climbing steeply on the left side across shelf rock and dense forest to the unsigned junction with the Spring Mountain Trail, in a burned-out saddle, at 20.1 miles. The upper 2 miles of the steep South Diamond Trail are in good condition, with some downfall but only a few switchbacks toward the top.

This completes the loop at the far end of the long stem of the lollipop. Turn right for the remaining 0.6 mile to Diamond Peak Spring. After filling up with whatever water is available, hike the remaining 11.5 miles north along the Continental Divide and Caledonia Trails back to the trailhead. It's best to get an early start for this long, dry stretch of the CDT.

Options: The Spring Mountain–South Diamond loop is the outer 8.6 miles of the overall hike. It can be done either as a day hike from a two-night base camp near Diamond Peak Spring or backpacked with a second night camp along South Diamond Creek. The additional weight of backpacking adds to the difficulty of the trip; when spread over two days, however, it isn't much more strenuous than a long day hike. If camping along South Diamond, the drainage can be explored farther downstream from the lower end of Trail 308.

The return trip can also be varied by dropping down Fisherman Canyon to Diamond Creek and then connecting back up on the Caledonia Trail (see Hike 50). This double lollipop loop would add about 1.5 miles to the length of the hike, along with a modest amount of elevation loss and gain.

52 CDT

Highlights:	The high points of Diamond and Reeds Peaks, rocky overlooks along the divide with outstanding views of surrounding canyons and rugged rock formations
Type of hike:	Three- to five-day backpack shuttle
Total distance:	34.1 miles
Difficulty:	Strenuous
Best months:	May through October
Maps:	Forest Service Aldo Leopold Wilderness Map; Lookout Mountain, Reeds Peak, Bonner Canyon, and Hay Mesa USGS quads
Special considerations:	FR 226 east of the beginning trailhead, between Monument Park and Chloride, is not recommended by anyone. Check with the Mimbres Ranger District regarding road conditions on FR 150 in early spring. The road is not plowed or maintained in the winter. Portions of the original CDT in recently burned areas could be brushy and blocked by downfall. Most of the CDT is dry, so fill up at every opportunity.

Finding the trailheads: *Beginning trailhead:* From paved New Mexico 59, 16 miles east of the Beaverhead Work Center, or 14.5 miles west of the junction with NM 52, turn south on signed Forest Road 226, located at Burnt Cabin Flat, which is also identified with a sign. This turn is between mileposts 14 and 15 on NM 59. Go south on FR 226, an improved gravel two-wheel-drive high-center road. At 4 miles 226A intersects on the left; stay on 226 south. After another 3 miles, turn left (east) to remain on FR 226. Drive 9 miles to the large Caledonia Trail signboard adjacent to the road on the right (south), right after you cross the usually dry Chloride Creek.

Ending trailhead: From NM 35, 4.5 miles north of the Forest Service Ranger Station in Mimbres, right after milepost 15, turn right on FR 150, also called North Star Mesa Road and NM 61. Cautionary signs at the junction on NM 35 warn of difficult terrain and lack of food, lodging, and gas for 120 miles. Actually the road is graded annually and gets rough only when it dives into or climbs out of canyons via tortuous switchbacks. A high-center two-wheel-drive vehicle can safely negotiate this road. With any vehicle, 10 mph is the average speed. Drive north on the improved gravel road 8 miles to the sign for Mimbres Trail 77 and Continental Divide Trail 74. Turn right and drive on the deeply rutted road for 0.75 mile to the corral and primitive campsites on the flat pinyon-juniper mesa at the signed trailhead.

To reach the trailhead from the north, travel west 16 miles on NM 59 from Burnt Cabin Flat to the Beaverhead Work Center. Turn left (south) on FR 150, and drive about 50 miles to the signed CDT/Mimbres River trailhead on the left. Turn and drive 0.75 mile on the rutted road to the parking area.

The driving distance between the two trailheads around the west side of the Aldo is 84 miles, only 16 of which are paved. The roads are slow, rough, and winding, so allow plenty of time for the car shuttle.

Parking and trailhead facilities: *Beginning trailhead:* There is very limited parking at the trailhead. There is room for one vehicle in a flat spot 0.1 mile west of the trail, back near the creek crossing. Lovely campsites are plentiful in Monument Park, 1.0 mile east of the trailhead. The park also has a pit toilet; the cabin there is closed to the public. To get water from the cistern, you will need a bucket and a rope.

Ending trailhead: There is spacious parking and campsites on a level mesa amid juniper trees, along with an information board, wilderness sign, and trail signs. There is no water.

Key points:
0.0   Caledonia trailhead.
2.6   Sign for NEW TRAIL NO. 42; begin switchbacks.
3.8   Junction with CDT Trail 74 in saddle; turn left.
5.1   Wilderness boundary sign.
5.6   Unsigned junction with Byers Run Trail.
7.8   Junction with North Fork Palomas Trail and Fisherman Canyon Trail.
11.3   Junction of CDT and Circle Seven Creek Trail #106.
11.5   Diamond Peak sign, fence, and spring.
11.8   Diamond Peak (9,850 feet).
13.5   Junction of CDT and Burnt Canyon Trail 69.

CDT

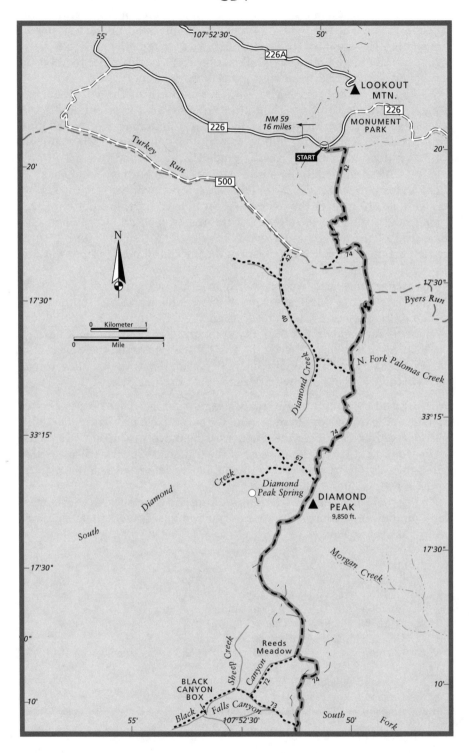

CDT

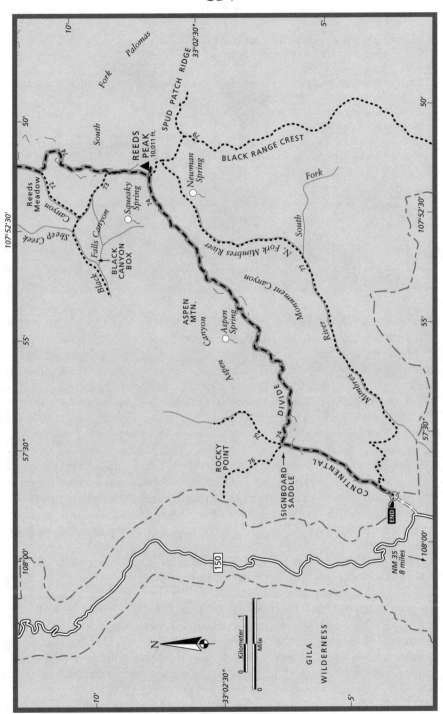

15.3	Junction of CDT and Sheep Creek Trail 481.
16.8	Junction of CDT and Black Canyon Trail 72.
19.1	Saddle on Continental Divide directly above and northeast of Whitmore cabin ruins.
19.6	Junction of CDT and Falls Canyon Trail 73.
19.7	Unsigned trail to Squeaky Spring.
19.9	Squeaky Spring.
20.3	Four-way trail junction on west ridge of Reeds Peak; turn left to peak.
20.6	Reeds Peak (10,011 feet).
20.8	Four-way trail junction on west ridge of Reeds Peak; go straight on CDT.
26.3	Aspen Spring site.
30.8	Signboard Saddle; stay on CDT 74.
33.7	Signed junction of CDT 74 and Mimbres River Trail 77.
34.1	CDT 74 trailhead.

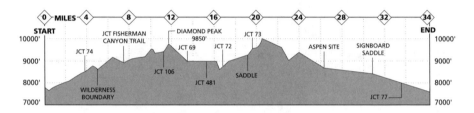

The hike: By traversing the entire CDT within the wilderness, this is truly the ultimate CDT "through hike" in the Aldo.

From the large new CALEDONIA TRAIL #42 sign, pick up the well-marked trail that drops along Chloride Creek before it turns south, within a mile. The well-marked pathway leads you up a gentle streambed to mile 2.6. At this point, you begin climbing via switchbacks through a burned area, rising from the stream to the high ridge that takes you to the Continental Divide and the intersection with CDT Trail 74. See Hike 48 for details on this segment of the hike.

Turn left along the ridge line on the CDT Trail, winding along the wild divide for 8 miles to Diamond Peak. You will pass several trail junctions on your way to the peak, as well as the spring shortly before the peak. See Hike 49 for details on this segment of the hike. The CDT climbs just west of the Diamond Peak summit to a CDT trail sign pointing south to Reeds Peak.

Most of the 9 miles of the CDT Trail between Diamond and Reeds Peaks have burned over in recent fires, so that this mainline trail is blocked by downfall, mountain locust, and other brush. Fallen trees are especially prevalent on high ridge-top trails, such as the CDT, and the presence of the burn ensures that there will be a source of continued blowdown for years to come, no matter how often the trail is cut out. The Forest Service tries to maintain this stretch of the CDT every two years. Of course, a lot can happen to a trail in two years, and even this modest schedule depends on funding, which varies from year to year.

The trail drops steadily along the Continental Divide in mostly green Douglas fir forest for about 1 mile before entering the burn, where there is some blockage from blowdown. The CDT follows a side ridge to the west and then angles around to a saddle between Burnt Canyon and Morgan Creek at 13.5 miles. This is also the junction between the Burnt Canyon Trail and the CDT. Burnt Canyon is well named. Its namesake trail isn't cut out on a regular basis and therefore isn't recommended as a means of going to or from the CDT, nor is the next trail south down Sheep Creek.

The next 1.8 miles to the head of Sheep Creek are rough because of fire damage and a lot more up-and-down travel. The trail rapidly gains 300 feet in about 0.4 mile, then follows the divide with views down Morgan Canyon. After sidehilling across the steep headwall of Morgan Canyon, drop gradually to the burned-out head of Sheep Creek. This small grassy opening at 15.3 miles is the CDT junction with Sheep Creek Trail 481 (signed as Trail 71 at the lower junction), indicated only by the burned remains of an old sign lying on the ground, along with a tiny CD sign on an old snag. Downfall and thorny locust might block the trail, but judging from abundant sign, the elk have certainly benefited from the additional forage produced by the fire.

From here the trail climbs for 0.2 mile to the Continental Divide and then gradually descends through a ghost forest of burned snags to a grassy swale with elk wallows. Look ahead for blazes wherever the trail becomes faint in the meadow. The tiny tributary to upper Morgan Creek may be flowing. Some of this trail section is rough, but the slower pace gives you a chance to look for blackbacked woodpeckers on the charred trees.

The trail rejoins the divide at 16.2 miles for a magnificent view into Morgan Canyon, and then begins dropping southward to the upper end of spacious Reeds Meadow at the head of Black Canyon Creek. The trail stays high and to the right of the meadow in a pine forest. This is a tricky stretch: There

Scenic tuff cliffs form the head of Morgan Creek on the east side of the Continental Divide.

are no blazes, and the trail can be hard to find. This wide upper end of the meadow narrows to the Reeds Ranch site, of which little remains. Elk sign includes a wallow and antler rubs on nearby trees. The widest part of the meadow is the upper end of the rugged Rattlesnake Canyon Trail, which plunges steeply to Morgan Creek on the east side. The unsigned trail, not shown on the quad map, has been essentially erased by fire where it meets the Continental Divide.

Although faint in the grassy meadow, the CDT is easily found by hiking on the right side of the sloping meadow, along the edge of the forest. The green, aspen-lined opening provides a welcome respite from the surrounding burn. Shortly after leaving the lower end of the meadow, the signed junction with the Black Canyon Trail is reached at 16.8 miles.

At the junction, turn left (east) onto the CDT. At first the good trail is well blazed, but it might be obstructed with blowdown at the lower end where it wraps around the south end of Reeds Meadow. The trail improves for about 0.6 mile, then deteriorates in a burned area before reaching the Continental Divide at 17.7 miles. It climbs around the head of the South Fork Palomas Creek and reenters the burn, where brush and downfall again take over. This rough stretch of trail is well constructed but seriously impacted by the burn. It's cut into a steep slope below cliffs and rock outcrops on the east side of the divide, where it mostly contours around the heads of several upper tributaries to the South Fork of Palomas Creek. An early season spring is passed at mile 18.6. The trail continues up to a saddle at 19.1 miles and then climbs steeply over the next 0.5 mile through more burn and into a green spruce-fir forest to the signed junction with the upper end of the Falls Canyon Trail.

Continue right (south) on the CDT to a broad, grassy park draping the divide after 0.1 mile. From here there are two ways to reach the summit of Reeds Peak. The first is to take the main left-hand trail straight up the divide and into the burn, where it's marked with rock cairns. The better choice is to take the trail to Squeaky Spring for water and then contour south to the Continental Divide just west of the peak.

The bypass to the spring is hard to find. The trail is unsigned and indistinct. To find it, head southwest across the meadow. The trail becomes obvious toward the edge of the meadow, near an aspen thicket suitable for camping. An old corral encircles the head of Squeaky Spring just below the aspen, where you'll find a small cement-lined cistern filled with water. And sure enough, the broken pipe faucet squeaks. This is an essential side trip to fetch water; don't forget to replace the heavy cement lid on the cistern.

From the spring at mile 19.9, an old trail climbs uphill about 50 yards and intersects the bypass trail. This trail is well constructed, but expect some downfall where it passes through the burn. It climbs gradually, reaching the Continental Divide at 20.3 miles. This is also the west ridge of Reeds Peak and a signed four-way trail junction. Significantly, the junction marks the intersection between the two main "high-line" trails of the Aldo: the CDT and the Black Range Crest Trail. From here the Continental Divide turns sharply west, as does the CDT. This point is also the northern terminus of the Black Range Crest Trail. Of course, the actual topographic turning point between the Continental Divide and the crest of the Black Range is Reeds Peak—230 feet higher and 0.25 mile to the immediate left (east).

The peak's open, rocky apex is surrounded by locust, aspen, and Douglas fir, preventing a complete 360-degree view from the ground. For a commanding view of the entire Aldo Leopold Wilderness and far beyond, climb a few levels of the unmanned lookout tower. The platform just below the lookout cabin has been removed, but if you're looking for a grand view, there is certainly no need to climb the very top of the lookout. The roomy cabin next to the lookout, complete with table, chairs, six bunks, and a woodstove, is open to the public. The cabin is in first-class condition thanks to responsible visitors who clean up after themselves. While relaxing in the cabin, out of the wind, take time to read the Reeds Peak cabin log. More than one grateful person thanked Aldo Leopold for his visionary gift of wilderness.

The 10-mile segment of the CDT between the west slope of Reeds Peak and Signboard Saddle is the longest high divide trail in the Aldo without a trail junction and without water. From the signed junction, continue west on the CDT. This portion of the CDT is on a biennial maintenance schedule, but the reality of funding and staffing may stretch this out a bit. At least the trail is well marked and well constructed.

The CDT quickly passes through an old stock fence and switchbacks down to rejoin the divide. The up-and-down nature of high ridges is well represented in this upper segment, where the trail loses and regains elevation before dropping steeply down the open divide, only to regain elevation by mile 22.6. After passing through an open-grown pine forest, the trail drops steeply to 22.8 miles, followed by a long pleasant section through old-growth Douglas fir. At 23.0 miles the trail cuts right and passes next to large mounds of granite outcrops. After another mile of long steep switchbacks in the Douglas fir forest, the trail gains nearly 400 feet of elevation along the narrow, open ridge top. Look back for a clear view of the Reeds Peak lookout.

The CDT begins a long descent by sidehilling around the head of Monument Canyon below Aspen Mountain. The woodland of pine and oak is drier, with broad views of the Mimbres River drainage. In places the trail tread is side sloped, but continues to be well marked. Follow a side ridge above the head of Aspen Canyon, then switchback down to a long contour through a picturesque ponderosa pine park to the bottom of a draw at the head of the canyon. After paralleling the draw, the CDT passes by the Aspen Spring site in an aspen–Douglas fir forest at 26.3 miles. The hard-to-find spring is well concealed in dense brush above the trail and is no longer flowing. The site consists of a concrete cistern sunk deep into the ground with broken pipe—and no water—next to some old mining debris.

The next 4.5 miles to Signboard Saddle are very pleasant, with only minimal climbing. The trail drops gently through a mixed forest of pine, gambel oak, and Douglas fir, with only the sound of the wind, the chatter of gray squirrels, and the resonating of woodpeckers for company. Every so often the direction of the trail changes abruptly, but it's merely following the serpentine path of the Continental Divide. The soft dirt trail is well blazed and easy to follow. After climbing up and down and around a series of grassy pine park draws that feed into Aspen Canyon, the CDT reaches Signboard Saddle at 30.8 miles. True to its name, the saddle is well signed, with the CDT continuing to the left.

The CDT climbs gently through a grassy pine park, weaving pleasantly on both sides of the divide. About 1.3 miles from the saddle, the trail begins a steep switchback descent on a rough, rocky tread for nearly 0.5 mile. Broad vistas open to the crest of the Black Range and to rugged rock formations as the rocky trail drops more gradually in a pinyon-juniper woodland. The signed junction with the new section of Mimbres River Trail 77 is reached at 33.7 miles. From here, an easy 0.4 mile on the wide-track trail brings you to the ending trailhead and the grand conclusion of this epic trans-Aldo CDT hike.

Option: From a saddle on the CDT at mile 19.1, descend to the right through an aspen grove, reaching the Whitmore cabin site and the Falls Canyon Trail in a grassy meadow after about 0.2 mile. The meadow offers good campsites, especially if the small stream is running. For a scenic overlook above the waterfall and down into Black Canyon, continue to the right on the Falls Canyon Trail for 1 mile.

53 Caledonia–Emory Pass

Highlights:	The longest shuttle hike in the Aldo, covering the four major peaks, along with high divide country the entire distance; grand vistas, rugged canyons, and perennial streams; the ultimate trans-Aldo hike
Type of hike:	Six- to eight-day backpack shuttle
Total distance:	51.4 miles
Difficulty:	Strenuous
Best months:	May through October
Maps:	Forest Service Aldo Leopold Wilderness Map; Lookout Mountain, Reeds Peak, Victoria Park, and Hillsboro Peak USGS quads
Special considerations:	The key consideration is water availability. There are long dry distances between reliable springs and streams, particularly later in the season. Portions of the CDT and Black Range Crest Trail are especially vulnerable to fire and windstorms, so expect some sections to be blocked by brush and blowdown. Frequent stream crossings on Holden Prong require wading during high-water periods.

Finding the trailheads: *Beginning trailhead:* From paved New Mexico 59, 16 miles east of the Beaverhead Work Center, or 14.5 miles west of the junction with NM 52, turn south on signed Forest Road 226, located at Burnt

Cabin Flat, which is also identified with a sign. This turn is between mileposts 14 and 15 on NM 59. Go south on FR 226, an improved gravel two-wheel-drive high-center road. At 4 miles 226A intersects on the left; stay on 226 south. After another 3 miles, turn left (east) to remain on FR 226. Drive 9 miles to the large Caledonia Trail signboard adjacent to the road on the right (south), right after you cross the usually dry Chloride Creek.

Ending trailhead: From Interstate 25, 12 miles south of Truth or Consequences, take NM 152 (the Geronimo Trail Scenic Byway) west 34 miles to Emory Pass. Turn right (north) at the pass to the vista parking lot. The faded sign for Trail 79 is located immediately south of the pit toilet on the west side of the 0.2-mile paved road to the parking area.

The driving distance between the two trailheads, around the east side of the wilderness, is 123 miles, 107 of which are paved. The roads are slow and winding, so allow plenty of time for the car shuttle.

Parking and trailhead facilities: *Beginning trailhead:* There is very limited parking at the trailhead. There is room for one vehicle in a flat spot 0.1 mile west of the trail, back near the creek crossing. Lovely campsites are plentiful in Monument Park, 1.0 mile east of the trailhead. The park also has a pit toilet; the cabin there is closed to the public. To get water from the cistern, you will need a bucket and a rope.

Ending trailhead: The trailhead has a paved parking area, picnic table, pit toilet, and an interpretive display of the area's history and geology. There is no water.

Key points:

0.0	Caledonia trailhead.
2.6	Sign for NEW TRAIL NO. 42; begin switchbacks.
3.8	Junction with CDT Trail 74 in saddle.
5.1	Wilderness boundary sign.
5.6	Unsigned junction with Byers Run Trail.
7.8	Junction with North Fork Palomas Trail and Fisherman Canyon Trail.
11.3	Junction of CDT and Circle Seven Creek Trail 106.
11.5	Diamond Peak sign, fence, and spring.
11.8	Diamond Peak.
13.5	Junction of CDT and Burnt Canyon Trail 69.
15.3	Junction of CDT and Sheep Creek Trail 481.
16.8	Junction of CDT and Black Canyon Trail 72; turn left on CDT.
19.1	Saddle on Continental Divide directly above and northeast of Whitmore cabin ruins.
19.6	Junction of CDT and Falls Canyon Trail 73.
19.7	Unsigned trail to Squeaky Spring.
19.9	Squeaky Spring.
20.3	Four-way trail junction on west ridge of Reeds Peak; turn left to peak.
20.6	Reeds Peak (10,011 feet).
20.8	Four-way trail junction on west ridge of Reeds Peak; turn left.
21.3	Junction of Black Range Crest Trail 79 and North Fork Mimbres Trail 77.
22.0	Newman Spring on the right, south of trail.
22.2	Junction of Black Range Crest Trail 79 and Spud Patch Trail 111.
23.1	Willow Spring (don't expect to find water).

Caledonia–Emory Pass

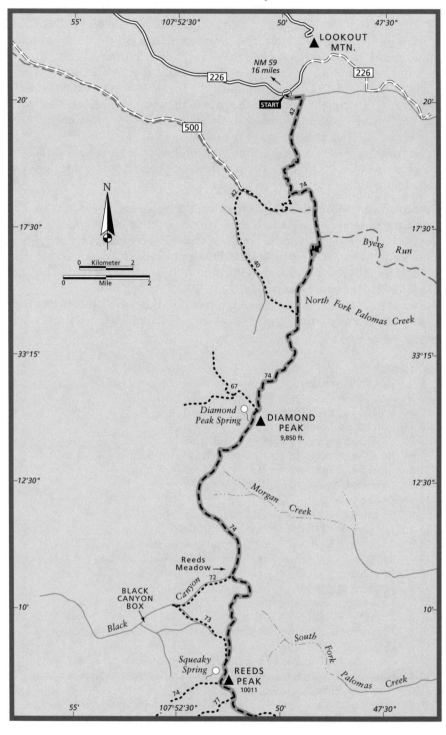

Caledonia–Emory Pass

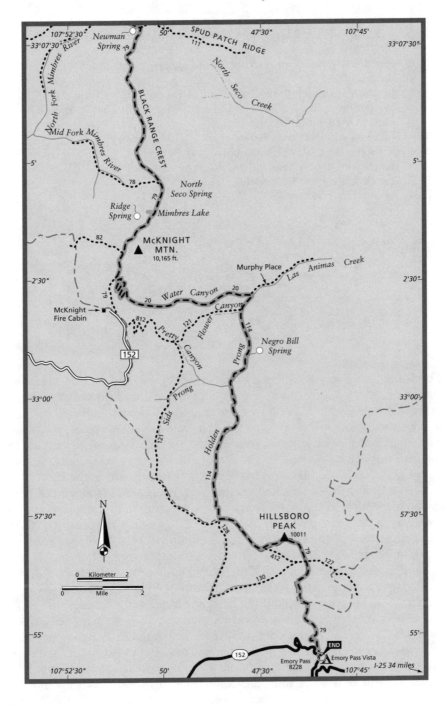

27.0	Junction of Black Range Crest Trail 79 and Middle Fork Mimbres Trail 78.
27.6	Mimbres Lake; junction of Black Range Crest Trail 79 and Lake Trail 110.
29.5	Junction of Black Range Crest Trail 79 and Powderhorn Ridge Trail 82.
29.6	Summit trail to McKnight Mountain (10,165 feet).
30.8	Junction of Black Range Crest Trail 79 and Water Canyon Trail 20; turn left.
36.0	Junction of Water Canyon Trail 20 and Holden Prong Trail 114; turn right.
36.5	Junction of Holden Prong Trail 114 and Flower Canyon Trail 121.
43.4	Holden Prong Saddle, junction of Black Range Crest Trail 79 and Railroad Canyon Trail 128; turn left.
45.0	Junction with Hillsboro Peak Bypass Trail 412.
46.4	Hillsboro Peak (10,011 feet), lookout, and cabin.
47.8	Junction of bypass Trail 412 and Ladrone Canyon Trail 127.
51.0	Pass by Forest Service heliport.
51.4	Emory Pass trailhead.

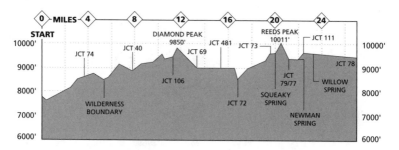

The hike: We've saved the longest (and arguably the best) for last. From the large new CALEDONIA TRAIL #42 sign, pick up the well-marked trail that drops along Chloride Creek before it turns south, within a mile. The well-marked pathway leads you up a gentle streambed to mile 2.6. At this point, you begin climbing via switchbacks through a burned area, rising from the stream to the high ridge that takes you to the Continental Divide and the intersection with CDT Trail 74. See Hike 48 for details on this segment of the hike.

Turn left along the ridge line on the CDT Trail, winding along the wild divide for 8 miles to Diamond Peak. You will pass several trail junctions on your way to the peak, as well as the spring shortly before the peak. The CDT climbs just west of the Diamond Peak summit to a CDT trail sign pointing south to Reeds Peak. See Hike 49 for details on this segment of the hike.

Most of the 9 miles of the CDT between Diamond and Reeds Peaks have burned over in recent fires. Fallen trees are especially prevalent on high ridge-top trails, such as the CDT, and the presence of the burn ensures that there will be a source of continued blowdown for years to come, no matter how often the trail is cut out. The Forest Service tries to maintain this stretch of the CDT every two years. Of course, a lot can happen to a trail in two years, and even this modest schedule depends on funding, which varies from year to year.

The trail drops steadily along the Continental Divide in mostly green Douglas fir forest for about 1 mile before entering the burn. The CDT follows a side ridge to the west and then angles around to a saddle between Burnt Canyon

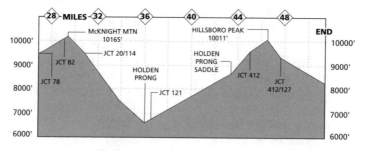

and Morgan Creek at 13.5 miles. This is also the junction between the Burnt Canyon Trail and the CDT. Burnt Canyon is well named. Its namesake trail isn't cut out on a regular basis and therefore isn't recommended as a means of going to or from the CDT, nor is the next trail south down Sheep Creek.

The next 1.8 miles to the head of Sheep Creek are rough because of blow-down and a lot more up-and-down hiking. The trail rapidly gains 300 feet in about 0.4 mile, then follows the divide with views down Morgan Canyon. After sidehilling across the steep headwall of Morgan Canyon, the CDT drops gradually to the burned-out head of Sheep Creek. This small grassy opening at 15.3 miles is the CDT junction with Sheep Creek Trail 481 (shown as Trail 71 at the lower junction sign), indicated only by the burnt remains of an old sign lying on the ground. Downfall and thorny locust may block the trail, but judging from abundant sign, the elk have certainly benefited from the additional forage produced by the fire.

From here the trail climbs 0.2 mile to the Continental Divide and then gradually descends through a ghost forest of burned snags to a grassy swale

Extensive burn at the head of Sheep Creek on the CDT.

with elk wallows. Look ahead for blazes wherever the trail becomes faint in the meadow. The trail rejoins the divide at 16.2 miles for a magnificent view into Morgan Canyon, and then begins dropping southward to the upper end of spacious Reeds Meadow at the head of Black Canyon Creek. The trail stays high and to the right of the meadow in a pine forest. This is a tricky stretch. There are no blazes, and the trail can be hard to find. This wide upper end of the meadow narrows to the Reeds Ranch site, little of which remains. Elk sign includes a wallow and antler rubs on nearby trees. The widest part of the meadow is the upper end of the rugged Rattlesnake Canyon Trail, which plunges steeply to Morgan Creek on the east side. This unsigned trail, not shown on the quad map, has been essentially erased by fire where it meets the Continental Divide.

Although faint in the grassy meadow, the CDT is easily found by hiking on the right side of the sloping meadow, along the edge of the forest. The green, aspen-lined opening provides a welcome respite from the surrounding burn. Soon after leaving the lower end of the meadow, the signed junction with the Black Canyon Trail is reached at 16.8 miles. At the junction, turn left (east) onto the CDT. At first the good trail is well blazed, but it might be obstructed with blowdown at the lower end where it wraps around the south end of Reeds Meadow. The trail improves for about 0.6 mile, then deteriorates in a burned area before reaching the Continental Divide at 17.7 miles.

The CDT climbs around the head of South Fork Palomas Creek and reenters the burn, where brush and downfall again take over. This rough stretch of trail is cut into a steep slope below cliffs and rock outcrops on the east side of the divide, where it mostly contours around the heads of several upper tributaries to South Fork Palomas Creek. An early season spring is passed at mile 18.6. The trail continues up to a saddle at 19.1 miles and then climbs steeply over the next 0.5 mile through more burn and into a green spruce-fir forest to the signed junction with the upper end of the Falls Canyon Trail.

Continue right (south) on the CDT to a broad, grassy park draping the divide after 0.1 mile. From here there are two ways to reach the summit of Reeds Peak. The first is to take the main left-hand trail straight up the divide and into the burn, where it's marked with rock cairns. The better choice is to go first to Squeaky Spring for water and then contour south to the Continental Divide just west of the peak.

The bypass to the spring is hard to find. The trail is unsigned and indistinct. Head southwest across the meadow and you'll quickly find an obvious trail on the edge of the meadow, near an aspen thicket suitable for camping. An old corral encircles the head of Squeaky Spring just below the aspen, where you'll find a small cement-lined cistern filled with water. And sure enough, the broken pipe faucet squeaks. This is an essential side trip to fetch water. Don't forget to replace the heavy cement lid on the cistern.

From the spring at mile 19.9, an old trail climbs uphill about 50 yards and intersects the bypass trail. This trail is well constructed, but expect some downfall where it passes through the burn. It climbs gradually, reaching the Continental Divide at 20.3 miles. This is also the west ridge of Reeds Peak and a signed four-way trail junction. Significantly, the junction marks the intersection between the two main "high-line" trails of the Aldo: the CDT and the Black Range Crest Trail. From here the Continental Divide turns sharply west, as does the CDT. This point is also the northern terminus of the Black Range Crest Trail. Of course, the actual topographic turning point between the Continental Divide and the crest of the Black Range is Reeds Peak—230 feet higher and 0.25 mile to the left (east).

A good trail takes you to the open, rocky 10,011-foot summit, which is ringed by locust, apsen, and Douglas fir. For a commanding view of the entire Aldo Leopold Wilderness and far beyond, climb a few levels of the unmanned lookout tower. The platform just below the lookout cabin has been removed, but you don't need to climb to the top of the tower for this top-of-the-world view. The roomy cabin next to the lookout, complete with table, chairs, six bunks, and a woodstove, is open to the public. The cabin is in first-class condition thanks to responsible visitors who clean up after themselves. While relaxing in the cabin, out of the wind, take time to read the Reeds Peak cabin log. More than one grateful person thanked Aldo Leopold for his visionary gift of wilderness.

From the Continental Divide junction just west of Reeds Peak, the Black Range Crest Trail angles left around the south slope of the peak with vistas to the south. The good trail switchbacks down to the burn at the head of the North Fork Mimbres River and trail junction. Because of the recent fire, you can expect some blowdown of large blackened Douglas fir trees across the trail up to the hill just south of the trail junction. The wide trail follows the crest through a thick Douglas fir–aspen forest sprinkled with stately Southwestern white pine. Along the way, the sloping meadow of Newman Spring opens to an expansive view westward, providing a pleasant break in the otherwise dense forest. The spring might be little more than a wet meadow seep, but is usually a reliable water source, except later in the summer during a particularly dry year. Just beyond, at mile 22.2, the upper end of the Spud Patch Trail drops steeply to the east. Rocky overlooks at this point provide spectacular views of North Seco and Massacre Canyons, along with Animas Ridge all the way to Hillsboro Peak.

Dense forest continues south from the Spud Patch junction as the crest begins to level off. Willow Spring will most likely be disappointing if you want water; the encroaching forest has erased it.

Along the divide you'll find some sporadic fire damage, blowdown, and mountain locust, but for the most part the well-defined trail remains in good condition. Much of the High Crest Trail is closed in with old growth, a "hall of trees" with towering monarchs lining the trail. But every so often this Gothic cathedral of nature opens to clear views in both directions that show the amazing contrast between the rugged canyons and rock formations to the east and the softer wooded slopes on the west side. When you come across one of these "windows," whether due to a rock outcrop or lightning-caused fire, drop your pack and soak up the scenery. Or pause in the deep woods and sit a while. Only the singing wind, the rustle of squirrels, and the calls of the birds break the stillness.

The trail maintains an overall moderate grade south of Willow Spring, with only a few short steep ups and downs. Dropping into saddles and contouring around steep side slopes keeps the trail between 9,400 and 9,700 feet for most of the distance. At mile 27.0 the trail makes a gradual descent in a mature old-growth forest to the signed junction with Mid Fork Mimbres River Trail 78.

The wide trail, a former jeep road, is clear, winding to the south as it rises to Mimbres Lake. Lake Trail 110 drops eastward from the lake. Mimbres Lake is a swampy stock pond bounded on three sides by a forest of aspen. It looks lovely from the trail, reflecting the sky and the forest, glistening in the sun. A disintegrating fence surrounds the pond, but no longer creates much of a barrier. The stagnant waters are enjoyed now by wildlife. Look for a variety of tracks in the soft earth near the pond. Mimbres Lake is a pleasant camping spot, but getting water, which requires treatment, is challenging. Wading in to the proper depth inevitably stirs up silt from the bottom.

South of Mimbres Lake, the wide Crest Trail curves east of the divide. The spring indicated on the quad map, 0.2 mile from the lake, has vanished in a dense slope of aspen, and there is no trace of a trail. The second spring, on the west side of the crest a mile from the lake, is 0.5 mile and 400 feet below the crest. Watch for log cuts and an opening in an old fence on your right.

In early spring you can expect scattered snowbanks on the northwest slopes of the Crest Trail. You also will encounter a bit of winter downfall if you are here ahead of the trail crew. Otherwise, the undulating trail is usually clear. Openings in the forest provide exhilarating views, such as when the trail switchbacks up the north side of McKnight Mountain. Excellent seating is available on a rock outcropping right next to the trail, with views to the east. Continuing to climb another 200 feet, the trail reaches a junction with the Powderhorn Ridge Trail.

Just south of the junction is the top of McKnight Mountain. The signed trail to McKnight Summit is located in an aspen grove. Drop your pack and hike the short distance to the grassy mountaintop, complete with perfectly contoured rocks so you can enjoy the view in comfort. At 10,165 feet, McKnight Mountain is the highest point in the Aldo.

From McKnight Summit, the trail south loses its jeep-road quality. There are several narrow rocky sections as it winds east of the divide and then to the west along rocky ridges. A little over a mile from the mountain, drop through a minor saddle at mile 30.8 to the signed junction with Water Canyon Trail 20 to Las Animas Creek. The trail is shown on the wilderness map, but not on the 1963 USGS quadrangle.

The Water Canyon–Holden Prong bypass, which comes next, avoids the monotonous 3 miles of the upper McKnight Road as it follows the crest between trailheads. With streams cascading through rugged canyons, it also adds scenic diversity to this mostly high crest route. Turn left, down Water Canyon, and descend a series of long, well-graded switchbacks through an aspen forest on the north side of Water Canyon, losing almost 900 feet in a mile. A small grassy spring is followed by giant rock fins and balancing rocks at mile 33.2. Soon a major fork is reached in the narrow, deepening canyon. The trail improves as it weaves back and forth across the creek. By mile 34.5

the neck-craning canyon closes in with towering rock spires and buttresses. The stream cascades over shelf rock into deep pools, creating a spellbinding effect. The deep, narrow canyon continues, with higher walls on its north side. A diverse forest of pine, oak, and fir gives way to a pine park as the valley widens. The trail crosses Holden Prong at 36.0 miles just below the mouth of Water Canyon.

Turn right (upstream) onto Holden Prong Trail 114. The rugged rocky streambed has little stairstep cascades between its deep spellbinding pools. The prong valley is broader here than in the rocky ravine upstream, so there are several locations suitable for camping. There are frequent stream crossings, some of which may be to midcalf in the early spring; be prepared with appropriate footwear. After another 0.5 mile, a faint trail heads to the right up Flower Canyon; continue left along the stream. Towering stone obelisks stand starkly against the sky upstream from the junction. At 1 mile from the beginning of the Holden Prong Trail, there is a rare 0.15-mile stretch of straight, flat trail on the west side of the prong. Watch for a stream or a trickle on the east bank of the prong, indicating the source of Negro Bill Spring.

At this point, the trail cuts through a lumpy grass meadow west of the creek, so you could easily miss it. Another hint of the spring is a defunct signpost standing next to the trail. Only the rusty bolts remain; the sign to this politically incorrect spring is gone, as is the trail. Trail 309, although still on the wilderness map, is unmaintained and has been erased by the wilderness. To visit the spring, cross the prong on the barely visible pathway and climb about 100 feet above the stream on the east bank into the rolling ponderosa pine park. Follow the little stream to its source at the spring, about 0.1 mile from the prong. There is no trail beyond the spring, just a few stray old blazes.

Continuing upstream on the prong, the trail departs from streamside on two occasions when a narrowed bed and rocky gorge don't allow for a trail. During these short hillside interludes, the tumultuous sound of falls and rapids fills the narrow canyon. At 1.4 miles above Negro Bill Spring, the rocky mouth of Sids Prong is on the right. The journey up Holden Prong is scenic as it travels along the stream through the dense forest. The stream crossings, especially in early spring, can be challenging; the water could be above your knees at some crossings. As a result, it is slow going, but this is beautiful country, so why rush it?

You will no doubt notice interesting blazes on the route: They've been painted on the tree trunks and boulders along the trail with white paint and a 4-inch brush. Perhaps this technique of trail marking is kinder than the traditional gouges in the bark, and they sure stand out, but they are sort of garish in this dark, woodsy canyon. Because we didn't see them elsewhere in the Aldo, apparently it was only an experiment that was not repeated.

Campsites become less frequent as you ascend this narrow canyon. Don't put off your selection until late in the day. There are long stretches of the trail with no clear level spots at all. The narrow rocky canyon is cluttered with downfall, although the trail is clear and well maintained. The dampness of the shady canyon has protected it from the fires that are common elsewhere in the Aldo; here the old-growth forest is reminiscent of the Germanic forests described by the Brothers Grimm.

After following the stream for 6.5 miles, the trail begins to switchback up the steep slope at the head of the valley, climbing through thickly bunched aspen to reach the Black Range crest. The 8,716-foot-high Holden Prong Saddle, on the crest of the range, consists of a grassy opening ringed by aspen, southwestern white pine, spruce, and fir.

Turn left (east) at the saddle and continue along the crest to the junction with the Hillsboro Peak Bypass Trail, another 1.6 miles. Taking the bypass route allows you to omit some elevation gain, but you'll also miss a potential water stop (if there is snow, the spring might be buried) and a wonderful view from the peak. It's a 1,300-foot elevation gain in 1.3 miles, slightly softened by switchbacks. And after all, if you're doing the Crest Trail, you need to include Hillsboro peak. It's worth it!

A friendly Forest Service sign welcomes you to the top, as will a friendly lookout ranger if you visit during the fire season when the lookout is manned. The ranger lives in the west cabin, but the east cabin is left open for the public to use, both for safety purposes and as a practical way to avoid break-ins. The east cabin was built in 1925 and remains in good condition, thanks to responsible people who are careful to clean up after they leave. In addition to providing refuge from an almost constant wind, the cabin has a sheltered front porch with a fabulous view eastward. The cabin logbook is entertaining to read, with many entries extolling the beauty and solitude of the Aldo.

The lookout and ranger cabin were constructed in 1934, replacing the previous wooden lookout. For an incredible 360-degree view of the entire Black Range and surrounding valleys and mountains, climb to the lookout cabin. The metal stairway is sturdy and guarded by railings, but those with a fear of heights would probably be happier on the ground. With permission from the ranger, you can fill up your water bottles from an otherwise locked rain cistern near the cabin. You might also be able to obtain water from a spring some 600 feet below and to the north of the lookout.

Trail 79 from the lookout drops steeply, with switchbacks, passing through a couple of stock fences and reaching a trail junction in a saddle at mile 47.8. Here a sign announces the wilderness boundary and commemorates the one hundredth anniversary of Aldo Leopold's birth in 1887. Continue along the seesawing Crest Trail, heading south 3.6 miles to Emory Pass. The trail shifts from a narrow footpath to a wide old jeep trail, and eventually to a road when you get close to the heliport. Watch for a sign on the left after the heliport that will direct you down to your destination at the Emory Pass parking lot.

The grand conclusion of this challenging high-country traverse calls for a celebration that evening, if you've got any leftover energy.

Option: From a saddle on the CDT at mile 19.1, descend to the right through an aspen grove, reaching the Whitmore cabin site and the Falls Canyon Trail in a grassy meadow after about 0.2 mile. The meadow offers good campsites, especially if the small stream is running. For a scenic overlook above the waterfall and down into Black Canyon, hike down the Falls Canyon Trail for 1 mile.

Appendix A: For More Information

FOREST SERVICE OFFICES

USDA Forest Service
Southwestern Region
Public Affairs Office
333 Broadway SE
Albuquerque, NM 87102
(505) 842-3292

Gila National Forest
3005 East Camino del Bosque
Silver City, NM 88061
(505) 388-8201

Wilderness Ranger District
HC 68, Box 50
Mimbres, NM 88049
(505) 536-2250

Black Range Ranger District
P.O. Box 431
1804 Date Street
Truth or Consequences, NM 87901
(505) 894-6677

Note: The Aldo Leopold Wilderness is administered by two ranger districts, with the Continental Divide and Black Range Crest south of Reeds Peak forming the district boundary. The west side of the divide north of Reeds Peak is in the Wilderness Ranger District, as is the west side of the Black Range Crest south of Reeds Peak. The east side of the crest and divide is within the Black Range District. General information about the Gila National Forest and the Aldo Leopold Wilderness is easily accessible on the Internet by typing "Gila National Forest" in whatever search engine you choose.

PUBLIC LANDS CONSERVATION GROUPS

Gila Watch
P.O. Box 309
Silver City, NM 88062
(505) 388-3449

New Mexico Wilderness Alliance
P.O. Box 13116
Albuquerque, NM 87192
(505) 255-5966, ext. 106
E-mail: nmwa@earthlink.net

Wilderness Watch
P.O. Box 9175
Missoula, MT 59807
(406) 542-2048
www.wildernesswatch.org
E-mail: wild@wildernesswatch.org

The Wildlands Project
1955 West Grand Road, Suite 145
Tucson, AZ 85745
(520) 884-0875
www.twp.org
E-mail: wildlands@twp.org

The Wilderness Society
900 Seventeenth Street, NW
Washington, D.C. 20006-2506
(202) 833-2300
www.wilderness.org

The Wilderness Society Wilderness
    Support Center
E-mail: wsc@tws.org

The Wilderness Society
Four Corners Regional Office
7475 Dakin Street, #410
Denver, CO 80221
(303) 650-5818

FINDING THE RIGHT MAP

To explore the Aldo Leopold Wilderness, you need two basic types of maps. First, the large-scale 1:24,000 topographic maps (2.6 inches/mile with 40-foot contour intervals) listed in the map information block for each hike. These detailed USGS quads are essential for on-the-ground route finding. Second, the 1984 1:63,360 Aldo Leopold Wilderness Map (1 inch/mile with 200-foot contour intervals) shows forest road access to trailheads, numbered Forest Service trails, and major features. Minor revisions to this map were made in 2000. This small-scale map, along with the 1997 Gila National Forest Map (0.5 inch to the mile on a planimetric base) are useful for overall trip planning and for finding your way to trailheads and at trail junctions. The Forest Service signs in the wilderness do not use the trail numbers but instead show the destination names.

The Aldo Leopold Wilderness map costs $7.00; the Gila National Forest map can be purchased for $6.00. They can be obtained from the Forest Service offices listed above. In addition, the Forest Service has a free Gila National Forest pocket guide, revised in 1998, that provides useful general information about major road access, campgrounds, and points of interest.

The USGS quads sell for $4.00 each. They may be purchased from USGS Information Services, Box 25286, Denver, CO 80225, or by calling (800) ASK–USGS. The USGS charges a handling fee of $5.00 for each order mailed.

Appendix B: Further Reading

Bookstores in Truth or Consequences, Gila Hot Springs, and Silver City have a good selection of titles on archaeology, natural history, settlers, ranchers, hunters, explorers, and miners of the Gila, Black Range, and southwest New Mexico. Many of the books are published locally and would be difficult to locate elsewhere. Listed below are relevant books that are widely available.

Bowers, Janice E. *100 Desert Wildflowers of the Southwest*. Tuscon: Southwest Parks and Monuments Association, 1989.

_____, *Shrubs and Trees of the Southwest Deserts*. Tucson: Southwest Parks and Monuments Association, 1993.

Brown, David E., and Neil B. Carmody, eds. *Aldo Leopold's Southwest*. Albuquerque: University of New Mexico Press, 1990.

Burke, Polly, and Bill Cunningham, *Hiking New Mexico's Gila Wilderness*. Guilford, Conn.: Falcon Publishing, 1999.

Leopold, Aldo. *A Sand County Almanac*. New York: Ballantine Books, 1966.

Little, Elbert L. *The Audubon Society Field Guide to North American Trees*. New York: Alfred A Knopf, 1980.

Lorbiecki, Marybeth. *Aldo Leopold: A Fierce Green Fire*. Guilford, Conn.: Falcon Publishing, 1996.

MacCarter, Jane S. *New Mexico Wildlife Viewing Guide*. Guilford, Conn.: Falcon Publishing, 1994.

McDonald, Corry. *Wilderness: A New Mexico Legacy*. Santa Fe: Sunstone Press: 1985.

Parent, Laurence. *Hiking New Mexico*. Guilford, Conn.: Falcon Publishing, 1996.

Peterson, Roger Tory. *Field Guide to Western Birds*. Boston: Houghton Mifflin Co., 1990.

Taylor, Ronald J. *Sagebrush Country: A Wildflower Sanctuary*. Missoula, Mont.: Mountain Press, 1992.

Appendix C: Hiker Checklist

Hiking in the Aldo Leopold Wilderness requires solid preparation. One of the first steps to being properly prepared is packing the right equipment for the type, season, and duration of the hike. We joke about carrying "Eighty pounds of lightweight gear," but in all seriousness, you are carrying everything on your back, so bring only what you really need. Use the checklist below before your trip into the Black Range country to ensure you haven't forgotten an essential item.

Core essentials for day hikes:

☐ Day pack (or "day and a half," climbing-style pack, if needed)

☐ Water: two quarts to one gallon per person per day in one- to two-quart Nalgene bottles or bladder

☐ Matches in a waterproof container

☐ Small first-aid kit: tweezers, bandages, antiseptic, moleskin or Second Skin or Spyroflex for blister prevention, first-aid tape, prescriptions, antibiotics, ibuprofen or acetaminophen, antacid tablets, bee sting kit (over-the-counter antihistamine or epinephrine by prescription), knee or ankle wraps, snakebite kit

☐ Head net and insect repellent (in season)

☐ Sunglasses, sunscreen (SPF 30 or higher), and lip sunscreen

☐ Pocketknife

☐ Whistle and signal mirror

☐ Flashlight with extra batteries and bulb

☐ Lunch and high-energy snacks, with bag for your trash

☐ Toilet paper in plastic bag

☐ Wilderness and quad maps and compass

☐ Rain gear that can double as wind protection (breathable water-repellent parka and/or rain suit with pants or chaps)

☐ Warm shirt, fleece, or polypropylene top (for layering)

☐ Sleeping pad (self-inflating type is best)

☐ Walking stick or trekking poles

☐ Backpack stove, fuel bottle (filled), repair kit with cleaning wire

☐ Collapsible bucket (for settling silty water)

☐ Water filter (with brush to clean in the field) and iodine tablets for backup

☐ Cooking kit, pot gripper, cleaning pad

☐ Eating utensils, including a cup, fork, spoon, and bowl with cover (three-cup size)

☐ Trowel

☐ Several small drawstring bags for odds and ends

☐ Biodegradable soap, waterless hand sanitizer, small towel

☐ Toothbrush, toothpaste, dental floss

☐ Nylon tape or duct tape

☐ Nylon stuffsack with 50- to 100-foot nylon cord for hanging food and drying clothes

- [ ] Plastic bags and a few smaller zipper-lock bags
- [ ] Small sewing kit
- [ ] Notebook, pencils
- [ ] Field guidebooks
- [ ] Compact binoculars
- [ ] Camera, film, lenses, filters, lens brush and paper (or keep it light and simple with a "point and shoot")
- [ ] Fishing tackle (fly and/or spinning)
- [ ] Thermometer
- [ ] Watch
- [ ] Sufficient food, plus a little extra

For overnight trips add the following:

- [ ] Backpack with waterproof pack cover and extra set of pack straps
- [ ] Tent with ground cloth (cut or folded to size of tent floor) and repair kit (including rip-stop tape)
- [ ] Sleeping bag (rated to at least 10 degrees F or as season requires)

Clothing (quick-dry fabrics preferred):

- [ ] Boots (medium weight recommended, broken in)
- [ ] Lightweight boots (sturdy enough for backpacking) for wading major streams during high water
- [ ] Neoprene socks (thermal protection for stream crossings)
- [ ] Several pairs of wool hiking socks and polypropylene or inner socks
- [ ] Shirt, sweater, pants, and jacket suitable for the season
- [ ] Extra underwear and shirt
- [ ] Warm skiing-style hat (balaclava, headband, or stocking cap)
- [ ] Windproof hat with broad brim for sun protection
- [ ] Mittens or gloves (weight depends on the season)
- [ ] Hiking shorts
- [ ] Swimsuit
- [ ] Gaiters, especially when snow is present
- [ ] Thermal underwear (wool or polypropylene/capilene, depending on the season)

About the Authors

Polly Burke and Bill Cunningham are married partners in the long trail of life. Polly, formerly a history teacher in St. Louis, Missouri, now makes her home with Bill in Choteau, Montana. She is pursuing multiple careers in freelance writing, leading group trips in wilderness, and working with the elderly. Polly has hiked and backpacked extensively throughout many parts of the country.

Bill is a lifelong "wildernut," as a conservation activist, backpacking outfitter, and field studies teacher for the University of Montana. During the 1970s and '80s, he was a field rep for the Wilderness Society. He has written several books and dozens of magazine articles about wilderness areas, based on extensive on-the-ground knowledge. Bill is the author of *Wild Montana*, the first in Falcon Publishing's series of statewide guidebooks to wilderness and unprotected, roadless areas.

Polly and Bill are the authors of *Hiking California's Desert Parks* (1996), *Wild Utah* (1998), and *Hiking New Mexico's Gila Wilderness* (1999), all published by Falcon Publishing. *Hiking New Mexico's Aldo Leopold Wilderness* is their fourth book and it truly reflects their love of Aldo Leopold's namesake wilderness.

The authors prepare for a long hike from the new Caledonia trailhead on FR 226.

WHAT'S SO SPECIAL ABOUT UNSPOILED, NATURAL PLAC

Beauty   Solitude   Wildness   Freedom   Quiet   Adventure

Serenity   Inspiration   Wonder   Excitement

Relaxation   Challenge

There's a lot to love about our treasured public lands, and the reasons are different for each of us. Whatever your reasons are, the national **Leave No Trace** education program will help you discover special outdoor places, enjoy them, and preserve them—today and for those who follow. By practicing and passing along these simple principles, you can help protect the special places you love from being loved to death.

THE PRINCIPLES OF **LEAVE NO TRACE**

- Plan ahead and prepare
- Travel and camp on durable surfaces
- Dispose of waste properly
- Leave what you find
- Minimize campfire impacts
- Respect wildlife
- Be considerate of other visitors

Leave No Trace is a national nonprofit organization dedicated to teaching responsible outdoor recreation skills and ethics to everyone who enjoys spending time outdoors.

To learn more or to become a member, please visit us at www.LNT.org or call (800) 332-4100.

Leave No Trace, P.O. Box 997, Boulder, CO 80306